DARING CHOICES

Stories From An International Life in Politics, Business, and Technology

BY JAMES B. KELLY III

DORRANCE
PUBLISHING CO
EST. 1920
PITTSBURGH, PENNSYLVANIA 15238

Dorrance Publishing Co
585 Alpha Drive
Suite 103
Pittsburgh, PA 15238
Visit our website at www.dorrancebookstore.com

ISBN: 979-8-89127-581-2
eISBN: 979-8-89127-079-4

DARING CHOICES

Stories From An International Life in Politics, Business, and Technology

ACKNOWLEDGMENTS

In early 2017, Max King and his wife, Peggy, came to our house for dinner. It was the second time I had met Max, and I regaled him and Peggy with some of my stories and he encouraged me to write them down. I'll never forget asking him why he thought these events in my life happened. He said, "Because you put yourself out there."

I thought to myself that when the former editor of the *Philadelphia Enquirer* and CEO of the Heinz and Pittsburgh Foundations, not to mention author of *The Good Neighbor* about Fred Rogers, tells you to write your stories down, you ought at least to give it a try. In the time since that dinner, I have seen Max every so often, and he always asks for a status report. If this book had a catalyst, it was Max.

Having written eighty thousand words, I had no experience turning them into a book. It was clear I needed a good editor to help me make sense of it all. Turning again to Max, he suggested I speak with his editor, Patricia Mulcahy. I did and, in turn, Patricia recommended editor Katie Hall. Katie and I have spent the better part of a year editing, reworking, and reediting the manuscript.

Thanks to Max for getting me started and to Katie for helping me finish!

Thanks to my wife, Janet, for her encouragement during the entire process.

And thanks to the Thunderbird School of Global Management. Had I not gone there, much of the story would likely have never happened. (That's the school emblem on the luggage tag on the cover).

CONTENTS

Preface xi

I. FOUNDATIONS 1

PITTSBURGH 1941–1947, THE EARLY YEARS 4

PITTSBURGH 1947–1957, SCHOOL YEARS 8

Dr. Jonas Salk 12

MIDDLESBORO, KENTUCKY 1956–1959, FIRST JOBS & HIGH SCHOOL 14

VA TECH 1959–1963, THE CORPS, DAD'S DEATH, AND A FRATERNITY 26

PHOENIX, ARIZONA 1963–1964, THUNDERBIRD GRADUATE SCHOOL 34

GREENVILLE, PA, DETROIT AND CHICAGO 1964–1965, CB&I TRAINEE 37

II. TRAINEE TO MANAGER 41

LONDON 1965, A BRIEF STOP IN SALES 43

ALGERIA 1965–1966, CB&I AND A LIFECHANGING SIX MONTHS 44

LA CORUÑA, SPAIN 1967, CB&I AND BREAKFAST WITH A KING 54

Don Juan, Elsie Hillman, Allegheny County Republican Party Chair 62

WASHINGTON 1968–1970, WITH PA SENATOR RICHARD S. SCHWEIKER 66

Congressman Richard S. Schweiker 66

Drew Lewis, Campaign Chairman 70

Richard M. Nixon, Presidential Candidate 74

Vice President Spiro Agnew 78

Governor Thomas Dewey 78

Senate Minority Leader Hugh Scott 78

Admiral Hyman Rickover, Father of the Nuclear Navy 78

Charles de Gaulle, Président of France 78

PITTSBURGH & HARRISBURG 1970–1976, PA HOUSE OF REPRESENTATIVES 80

Former Pennsylvania Governor William Scranton 82

Alice Cooper & Shep Gordon 90

Valery Giscard d'Estang, President of France 95

PITTSBURGH 1976, A RUN FOR CONGRESS, THE GENERAL AND THE IMPOSTER 96

General Mathew B. Ridgway 96

IV. THE INTERNATIONALIST 101
PITTSBURGH 1977–1980, ALGERIA (AGAIN), THE MIDDLE EAST, AND CHINA 103
CHINA 1977–1980, A PIONEER 108
Former Pennsylvania Senator Hugh Scott 109
Deputy Chief Liaison Han Xu, later Ambassador 109
PITTSBURGH 1980, A BRUSH WITH PRESIDENTIAL POLITICS 117
MILAN, ITALY 1980–1983, DRAVO ENGINEERS 120
Bulgaria 122
CLEVELAND AND HOUSTON 1983–1984, DAVY MCKEE 126
WASHINGTON 1984–1988, REAGAN ADMINISTRATION 128
Malcom Baldrige, Secretary of Commerce 129
Mohamed Sahnoun, Algerian Ambassador 132
Tariq Aziz, Iraq Foreign Minister, Deputy Prime Minister 134
Nizar Hamdoon, Iraq Ambassador to the U.S and U.N., Later Deputy Foreign Minister .. 134
George Schultz, U.S. Secretary of State 134
Iraq 135
India 137
Rajiv Gandhi, India Prime Minister 140
Algeria (Again) 142
Chadli Bendjedid, President of Algeria 142
Saudi Arabia 142
Zimbabwe 145
South Africa 146
Mozambique 150
Nigeria 151
1988–1990 WASHINGTON, SCIENCE APPLICATIONS INTERNATIONAL (SAIC) 154
Iraq (Again) 158
1990–1992 BRUSSELS, VALMONT, IRAQ (AGAIN), AND WAR 162
Iraq (Again) 163
Belgium and Holland 165
Poland 167
1992–1996 WASHINGTON AND GERMANY, CARLYLE'S BDM INTERNATIONAL 169
Frank Carlucci, Secretary of Defense 175
Pamela Harriman, U.S. Ambassador to France 175
Korea (Again) 179

V. THE ENTREPRENEUR........181

1996–2005 WASHINGTON, SYNXIS STARTUP........183

2003–2014 BLACKSBURG, VIRGINIA TECH BUSINESS SCHOOL........201

2005–2008 WASHINGTON, FLIGHT EXPLORER........203

2009–2012 WASHINGTON, LIFEDOX........213

Dr. Robert Kahn, A Founder of the Internet........214

VI. FINALE........217

2014–2016 WASHINGTON........219

2016–NOW WASHINGTON TO PITTSBURGH AND ONWARD........219

James Roddey, Allegheny County Executive........221

APPENDIX A........225

TEN–STEP SOFTWARE ENTERPRISE STARTUP ROADMAP........227

INDEX........231

ABOUT THE AUTHOR........241

PREFACE

I was forty-three when I joined the second Reagan Administration. By then, I had moved around. A lot. I grew up in Pittsburgh but finished high school in Kentucky. I attended college in Virginia and graduate school in Arizona. My first job, as an engineer, took me to London, North Africa, and Spain. After that, I deliberately returned to America to pursue political roles in Washington, D.C., and Pittsburgh. Catching my breath after working on Capitol Hill and in the Pennsylvania Legislature, I went on to work as a marketing executive in the Middle East, China, Europe, and Eastern Europe, before joining the Reagan International Trade Administration. I then spent several years in the Washington defense industry and, ultimately, started a couple of successful software companies.

I have come to describe my skillset as a unique three-legged stool: technology, government, and business, usually with an international focus. This was a rare combination, especially in the U.S., because few businesspeople understand government, just as few civil servants understand business. As a technology entrepreneur with government and international experience, I found myself in even rarer space.

Not surprisingly, my diverse experiences left me with stories I enjoy telling, especially about the people I met and those who helped me along the way. Many friends, colleagues, acquaintances, and students hearing these stories have asked me *how* I had such an eclectic career and so many diverse life experiences. I have written this book as an answer. I hope that people just starting out, and those looking to change their lives, may take from my stories insight into what it takes to build a successful multitrack life. In these pages, I offer up my own experiences as examples of what one can do by making daring choices. Often those choices led me across time zones and skillsets. I wanted to live an interesting life and to do so I pushed beyond my comfort zone. I chose paths and people I wanted to know and understand.

Encouraged by a friend who told me my life happened the way it did because I "put myself out there," I thought it was important to share how one does just that. I found that each experience informed the next, as I built my life deliberately and strategically. As a curious young man, I decided I wanted to see the world, and set out to do that. To make myself stand out among my peers, I set a goal of learning essential technical and management skills. I approached accomplished people I admired and asked for their help. In turn, I helped them. In this way, I initiated mutual relationships with extraordinary men and women who taught me significant lessons they had learned throughout their lives.

The stories in this book occurred within a rapidly changing world. In following along, readers will see why I made the decisions I did, and how I changed with the times, all the while staying focused on the things that mattered: my family, friends, colleagues, and bosses, all of whom contributed to my learning process. These stories, then, are not just about events and choices, but about the people who made them possible, including my father, who taught me how to lead, and my two grandfathers, who left not a word about their lives, but whose exemplary careers inspired me.

I hope readers, including today's people interested in government and business, will understand that much is possible if you push beyond what is expected, if you accommodate change and failure, and if you pay close attention to establishing fruitful personal bonds. It can be done!

Most importantly, though, I hope today's readers will set out to learn something new at every step in their lives! After all, it's your only life—make the most of it!

I. FOUNDATIONS

The year was 1965. I was twenty-four years old and headed into my new(ish) office in London. A dark rain worsened the commute and unusually heavy traffic clogged the streets as I made my way from my apartment in Chiswick to my Chicago Bridge & Iron Company office in the York House building next to Wembley Stadium. My office, high enough to see into the far end of the soccer stadium, was in the engineering department, where I had spent the previous months learning European engineering standards. This was my first job out of graduate school, and I had already been given my next assignment: I was to be promoted to the sales department, located in the other side of the building, an early step up for someone my age.

Just as I had taken my seat at my drafting board, Jess, the engineering manager, approached and said, “Don wants to see you right away.”

As I entered Don’s office, the twenty-nine-year-old managing director quickly came to the point: “The engineering manager has concerns you’re getting too big for your britches, so I am going to give you a choice: You either go to Africa as a project engineer, or you go home.”

He then briefly explained that a main ingredient of my job was to get along with my boss, not the other way around, and that without Jess’s recommendation I would not be going to sales anytime soon.

To say I was humiliated would be an understatement. As I reeled through all the possibilities in a near state of shock, it was quite clear that whatever I had done in the preceding months was not to be the subject of a negotiation. One thing was very clear to me: The longer I took to decide, the worse it was going to be for me.

I had absolutely no knowledge of any of the projects in Africa, but I knew that going to some yet-to-be-defined place would at least preserve the fragile beginning of my career. Going home to Pittsburgh with my tail between my legs, however, would mean starting over while trying to explain what had happened in London.

I decided to go to Africa!

PITTSBURGH 1941–1947, THE EARLY YEARS

"Hell with the lid taken off."

That is what the *Atlantic Magazine* had to say about Pittsburgh in 1868. Seventy-five years later, in the Second World War, the city doubled and even tripled down on that statement, becoming the industrial center of the "Arsenal of Democracy" by producing 95 million tons of steel. By the mid-1950s, Pittsburgh led the world in steel production, and accounted for nearly half of all American steel.

By 1970, Pittsburgh was the nation's third-largest corporate headquarters town, and hosted Mellon Bank, U.S. Steel, Gulf Oil, Westinghouse, Alcoa, PPG, Heinz, and Rockwell. Its parks, museums, libraries, universities, and hospitals were built and endowed by the enormous figures of the Gilded Age, including Andrew Mellon, Andrew Carnegie, George Westinghouse, and Henry Heinz.

Home to tens of thousands of immigrants who flocked to the industrial city for its jobs, its neighborhoods grew cultures all their own in Little Italy, Polish Hill, and Deutschtown. The downtown Hill District, where many Southern Black Americans settled after the Great Migration, became known for its music, establishing such artists as Erroll Garner, Billy Eckstine, and George Benson.

Pittsburgh's WQED became the nation's first community-supported television station and later featured a then-unknown Mr. Rogers. The developing networks brought stars like Bishop Fulton J. Sheen and Ed Sullivan to the city on promotional tours. During drive time, everybody listened to Rege Cordic on WWSW and then KDKA, the nation's first commercial radio station, where he was known for the creation of outlandish characters like Omicron from outer space and products like Frothingslosh Pale Stale Ale with the foam on the bottom.

Though Pittsburgh remained the third-largest corporate headquarters town in the country, and though the aluminum, glass, and food industries continued to grow, the deindustrialization of the '60s and '70s began to change everything in the city except the sports teams. While the Steelers, Pirates, and Penguins set about building winning franchises, manufacturing declined, corporations left, unemployment took hold, and the population receded. To stop the bleeding, the city's industrial and political fathers, including the Mellons, the Heinzes, and the Hillmans, stepped up and through such organizations as the Allegheny Conference on Community Development initiated a forward-thinking process that, over the '80s and '90s, led to the vital Pittsburgh of today.

Known as the City of Bridges—446, to be exact—Pittsburgh is now considered one of the most livable cities in the United States. But locals more often refer to it as the city of "Eds and Meds," as universities and the massive health campus of the University of Pittsburgh's Medical Center (UPMC) now form the heart of the city. Carnegie Mellon University and the University of Pittsburgh, with fifty thousand students between them, have established global reputations in the fields of Business, Technology, Robotics, Medicine, and Law. Pennsylvania's largest non-government employer, UPMC, has been the home of renowned leaders in vaccines (Jonas Salk) and transplants (Tomas Starzl).

Gone today are the steel mills, warehouses, and the corona of black smoke that used to mark the city for miles. Taking their place are technology centers hosting such companies as Uber, Google, and various driverless-car and robotic companies. The Pittsburgh sports teams occupy the latest and greatest facilities, comparable to any in the country, and at least one of the teams is usually a championship contender.

This is my city.

I was born in 1941, in the earlier, smoky version of Pittsburgh. In the same week of my birth, six months *before* the Japanese attack on Pearl Harbor, my dad was called up by the Army as a part of America's first peacetime conscription. Immediately after the attack on Pearl Harbor, President Franklin D. Roosevelt declared war on Japan, and Chancellor Adolph Hitler declared war on the United States. For America, it was the beginning of WWII.

My earliest memory is riding a troop train with my mother south to Jackson, Mississippi, where my father was in basic combat training. Ultimately, his first duty station would be with the Corps of Engineers in Anchorage; he would spend most of the rest of the war in the Aleutian Islands. A busy two-year-old, I dragged a large wooden toy train up and down the aisle of the train while all the soldiers patted me on the head and chatted up my attractive mother; at 5'7", blonde, and thin as a rail, she was a double for Lauren Bacall. Each time I returned to my seat, there was a crowd of soldiers talking to Mom. I was happy with all the attention but had no idea why.

During part of the war, I traveled around with my mother visiting friends and relatives. I was told later that I spent many a night sleeping in whatever sufficiently large dresser drawer happened to be handy. I suppose it was the same story for many of us whose fathers joined the service at the war's outset.

As the war was ending, Mom and I joined Dad in St. Louis, which was hotter than hell, while he completed a final Corps assignment. Neither parent ever said much about their war experiences, but on a couple of occasions my father made clear his dislike of the Japanese and Germans for his having to spend four years away from the family, a sentiment he certainly shared with many other WWII vets. My sister Molly was born in late 1945 and my brother Kevin in 1948. It was a big age gap between me and them when we were children, but one that closed as we grew older and closer.

When I compare notes with other sons and daughters of WWII soldiers, I find that many of us experienced similar scenarios. Dad and three or four of his neighborhood friends, who also had served, would meet up and have more than a few martinis. One of dad's friends had been a Marine company commander on Iwo Jima, another an infantry officer in Europe. Together, in someone's living room or den or in someone's garage, they would simply "get together."

Sometimes I was "around" to hear their conversations. They never seemed to talk about their war experiences, which was what I wanted to hear about, but just about everything else. Later I chalked it up to making up for lost time, never truly understanding.

My dad was a special man, and I hold him up as my greatest hero. When he entered the room, he took it over with his quick sense of humor that set everyone at ease. It didn't hurt that he was good looking and had an easy, graceful manner, or that he could make the best martini.

He walked gracefully and dressed elegantly, whether in khakis and boots, or a suit and tie always with a gold, knotted tie pin and an overflowing jacket handkerchief. He had a marvelous sense of humor, full smile, and occasionally a fierce temper. Friends and neighbors in Pittsburgh always told me what a wonderful guy he was, and how important he was to them. I wanted to be like him and tried mightily to emulate his ways, but never seemed, until later, to be able to put my finger on just what they were.

My childhood during the 1940s and 1950s was probably like that of many of my contemporaries in that most of us, including my younger sister and brother, had enormous freedom to do what we wanted and to go where we pleased. My parents were "very social"—again, perhaps making up for lost time—and I seldom spent time with them alone either during the week or on the weekend. Their friends were at our house, or our parents were at theirs, while we children played. There was only one rule in our house: Be home for dinner, which was usually at 7, and that was when the five of us caught up with each other.

Our three-story house was on Wightman Street in Squirrel Hill, a middle-class community bounded by a conservative Jewish community on one side and Shadyside, a walkable neighborhood surrounding a variety of shops, on the other. Saturdays were spent at the Manor Theater watching seventeen cartoons and a double feature, or at Forbes Field watching baseball played by the likes of Ralph Kiner and Stan Musial. At other times, I visited the Carnegie Museum or roamed on foot or bike around Pittsburgh's East End nooks and crannies, such as Panther Hollow.

What often slowed me down, and my first significant challenge, was a multitude of allergies and the consequent asthma that was exacerbated by living in a house where my parents and their friends smoked incessantly, and in the Steel City where the sun was blotted by mill smoke and office workers changed their shirts midday because of the soot around the collar.

Although I reported to an allergist every couple of weeks for ten or twenty shots in my back to reduce my sensitivity to just about everything, the asthma sometimes became unbearable. When I struggled for breath, my parents would put me in their double bed and call Dr. Ray Vilsak to stop by the house to give me a shot and pyrobenzamine pills, as my high fever brought on hallucinations. Once, I scraped off wallpaper thinking it was on fire, while another time I dreamed of ducking rolling boulders. The fever sometimes led to a hospital stay.

I have a bittersweet memory from one stay at West Penn Hospital, which is now a part of The Allegheny Health Network. It was evening, and Dad had come up to my room with an Army flashlight as a present for me. He said he was going to go downstairs to get something to eat and be right back. I turned out the lights to test the flashlight and promptly fell asleep, and so missed his return. To this day I feel bad, not so much about having fallen asleep and perhaps disappointing him, but more about having lost a rare opportunity to spend time alone with him.

PITTSBURGH 1947–1957, SCHOOL YEARS

More than anything else, I think of my childhood as that of a curious vagabond. As I started to outgrow my asthma, I began to walk all over my Squirrel Hill neighborhood with a friend or two. We'd inevitably assume the roles of soldiers, baseball players, hunters, or explorers. I often visited my cousin Roger Flannery in Fox Chapel, a suburb of Pittsburgh. His house was on thirteen acres and had a pond and a creek. Once we took our BB guns and brought my Aunt Sara a couple of birds—putting them in glass milk bottles before presenting them to her. We couldn't figure out why the birds didn't stand up straight like those in the Carnegie Museum.

Roger and I started first grade at Mount Mercy, which is now the site of Carlow University in the west end of the Oakland neighborhood. My fifth birthday had been in May, Roger's in June, and for some reason we were able to start in September. But it was not to last.

In December, we were told that because of our ages we would have to restart first grade the following September. For the rest of the winter and throughout the spring, I watched the bus go by our house each morning with mixed five-year-old emotions. On the one hand, I missed my new friends; on the other, I didn't understand why we would have to go back and do what we just did!

The next September, I restarted my education at St. Paul's grade school on Craig Street in the heart of Oakland. There, I met a lifelong friend, Jim Morris, whose zany and super-intelligent outlook on life hasn't changed one bit over the years. Today, he is the Dean Emeritus of Computer Science at Carnegie Mellon University, and we still fool around—on the tennis court.

I remember very little of my six years at Catholic school. I was taught how to hold a pen in penmanship, Sunday mass was a requirement, and all boys were expected to try out as altar boys. Alas, I failed the Latin memorization part of the altar boy exam and so was relegated to the choir. I do recall seeing some sort of report card, so if the nuns gave me grades, which they probably did, they must have been just enough to send me on to the next level. I don't recall any discussions with my parents about my performance. What I do remember was catching the streetcar up Fifth Avenue to my grandmother's apartment to drain her penny jar to help our grade win the bishop's charity drive. I don't remember if we did.

Outside the classroom, I wasn't always looking for trouble, but oftentimes it found me, like when a piece of sharp slate creased my head during a rock fight. I went home a bloody mess that certainly scared my mother, but she didn't say anything and just washed me off.

Mom wasn't one to worry, which was fine with me. I bashed my knee roller-skating, and she told me I was a hypochondriac. An x-ray years later showed a faint fracture of my kneecap. On another occasion I fell on icy steps and broke my arm. Mom said, "You'll get over it," before my grandfather insisted on taking me to the hospital, where I got a half-steel cast just in time to show it off at Christmas Mass.

My mother was a voracious reader and Sunday crossword puzzle aficionado, as was her best friend, whom we called Aunt Jane. Aunt Jane lived outside Pittsburgh in a small municipality called Sewickley and we visited her often, spending the weekend in her house that had an attached log cabin. Spending time at Aunt Jane's always reignited my asthma, but that was never a good enough reason not to visit.

When our parents traveled, my brother, sister, and I would stay with Aunt Jane. If my asthma got bad, she would put me in the guestroom and then find a book for me. She would often sleep in the other twin bed in the room. Thanks to her, I remember reading, among other things, the *Hardy Boys Adventure* series. But on one occasion, she gave me Jules Verne's *20,000 Leagues Under the Sea*. To this day, I view it as my first adventure into technology. With that book, I became fascinated with submarines. I have been ever since.

After Jules Verne, I began to read more seriously. Though I wasn't captivated by my studies at school, I made up for it by reading on my own. My

Grandfather Henry Yates gave me Sandburg's voluminous Lincoln biography, after which I read General Robert E. Lee's biography. Occasionally, my mother helped me with my reading and multiplication tables, but she and my father didn't seem concerned about what must have been less-than-average grades, at least no more than I.

When not exploring, I hung out in my third-floor bedroom down the hall from my chemistry lab table built for me by one of the managers in my uncle's department store display fabrication shop. I wasn't so successful experimenting with chemicals but managed to string wire to my two neighbors' houses so we could practice Morse code.

In the middle of the sixth grade, my parents transferred me to Shady Side Academy Junior School, a private boys' school in the East End of Pittsburgh, about a twenty-minute bike ride from home. It was a gutsy move for my father; upon learning of his decision, the bishop wrote him a letter that implied that he would go to hell for doing it. My Episcopal mother was not concerned.

I didn't feel one way or the other about the move, but quickly realized I was more than half a grade behind the other boys at my new school. Admittedly, transferring mid-grade is tough for anybody, but transferring from an urban Catholic school to a private boys' school exacerbated the situation. I also found that playing on the concrete playground at St. Paul's had been poor training for making a splash on the soccer and baseball fields at Shady Side. Rather than try to catch up and focus on my studies or athletics, I continued to do everything else, including get into trouble. Big trouble.

One day, several of my friends and I "found" dynamite caps at a construction site on the other side of our block. They were three-inch-long copper cylinders with wires that were used to ignite dynamite to break up old concrete foundations, which were then carted away to make room for new home construction. I hung these cylinders between our house and the house next door and ignited them with my train transformer. The explosion pitted the windows of both houses. Someone rightly concerned called the police. Eventually, the police arrived and relieved me of my stash. I don't remember my parents' reaction, but I doubt they were pleased.

As far as I was concerned, my relationship with my parents was much like every other kid's relationship with their parents. My mother and father each made clear to my sister, brother, and me that the other parent came ahead of us, and children are better seen than heard. As noted, we were free to roam so long as we were home for dinner. With such latitude we often had some explaining to do, but we could always rely on Idoza to bail us out. Idoza was the family maid and the only black person I was to know until an assignment in Greenville, Pennsylvania, in the '60s. It is hard to imagine today, but in the early '50s middle America, many children were largely unaware of race issues, although my sister recalls conversations with Dad about the inequality between our neighborhood and Idoza's.

Early in the summer between sixth and seventh grade, I was at Camp Kiski in Saltsburg, Pennsylvania, when one of the counselors approached and said, "You and Skip need to pack up quickly because there will be a car soon to take you home."

Skip and I were friends, but "Skip" was also my nickname, so I wondered if there had been a mistake. The look on the counselor's face, however, told me to get moving. Skip and I had known each other for many years; Skip's father, Seward, had been my parents' best man. His family lived on the other side of our block.

The car that picked us up dropped me off first. Meeting me at the door, Dad explained, "Seward and Skip's older brother are quite sick, so you and Skip need to be home in case whatever it is spreads."

Within hours Seward had died, and Skip's older brother wound up in a device to support his breathing, something known to everybody then as an iron lung. It was polio.

Though I had no symptoms, I tested positive and in short order I was quarantined. This meant I was required to stay home, although no one else in the family was. A poster was attached to our front door explaining that no one was to enter. After watching me grow more and more wan as the quarantine continued, Dad, who had been a swimmer at Carnegie Tech, built a small lap pool in the backyard to keep me occupied and to build up my endurance. He made me practice several hours a day whether he was there or not. I would rather have done anything else, but it did jumpstart my Virginia Tech swimming career.

After my quarantine ended, neighbors and friends stopped by the pool on weekends and Dad bought a slot machine to pay for pool supplies. My job was to clean the pool and service the dime machine.

DR. JONAS SALK

At the time I was quarantined, America was being held hostage by a polio outbreak, but help was on the horizon. My Shady Side class became an early recipient of Dr. Jonas Salk's vaccine, getting injections directly from Dr. Salk, who worked at the University of Pittsburgh developing the vaccine that would later bear his name. On the day we were to receive the vaccinations, we lined up in the gym carrying his *Time* magazine photo for an autograph; we knew he must have done something important!

After receiving the vaccination, I was taken by my Grandfather Yates on a trip to his and my mother's hometown, Springfield, Illinois. He was an insurance executive and drove a fancy gray 1949 Cadillac. My grandmother had died ten years before I was born and he had not remarried so, contrary to my life at home, I had his full attention as his first grandchild, and we became very close.

Midway through our trip, we stopped at a clinic to have my blood drawn per Dr. Salk's prescription and mailed the sample back to his lab in a paper tube, presumably to make sure my blood chemistry was in order and that I was immune.

The doctor and I would meet much later during my time in the Pennsylvania Legislature, when we were both speakers at a conference. After telling him that I had been one of the first recipients of the vaccine, he asked me what I had done to that point in my life. He later wrote me a kind note, of which all I have today is the signature. It seemed to me he was pleased to hear about the lives of us early recipients.

On the trip to Springfield, my grandfather showed me paintings of my great-great uncle, Richard Yates, who was the governor of Illinois during the Civil War (1860-1864), and his son Richard, also governor (1901-1905). This is my first memory of hearing about our family's Illinois history in politics and perhaps a stimulant for a later part of my future.

In addition to traveling to Illinois with Grandfather Yates, Mom, my brother, sister, and I spent a couple of summers with him in Castle Park, Michigan, while Dad stayed in Pittsburgh to work. I learned to ride there and care for horses and was a good enough jumper that my grandfather leased a horse,

Cricket, for me. Unfortunately, my sister was thrown by Cricket and suffered nine stitches, so that ended the lease and her riding career; however, this experience with horses would not be my last.

After seventh grade at the Junior School, our class transferred to the Shady Side Senior School for grades eight through twelve. The senior school was located outside Pittsburgh in Fox Chapel on a property next to my Flannery relatives. Most of the time I boarded at the school, staying in a dorm. Some weekends, I stayed with my aunt and uncle. My father, the disciplinarian of my two parents, had begun a new job managing a coal strip-mining operation in Kentucky and was absent much of the time. It's likely my parents thought my proximity to the classroom might improve my lackadaisical study habits.

Overall, my senior school grades continued below average—except for Mr. Cavalier's English class, where he encouraged us to diagram sentences and read Shakespeare and Walter Scott's *Ivanhoe*, all of which I liked. Yet I struggled with many of the other subjects, and my teachers seemed to be saying to me and my parents that I was lazy and not performing according to my abilities. I flat-out failed French, and in view of my get-by performance in everything but English, I would likely have to repeat ninth grade.

I was spending most time in the classrooms daydreaming about the weekends. After class, soccer was the only athletic option and I thoroughly disliked running up and down the field in heavy shoes with wood cleats.

The only sport I was good at was skiing. As a young teen, I learned to ski with my neighborhood friend whose family had a house at Seven Springs, a ski resort established by the Dupre family about an hour from Pittsburgh. Herman Dupre, later elected to the Skiing Hall of Fame for developing the artificial snowblower, was our instructor on the rope tow and T-bar well before there was a chairlift. When it was cold enough, we used to pour buckets of water down the lift lines to see how fast we could go on the ice.

While living in a Shady Side dorm, I became friends with Bede Foster and together we wasted late-night study time playing bridge with other like-minded students. At one point Bede introduced me to his sister, Polly, whom I later took to the ninth-grade prom.

In December 1956, I went to Stowe, Vermont, skiing with the Fosters. Skiing in the East was exciting in those days because the skis were wood, and the edges were screwed-on metal strips, and so we spent the evenings gluing and screwing the edges back on after they had been sheared off by rocks peeking out from the ever-present New England ice.

When not working on the skis we watched Warren Miller's stunning skiing films. All in all, watching the films and practicing in suboptimal conditions was a great way to learn, and perhaps why I eventually became a ski instructor. From skiing, I learned two very important lessons I applied throughout my life: If you want to be super good at something, learn to teach it; second, people will generally do well what they most like to do.

In 1957, before I turned sixteen, Bede drove us to New York City. I had $5 ($60 today) from my father but hadn't told him where we were going. We arrived in New York in time to have a late-night drink at Eddie Condon's jazz bar and turn around and drive back. We did have our picture taken while we were in New York, and looking at it now, I wonder how I had been served alcohol; I didn't look a day over ten! When later I told my father where we'd been, I reminded him he had gone to the 1933 Chicago World's Fair to chase my mother using $5 ($115 today) my grandmother gave him to get groceries. We were even!

Later that year, Bede and I thought his father's car would perform better if we added a heavily advertised mile-booster mechanism to the carburetor. With several hours labor we got the carburetor apart but couldn't put it back together. Mr. Foster wasn't impressed and had to engage a local mechanic to come and put it back together. I learned that being disciplined by a friend's father was even worse than the same treatment at home.

My extracurricular activities didn't help my grades and my studies continued to suffer.

MIDDLESBORO, KENTUCKY 1956–1959, FIRST JOBS & HIGH SCHOOL

My father, who was supervising a coal mine in Middlesboro, Kentucky, had become friends there with a local doctor who had a small stable of racehorses. When Dad mentioned my Michigan riding experience, the doctor suggested I spend the summer as his stable boy and exercise jockey, an idea that appealed to me. I believe Dad and I both saw the opportunity for me to have a work experience and make some money while spending more time with him.

Middlesboro, Kentucky, a town of about ten thousand people north of Knoxville, Tennessee, and a mile from Cumberland Gap, is home to the oldest-known continuously played American golf course. This was largely because the Scottish-born and Canadian-raised engineer, entrepreneur, and golfer, Alexander Arthur, established the town in 1888, naming it after the English industrial city of Middlesbrough, known then for steel production and ship building.

The Kentucky location evidenced substantial coal deposits and adequate, but low-quality, iron-ore deposits, perhaps because it was located within an enormous meteorite crater easily seen today from the air. Arthur's expectation was that the town would become the Pittsburgh of the South and would include, besides steel mills, running water, electricity, a large sporting common, and electric trams.

That never happened. Middlesboro (the name was Americanized by the post office in 1890) never came close to approximating Pittsburgh. A huge industrial fire downtown in 1890 and the Wall Street panic of 1893 made raising capital all but impossible and ended what little iron production had begun.

By the time I got there, sixty-five-years later, the summer of 1956, the town hadn't really grown beyond where it was at the death of Mr. Arthur's dream. Aside from the golf course, the coal industry became the city's main attraction. Most of the few businesses, including the United Mineworkers' Hospital, supported mining in one way or another. Notably, like much of Kentucky at the time, the Baptist-majority town was dry.

The town also hadn't really changed much since its inception and seemed disconnected from events of the time. It was even said that some people in the hollows still spoke a version of Old English. The biggest attraction in the '50s was the 1959 visit of Vice President Richard Nixon for the inauguration of the nearby Cumberland Gap National Historical Park. The doctor I was to work for ran a local hospital, where I was given a room, which was good, as Dad was in a hotel when he was there. Dr. Stelio Imprescia had gone to medical school in Louisville and worked as a general surgeon in New York City while studying lung diseases. At some point, he began serving as a pathologist and documenting black lung disease at various Appalachian Mine Workers' hospitals.

With a love of horses, he decided to move to Middlesboro, where he could help afflicted miners and raise horses. He had taken over a rundown four-story commercial building, with a rickety elevator and kitchen, near the center of town and converted it to a small hospital. He also bought a farm on the edge of town next to the airport and built horse stalls in the barn, and added a half-mile track and railing.

My daily responsibilities included running a brief morning workout session with one of the feisty thoroughbreds: Count Morris, Commemoration, Morning Melody, or Doc Will. The afternoons were spent on fence maintenance, feeding the horses, and cleaning the stalls. Once the chores were done, I returned to my room in the hospital.

I was excited to go to Middlesboro for several reasons. First, my brother, sister, and mother would remain in Pittsburgh, so I was hopeful about having more time with my father and, second, I was to be paid $25 ($275 today) a week, which in those days was a tidy sum for a fifteen-year-old. As for the work itself, I was only slightly worried about what would be my first encounter with true thoroughbred horses, but I figured I could handle that; ignorance is bliss!

The hospital was a couple of blocks from Dad's hotel at the center of town. I suppose my father thought the experience would settle me down and improve my attitude toward school, and I figured he planned to give me a little closer oversight. I kept a diary and noted that occasionally he and I would have dinner together, but I never saw as much of him as I would have liked and chalked it up to his long days at the mine. At fifteen, I wanted to talk to him about everything, especially mundane work issues like the fistfights I mostly lost with the older jockeys who resented my summer job horning in on their life's work. Dad was usually very busy with his own responsibilities, so I was pretty much on my own, learning from the experiences as best I could.

My room in the hospital had a bed and a bathtub, though there was no shower. Like the rest of the building, the floors were linoleum and the walls had peeling paint and windows with no shades (above street level). Because the hospital was understaffed, there were times I filled in as the doctor's nurse, helping to deliver babies or helping out in the operating room passing instruments for surgeries like cesarean sections or appendectomies in what were barely sterile conditions.

One of my hospital assignments was swatting flies and adjusting the air conditioners, turning them off when we used ether, which was volatile. On one occasion, a woman who had had a spinal tap (a local anesthetic) didn't believe the surgery was finished. The doctor showed her the appendix, and she promptly had an epileptic fit and knocked surgical instruments everywhere. The doctor raced out of the operating room and chewed out the husband for not telling him the woman was epileptic, and I wondered whether the husband even knew what that was. At the time, I didn't realize what an education this was for a fifteen-year-old, but it never convinced me to go into medicine.

Work was not always about horses and fights with the other jockeys. During down time, I loved talking with the stable boy about his experiences in the Korean War. My work in the hospital was interesting and it was fun to sit at the dinner table and kibitz with the nurses, who treated me like a younger brother. I didn't see much of Dr. Imprescia, who was always too busy at the track or hospital for small talk. Some evenings I was able to get away to a movie, read, or just walk around town by myself. There was a television in the hospital and occasionally the doctor and I played catch; I think it was his way to blow off steam.

On one occasion, the local paper came out to the barn to take pictures. Unfortunately, I wasn't in my riding gear, and the doctor handed me my helmet and told me to jump up before he lost the opportunity to show off his horses, so there I was in a front-page article riding Commemoration in my loafers and button-down shirt. At least I was wearing the helmet.

With my free time, generous earnings, and a burgeoning interest in airplanes (the 1950s being the advent of the "jet age"), I went to the Middlesboro Airport next to the exercise track and took flying lessons from instructor Jack Colson in a high-wing Piper J-3 Cub, which had two seats, one behind the other. There was seldom other airport traffic, so we had abundant airspace to practice figure-8s, rolls, stalls, and spins. Once I forgot to fasten my seatbelt and rattled around like a pinball. I got my student license at age fifteen, when my track riding weight was 116 pounds. I couldn't drive a car, but I could fly a plane … and a horse. I always thought riding horses gave me a good sense of balance, which I was able to apply in skiing and flying, both of which I enjoyed immensely.

At the end of that summer in Kentucky, I returned to Pittsburgh for my second trip through Shady Side's ninth grade and first-year French. But by the

My first job: exercise jockey. Embarrassed when the *Middlesboro Daily News* wouldn't give me time to put on my boots.

end of that school year, with no improvement in my grades, my parents were called in. They told me the headmaster suggested that "Skip might do better in another school." The core of the headmaster's decision was that Shady Side required competency in a foreign language, and I just didn't seem to have that ability in my supposedly limited toolkit—something we later learned was not true.

Dad, and presumably Mom, decided the family would move to Middlesboro and I would spend the summer of 1957 working in the coalmine. When the family house sold my mother, brother, and sister would move to Kentucky and the three children would continue school there.

In June, I flew to Knoxville alone and Dad picked me up at the airport, which was about an hour from Middlesboro. I had just turned sixteen and bravely asked if I could bum a cigarette. He didn't voice any objection, so I took that as a sign that I was being accorded adult status.

Again, I had hoped to be able to spend more time with Dad, but because of his frequent trips to Pittsburgh, we lived together like two ships passing in the night in the new house he had bought for the family's arrival after the Pittsburgh house sold.

I had just received my driver's license, so Dad drove a company car and gave me his 1949 black Mercury convertible; the family also had a Ford station wagon in Pittsburgh. At the mine, I was assigned a job by the foreman, just like any other new hire. I was to work as a dynamite specialist (not related to my previous experience on Wightman Street). The job involved moving a drilling machine and its accompanying drill bits along the side of an exposed coal seam, drilling a thirty-foot-long horizontal hole every forty feet on top of the seam, packing it with dynamite and a wire, sand, and dirt, and then attaching the wire between the holes to a transformer and, from some distance away, ducking and igniting it. It sounds dangerous, but it really wasn't, and looking back I realize that my father wouldn't have allowed me to work a dangerous job.

One time, carrying two fifty-pound augur bits on my shoulders and wading through a pool of muddy water runoff, I fell under the water into a ten-foot-deep pit, named a "coalhole." The hole had been made to measure the depth and direction of the coal seam. Luckily, the steam shovel operator saw me go in and blew the whistle, something only done in an emergency. But before anyone could locate the hole in the middle of the runoff, I walked up and out of the sloped side of the hole, still carrying the bits, to a crowd, including my father. From that point on, I became known among the miners as "Coal-hole Kelly."

Working for my father was less of a "situation" than I had thought it would be. Dad had high behavioral standards that I suspect stemmed from his strong Catholic mother. Even in his forties, he knelt every night by the side of his bed to say his evening prayers and I don't recall our missing Sunday Mass. His was an example I feel I have done my best to follow. No, I don't kneel for prayers before bed, and I don't go to mass every Sunday, but I do try to treat people as he would have.

When we worked in proximity in the mine, sometimes within eyesight, I watched him navigate with ease the diverse group of men under his care. Honoring the fact that most of the men had been working in the mines for a long time and knew their jobs, he saw it as his role to find ways within specific guardrails to make their jobs easier. Step outside those guardrails, like be late for your shift, and you knew you were in trouble. But do your job, and he would give you great latitude to succeed. Eventually, I began to realize that that was the way he treated me, my sister, and my brother. If we behaved well individually and with each other (and showed up for dinner on time), he left us alone. He was not one to express what today are called warm fuzzies, nor were there frequent mid-course corrections, but we always somehow knew where we stood.

Eventually the miners began to make positive, fulsome comments like those made by our Pittsburgh neighbors. With each man, he established a personal connection. With each man, he urged him forward to greater success. Even today, I can picture him telling the miners they could accomplish anything. Believing in your team—and sharing that confidence—is a great and effective style of leadership and it's something I have tried to replicate at each step in my career.

The most meaningful lessons he taught me (through my observations of him) were that a leader must be able to communicate well with people at the top and at the bottom—*and choose to do so.* A leader must be a good listener and give people their full attention. To this day, I have tried to incorporate these things into my daily life. Doing so shows that I value the other person and it's a powerful *and effective* way to lead.

As fall approached, and my family permanently relocated from Pittsburgh to Middlesboro after the sale of our house, I entered the Middlesboro public high school. Much to my surprise, when I presented my transcript, the principal decided I would skip the tenth grade and enter the eleventh with about 120 other students my age, many of whom were not much interested in or destined for college. The last piece of good news was that I only had to take a semester or two of Basic Spanish to graduate (foreign languages just weren't very popular in Appalachia).

During the summer after work and on the weekends, I palled around with brothers David and Penn Nicholson, and Geoff Mitchell. Penn and Geoff were top students in the class ahead of me; David would become my best friend in our class. All three would eventually go on to become lawyers. Geoff would become my company's chief counsel.

Throughout my childhood and into high school, I had been an indifferent student and at my worst when it came to French, but all that was about to change.

Eleventh grade was the game changer for me. As we started the year, Penn and Geoff invited me to be a part of the high school debate club. I agreed to go simply because these were two smart friends inviting me to join them in something challenging that they assured me I could handle. It also was something I had never tried and knew nothing about—I was always up for a challenge and for something new. Outside late-night bridge games, being invited by fellow students to participate in any school activity had never happened at Shady Side.

There were only a few students present when Miss Gladys DeMarcus, our English teacher and coach of the Debate Club, teamed us up, gave us a topic, and assigned us a side. We had a few minutes to prepare before speaking. I don't recall the topic, but I do recall standing up, looking only at my notes, trembling, inserting "ah" between every other word, and pressing my back against the blackboard imprinting a perfect copy of what was there on my dark sweater.

As I scrambled back to my seat, Miss DeMarcus looked over her glasses and simply said, "You did very well, but you can do better."

It was the first time I received a message like that…and believed it! I suppose it was her intuition, but she was telling me that yes, I could compete in something that required some intelligence, and she was helping by expressing confidence in me to do it.

To that point, all I had heard from my teachers at Shady Side, apart from my English teacher, was that I was a poor student and needed to work harder. I had never, never received any encouragement. I just assumed I was not as bright as the others. It turns out that although I studied as hard as many of the other students, I didn't do so with the proper focus. For me, studying more than enough-to-get-by had become a waste of time. With the debate team, all that changed.

From that first Debate Club meeting until I graduated, Miss DeMarcus worked with me and the Debate Club on diction, posture, eye contact, vocabulary, structure, and strategy. We learned to listen to our opponents instead of revising our presentations while they were speaking. She worked with me not only during our time in debate, but also during English class, where time was devoted to public speaking, to making radio announcements, and to our lengthy reading list that included Lincoln's speeches and Chaucer in Middle English.

I fully engaged in the debate society and prepared especially hard for statewide competition achieving success, but not quite the championship won by Penn and Geoff the previous year. We once debated the question "Should the United States adopt the English system of education?" The knowledge I gained of the English system would pay off later as I counseled my son on the complex British exam system before his English high school graduation.

I had finally found my own identity through something I could do well: public speaking. I thoroughly enjoyed it and the intellectual competition as well and observed again that people enjoy doing something they do well.

Based on my Shady Side French experience, I knew I had difficulty memorizing anything longer than a sentence, but thanks to my newfound confidence I earned lead parts in the junior and senior plays. I became an officer of the National Thespian Society and was elected to the National Forensic League, where the requirement was to be in the top third of your class. I even got a top grade in Spanish! All in all, it was a 180° turnaround from Shady Side, and I began to think of myself as a more capable person in all respects and managed to get sufficient grades to apply for college.

Some might gauge Middlesboro to have been a lower bar than Shady Side, and that would be true. But the fact remains that in that environment, after having worked a summer in the mine, I began to see life differently and to exercise my abilities encouraged by my teachers and fellow students, to whom I am especially indebted.

Penn and Jeff went on to win the state debate championship, which was celebrated with a town parade, and my partner and I made the finals the following year. I thoroughly enjoyed the experience and continued with debate in college.

As for Miss DeMarcus, she was elected, among other honors, to the Kentucky High School Speech League Hall of Fame. She was an outstanding English teacher and coach who challenged me to overhaul my limited view of school while shaping my performance at the podium. Years later, as I was driving from Houston to Washington to join the Reagan Administration, I stopped by Middlesboro and Miss DeMarcus' house to thank her for all that she had done for me. I think she was genuinely pleased.

Southeast Kentucky, as I knew it in the '50s, was more Southern than Northern and consequently subscribed to the racial policy of "separate but equal," which I knew nothing about. Coming from all-white Pittsburgh Catholic and private schools, I was oblivious to the fact there were no black students in Middlesboro High. Nor had I realized they were being educated in a separate but supposedly equal facility on the other side of town. Not until my 50th reunion did this situation become clear to me.

Outside the school, in the center of town, I do remember seeing two water fountains with the words "Whites Only" and "Colored Only" and thinking that those must have been left over from the Civil War.

Kentucky, though known for bourbon, is today a patchwork of wet and dry counties. In the '50s Middlesboro's Bell County and the surrounding counties were dry as dust, so with my '49 Mercury convertible and later my family's '56 Ford station wagon, I and others would drive to Tazwell, Tennessee, for moonshine, and to Big Stone Gap, Virginia, for bourbon both for our parents and our friends. We sometimes had delusions of ourselves as the real-life moonshine runner played by Robert Mitchum in *Thunder Road*.

In the real world, one night I was at the local drive-in movie with my girlfriend and as we were leaving it appeared as if lightning were streaking across the sky behind the screen. What it turned out to be was a car careening end over end, the headlights striking the low clouds. When we drove past the scene, we found the ground littered with bourbon half-pints, which had flown from the trunk as the car flipped end over end. I didn't hang around to "help" pick up the bourbon bottles, but later learned the deceased driver was a Kentucky State Trooper running bourbon who was being pursued down Pinnacle Mountain by other troopers and couldn't hold the curve past the drive-in's exit.

One of my friends in the class ahead of me loved fishing and had been making impressive rods that he sold to other fishermen in town. I gave him some help winding the eyes on the rods and got the idea we could sell them beyond Middlesboro. Dad gave me a bus ticket and I took some samples to a large upstate sporting goods store. Although the manager liked the handmade samples, I think both of us realized there was no way my friend and I could meet market demand from his basement, and neither my friend nor I had any idea of how to ramp up production without a small army of winders who were just not available. So my first "let's build something" entrepreneurial venture never took off.

Middlesboro is in the very southeastern tip of Kentucky, not far from "Bloody" Harlan, Kentucky, just to the north in the heart of Appalachia. Because of the friction among various groups of miners, employed and unemployed, and various families like the well-known Hatfields and McCoys, life there was never a bed of roses. Although my father didn't sanction it, I sometimes carried his WWII Colt .45 in the car and on one occasion stuck it under the nose of one nasty miner. He approached me and Geoff Mitchell in the Mercury convertible and was about to smack me with a coal shovel because he somehow thought I was after his perfectly ugly girlfriend. It was a situation my parents never heard about.

The Mercury unfortunately met its death while Geoff and I were heading for a Kentucky/Tennessee football game in Knoxville. The overdrive unit, a fourth gear in a casing attached to the back of the transmission, common in those days, had a design flaw that frequently caused the main transmission to fail, and it did at the busiest intersection outside the stadium.

Although I carried a spare transmission and an engine jack, the amused policeman was not about to let two high schoolers repair the car during game traffic; he called a tow truck. When we found the car after the game, the tow company had phoned my father requesting he Western Union them $67 ($710 in today's dollars; no credit cards in those days). Dad told them to sell it and keep the change. At that time, most people didn't keep cars for more than three or four years, and that one, at nine, was well past its prime. We hitch-hiked home and at one point had to jump over a guardrail to avoid a speeding car and wound up in a ditch covered in mud. My father greeted us with a drawing he made of the Mercury with the transmission hanging out and dollars flying away above it that I still have on my wall.

During my senior year, Dad's business partner died unexpectedly. When the man's wife insisted on cashing out company assets, Dad decided to give up the mining business and make plans for our return to Pittsburgh. While he was traveling back and forth from Pittsburgh, I was busy thinking about college. Not until much later did I realize how difficult giving up on the mine must have been for him.

That spring, my last year of high school, I applied to Virginia Tech (which was called VPI then), following in the footsteps of an influential friend in a class above me. I was accepted to the engineering school on the basis that I complete some additional math credits, which I did at nearby Lincoln Memorial University (LMU) over the summer. Virginia Tech is one of the United States' six senior military colleges and provided a military experience like that of the service academies. At that time, 1959, it required enrollment in its Corps of Cadets. Although my father had been successful as an officer in the military during wartime, I had the impression he considered it no more than "doing his duty" and was surprised that I wanted to attend a military college in peacetime.

Why Virginia Tech? My college search and application from Middlesboro was very different from what it might have been today or even then at Shady Side in Pittsburgh. There was no such thing as a guidance counsellor, so of 114 in my class only a few applied to and went to college; most of these went to nearby schools in Kentucky or Tennessee. Like the others, I applied to the University of Kentucky and the University of Tennessee but, from the beginning, I was most interested in Virginia Tech because it had strong credentials in aeronautical engineering and an Air Force ROTC (Reserve Officer Training

Corps). We still had the draft in those days, and my thought was that if it came to my "doing my duty" I wanted to do it as an officer like my father.

I also wanted to fly. Based on my Middlesboro flying experiences, I was interested in anything having to do with airplanes and thought seriously about the possibility of flying in the Air Force. In deference to my father and grandfather, both of whom were engineers, I was applying to the engineering school. In truth, I didn't understand the difference between flying planes and engineering them, and time would show I had different interests.

VA TECH 1959–1963, THE CORPS, DAD'S DEATH, AND A FRATERNITY

We moved back to Osborne (Sewickley) near Pittsburgh in August 1959, and I made plans to head for Virginia Tech in Southwestern Virginia in early September. One day, Dad interrupted my packing. My first thought was *Uh-oh, here comes a lecture.* Instead, he sat down and gave me a four-hour college-level poker lesson. Later in the month, my parents drove me to Blacksburg, Virginia, in what was then about a twelve-hour drive, without interstate highways, twice the time it would have been from Middlesboro.

Virginia Tech today has around thirty thousand students and Blacksburg a population of forty-four thousand; then it was about seven thousand students in a town of seven thousand locals—quite a change!

My room was in Shanks Dorm in "S" Squadron on the upper quad. Although Virginia Tech today has a 1,200-member volunteer corps of cadets, when I arrived in 1959, membership in it and ROTC was required for all but veterans during freshman and sophomore years. (First-year cadets were called rats.) The Corps then probably numbered about 1,600. As I found my room and started to unpack, the squadron executive officer began the "rat" treatment, and I was aggressively told to brace (come to attention). My father, an Army Reserve major, came in the door at that instant and said, "He's mine 'til I leave, then he's yours!"

As one of roughly thirty freshmen, at the bottom of a cadet Air Force squadron for nine long months, I got an extra dose of discipline in everything from cleaning my room to eating, studying, or walking on campus. Importantly, I learned to do everything as a member of a team, including competing with other similar teams. The essentiality of teamwork was a mantra I adopted

Photo by my mother. I'm second from left during my sophomore year in the Va Tech Corps of Cadets.

then and held throughout my career, treating colleagues and staff as fellow team members. I always saw it as my job not only to do my assignment, but also to help my teammates do theirs.

There was a stringent honor code in the Corps: *I will not lie, cheat or steal, nor tolerate those who do.* I once served as an honor court juror on a case where the student was found guilty and drummed out in the middle of the night. The code was not new to me; my father delivered that message long before I got to Virginia Tech. Had I not been truthful during my grade school dynamite caper, my backside would still be sore.

As far as I was concerned, both in school and later in my career, honesty was the *only* policy. For my rigid beliefs, I was sometimes called "straight-arrow" by my squadron mates and fraternity brothers.

Virginia Tech's Latin motto, *Ut Prosim*—"That I May Serve"—was not lost on me. It left my friends and me with a clear sense that we were being prepared to serve a larger purpose. For some, it would be in Vietnam, for me it is the rest of this story.

~~~

I began to realize Dad wasn't feeling well during the trip driving to Blacksburg, but I didn't really know what was wrong. I saw him next at Thanksgiving when he picked me up in his new company Volkswagen at a turnpike exchange where friends had dropped me on their way past Pittsburgh. During the ride home he talked about my eleven-year-old brother, Kevin, who wasn't doing well in school and was constantly getting into one kind of trouble or another. Dad expressed concern for Kevin's future. While he did not ask me to do anything, he seemed to take pains to make sure I was aware of his feelings. I parked that conversation only to visit it five months later, when Dad died.

The next month, over Christmas vacation, Dad had surgery, which revealed he had lung cancer that was later determined to have started in his pancreas. Although he expressed hope for the development of a cure, that was 1959 and doctors were clear there was no hope. After he came home, I remember sitting outside his room while he was sleeping, shining my cadet shoes, and smoking a cigarette with no thought that smoking had likely contributed to his illness or that it was bad for me. He and my mother insisted I return to school even though Mom admitted to me she was in for one hell of
~~~

a bad time, telling me, "I have no idea how I will get along without him." I tried, but couldn't talk them into letting me stay.

He died in April. As fate would have it, it was the same squadron executive officer who came to my room at about 4 that morning. I was sleeping with my M1 rifle to work off demerits and as the two of us came clattering out of the upper bunk, the exec said, "At ease, you have privileges," which basically meant that for the moment I had the same privileges as an upper-class cadet. Any "rat" would give his eye teeth to hear those words any time day or night, except me: I knew they meant my father had died.

In the morning, I stood formation as best I could and marched to and from the mess hall. I didn't take privileges because I didn't want to have to explain things to the upperclassmen. After breakfast, I went to the campus airport. Blacksburg is in the middle of nowhere and the nearest commercial airport was in Roanoke, an hour away, so my uncle and godfather, Rogers Flannery, sent a small twin-engine plane for me. Grandfather Yates met me at the Pittsburgh Airport.

The viewing was at Indian Hill, the Flannery residence in Fox Chapel, where I stayed during the funeral. I spent most of both nights sitting next to the casket watching for a sign of life, something I obviously knew was not going to happen. Three of my grandparents were still alive and the fourth I had never known; this was my first encounter with death, and at such close range.

In Catholic grade school, the Sisters of Mercy had taken us to say goodbye to one of their departed, but it hadn't meant much to us six-year-olds. At eighteen, as a college freshman, sitting by my father's casket, I alternately experienced denial and acceptance while trying to focus on how my mother, brother, and sister must have felt being with him those last few days. I also knew that although Dad preferred to let me make my own choices, I would now return to my freshman year without his living example, my North Star. I would also have to begin to figure out, without his counsel, where I was headed, and what I could do to help my mother.

I suppose it was to show some fortitude that I wore my cadet uniform through the funeral at St. Paul's Cathedral; I may not even have had a suit. Walking out of the cathedral by myself, Kevin and Molly were on either side of Mom, I remembered my Thanksgiving conversation with Dad about Kevin and concluded he must have had a premonition of what he was in for.

A day or so after the funeral, I flew to Roanoke and got a lift to Blacksburg and Virginia Tech. As I sat and watched the rain during the Allegheny Airlines flight, I wondered what my own life trajectory would bring, but mostly I just thought about my father and how short his life had been and how little time we had had with him.

I enjoy reading biographies. Recently, I have read powerful stories about Andrew Carnegie, and by Ambassador Samantha Power, and TV anchor Megyn Kelly, all of whom lost their fathers at an early age. In those stories, the writer looked to understand what it was about their father's death that most influenced or impacted their lives. In my own life, it was my father's early death (he was forty-five and I was eighteen) that undoubtedly most influenced my life. Though it was a change I could barely understand, what resonated over and over was that now I was entirely on my own, and that time is short.

Dad's life and early death impacted me in many ways, but two of those ways stand out. First was his confidence in relating to others, which was based on an empathetic way of listening to other people's points of view before offering his own. His was never the direct approach; rather, he would ask, "Have you tried looking at it this way?" This was a leadership trait I spent a lifetime trying to emulate. It later occurred to me that nearly all the people I enjoyed working for and with also utilized such an approach. It fosters innovation and improvement without blighting criticism. Secondly, because he died so young, I never assumed my life would last any longer; as such, I have always been in a hurry!

Dad's commanding officer in Alaska during WWII in the Army Corps of Engineers, commenting on Dad's assignment as a twenty-nine-year-old chief of operations for construction projects (which supported a prospective attack on Japan), described him as a future flag officer (a general): "He has impressed everyone with his absolute confidence in his ability to accomplish results under the most trying circumstances. Loyalty, tact, personality and leadership are his outstanding qualifications."

These words were not lost on me.

My dad was my first role model. In counseling students at Virginia Tech, Thunderbird, and the University of Pittsburgh, I have been asked why my life took the turns it did. My response has been: "Given options, I chose bosses, mentors, and role models carefully. I observed them closely and followed their example. It is important to work with and for people with admirable qualities."

For me, those were people who had the same qualities I admired in my father, and they were people who cared about me as much as I cared about them, which may in the end have been the reason they gave me the responsibilities they did.

I suppose Dad's genuine respect for others speaks most tellingly of his profoundly good character. His deep respect for the men he encountered at his worksites and across the backyard fence and in his daily life impacted my life; it gave me the model I follow.

After my father's death and my return to Virginia Tech, part of me remained in Pittsburgh. My lack of focus and attention showed in my studies. My grades fell off the cliff, especially chemistry and differential equations; they fell so precipitously that semester that I thought I would be dismissed. Fortunately, one of my professors understood the situation and told me, "You take care of your head, and we'll worry about your grades." With the help of a sympathetic faculty, I made it through my freshman year.

Encouraged and motivated by the faculty, I reevaluated my coursework. At the beginning of my sophomore year, I changed the focus of my studies from Aeronautical Engineering to the more businesslike Industrial Engineering. In the following trimester, I changed it again to Public Administration (which is what I seemed to lean toward) in the business school. Although I had not up to that moment begun to think seriously about politics, I did see public administration as enabling employment options within two distinct worlds: business and government.

In the fall of 1960, during my sophomore year, Grandfather Yates was hospitalized. He suffered from rapid-onset dementia brought on by thirty-five years of type 2 diabetes and died shortly after I got home from school in December. I had always thought of us as being close—I decided I was his favorite, since I was five years ahead of my sister and seven ahead of my brother. As I was growing up, he often took me in my one and only coat and tie to Sunday brunch at the Pittsburgh Athletic Association (PAA), where he sat patiently through my enthused stories of friends and adventures. Now that I have grandchildren of my own, I've come to find that they may get bored with me, but never me with them.

On our trip to Springfield, years earlier, Grandfather Yates proudly introduced me to all his friends and relatives still living there. I met his brother, who looked just like him, and later found out from my mother that working in construction he had suffered a head injury at an early age and was never able to work again; my grandfather supported him and his wife much of his life.

After his death, my mother and I accompanied his casket on a train from Pittsburgh via Chicago to Springfield, Illinois, where he was buried next to my grandmother, who had died in 1930 and not far from President Lincoln. She and I stayed up all night talking. I often thought about what my mother must have been going through during this period, having lost her husband and her father in the same year. There were many tearful evenings that Christmas.

Mom developed a relationship the following year with Erwin Schuette, who owned a farmhouse and kennel named Season Hill, in Sewickley Hills Borough, and they were married during my junior year. My roommate and I came for the wedding. I recognize that many children have issues with a parent who remarries, or with the partner of that parent, but my brother, sister, and I took the event in stride with a sense that this would be good for Mom.

Erwin, quiet and softspoken, dressed in rumpled khakis and button-down shirts, without an ounce of flair, was nothing like my father, so for that reason I was surprised at the marriage. At the time, I assumed my mother just wanted to get away from the extrovert life she had had with my father and lead a more sedate life. Erwin made that happen and I think they were very happy together. They had met in the "dog world," perhaps as far back as when she was showing my childhood friend Mimi a standard poodle, so they had known each other for some time and had a common interest in dogs. After the wedding, they revamped the farmhouse and added a pool. It became home for my brother and sister and an address and storage space for me.

Virginia Tech in those days was about twelve hours from Pittsburgh by car, so I didn't get to Season Hill very often. But with help from Mom, I did buy a two-seat 1959 MG and, before my senior year, a 1956 Ford Thunderbird. Both cars served me well in college, as trips to Virginia's women's colleges were regular outings.

My first two years at Virginia Tech, I was in the Corps of Cadets. However, since I didn't have the 20/20 eyesight to pass the Air Force flight physical, tough in the days before Vietnam, I opted out of the Corps knowing that those two years would position me well for Officer Candidate School were I ever to go into the service. My last two years of school I focused on a fraternity.

Sigma Omega Tau, later the national fraternity Lambda Chi Alpha, got a fair amount of my attention. Toward the end of my sophomore year, I led the purchase of a fraternity house on Roanoke Street in Blacksburg and in my senior year was treasurer of the fraternity.

I was honored to be appointed to the Ring Committee, prestigious in the military schools, by the '63 class officers. I spent time with several other classmates helping design the class ring with prospective suppliers. In deference to tradition, we included the Confederate battle flag in the design, something that would not happen today. I was also active in the Debate Society and continued to hone my public-speaking skills.

I had scored well on the ROTC leadership exam at the end of my sophomore year. Because I was considering all options for life after college, I interviewed with the military my senior year. It was just before the Vietnam ramp-up, so the services weren't offering the sun, the moon, and the stars they did later. The Army thought I'd make a great artillery officer (I didn't agree), while the Air Force suggested the intelligence branch. The most interesting and interested was the Navy (more about that in a minute).

During the final term of my senior year, although my grades had improved year over year, I still didn't rank high enough in my class to snag interviews with the top companies. As such, I was invited to interview with only a small number of potential employers. As well, at the time, Virginia Tech was known for engineering (which I had transferred from); its business school (from which I would graduate) didn't have the cachet it has today.

One afternoon, looking at the announcement board (no internet then), I saw a notice promoting the American Institute for Foreign Trade (AIFT), also known as Thunderbird, and affiliated with the American Management Association, that offered a one-year Bachelor's degree in Foreign Trade at a cost I thought I could afford.

Thunderbird? Reading the announcement, two thoughts struck me. First, I knew that if I were to have a meaningful career, I was going to have to differentiate myself from other business school graduates. At Thunderbird, I reasoned, I could develop a skill in international business, unusual in those days, and master it. I figured if I did well, I would stand out, and meaningful job opportunities would follow. Second, having done well in history, I had always wanted to see the places I read about, especially Europe; I wanted my life to be about more than Pittsburgh, Middlesboro, and Blacksburg.

I applied and was accepted. Going to Thunderbird was a big step, especially since I would be expected to become fluent in a foreign language by graduation. On my application, I selected, of all things, French.

PHOENIX, ARIZONA 1963–1964, THUNDERBIRD GRADUATE SCHOOL

When I was there, and until recently, Thunderbird was located on a former airbase in Glendale, Arizona, well outside Phoenix, in the middle of nowhere. Today, Glendale is a major Phoenix suburb. Then, the Phoenix population was 668,000; today it is 4.5 million.

The Glendale airbase was envisioned by several Hollywood notables in 1939 as a collaborative project to train WWII pilots. Its early 1941 construction was backed by such stars as Jimmy Stewart, Cary Grant, and Henry Fonda, who foresaw America's entry in the war. Between 1941 and 1945, ten thousand pilots from thirty nations were trained at the field, and in 1942 the popular movie *Thunder Birds* was filmed there. After the war, the field was acquired from the government for one dollar by former Air Force Lt. General Barton Kyle Yount on the promise it would be used for educational purposes.

As the former three-star head of the Army Air Force Training Command, General Yount then created the American Institute for Foreign Trade, opened in October 1946, for the purpose of training American business executives to serve successfully overseas. Today it is known as the Thunderbird School of Global Management and is housed in a new five-story facility in Downtown Phoenix as part of Arizona State University (ASU).

Having selected French over Spanish, and since one of the graduation requirements was fluency, I figured two years of failed French at Shady Side would serve me better than one semester of Middlesboro High School Spanish. The other choices to be made were a geographical focus, and a business major. I chose European Area Studies over Central and South America studies, and Marketing rather than Finance. Other languages, regions, and disciplines were not yet a part of the curriculum.

As it turned out, I ranked at the top of my French class because it was taught by the "Monterey" method, which is without books, but through incessantly memorizing recorded dialogue. It turned out that I learned languages with my ears, not my eyes.

Early in the term, Marketing-major students were required to take a class in advertising in which we acted as a team pitching a media campaign. Because of my presentation skills learned in Debate, I was designated as the account executive, and we pitched GE executives the idea of selling American-sized refrigerators in the UK, where customers traditionally bought smaller ones. We won the competition, and I was invited to San Francisco for an interview with J. Walter Thompson, then one of the largest media advertising companies.

Phoenix had a relatively small airport with an equally small bar. As I settled into a seat, the fellow next to me announced that he was going to break the record, posted behind the bar, of four martinis before takeoff. I think he drank six and, in the process, gave me two. I could barely see getting on the plane and shortly after takeoff he came from first class with a bottle of champagne looking for his friend Kelly. I never forgot him, the president of a national printers' union.

When I arrived, I went to the hotel in San Francisco, flopped on the bed, and slept in my clothes. The next day I had eight interviews; I passed seven successfully, but in the last, I was asked by the top executive to explain man's relationship to his fellow man and God. I gave it little thought and gave the immature answer, "You're kidding," and immediately failed out!

Later in the year, as Thunderbird students were in the job-interview process, I gave a talk based on my debate experience to some of my fellow students on how to be an effective public speaker. Sam Johnson, at Thunderbird to interview students, was in the back of the room and asked if I would be interested in interviewing with his company, Chicago Bridge & Iron, Inc. (known then and today as CB&I or just Chicago Bridge). Sam had come up through the construction side of the business and, as we spoke, he reminded me of my Grandfather Kelly.

At that time, I had an interview scheduled with Cummins Engine Company in Columbus, Indiana, suggested by my classmate and good friend Richard Aguirre, so I agreed to stop in Chicago on the way back to Phoenix. In Indiana, I got caught in the rain and high water on the road, so when I arrived in Chicago, I looked like what the cat dragged in.

Despite that, and shortly thereafter, CB&I made me an offer I was pleased and excited to accept. Though I had been bartending and selling clothes while at Thunderbird, this was my first real job. My starting salary was approximately what my father was making on his last job four years before. Frankly, I didn't know what to make of that but was pleased that it put me in his league.

Why Chicago Bridge? First, these were contractors like my father and grandfather, and I easily understood their language. Second, they had major steel-fabrication and erection projects around the world and assured me I would be assigned overseas after a brief training program (we all wanted to be quick to go overseas). And third, this was a company where my one-year-plus of engineering studies at Virginia Tech would serve me well.

Parenthetically, I had had discussions with a Navy recruiter in Blacksburg while at Virginia Tech. I considered the Navy a viable option after graduation and was accepted to Newport, Rhode Island, Officer Candidate School (OCS) but, having always been fascinated by airplanes and submarines, boldly asked for a guarantee of submarine service.

In an interview visit to Newport, Virginia, an admiral advised me that submarine school at the time, and with few exceptions, was reserved for Naval Academy engineering graduates. Furthermore, it would be hard to guarantee an assignment before OCS graduation. He said he thought highly of Thunderbird and would let me know while I was there in the event of potential submarine openings.

As it turned out, a naval officer came to Thunderbird as I was packing out after graduation to let me know I had been provisionally accepted for submarine service, assuming I did well at Newport. I apologized and explained that I had already accepted a position in the private sector (my dermatologists have since told me I should have chosen submarines).

I have sometimes wondered how my life would have turned out had I pursued a career in the Navy, perhaps even the Submarine Service. Years later, an Air Force general told me that though my eyes were not quite 20/20 when I tested during Virginia Tech ROTC, had I applied for Air Force flight status during the height of the Vietnam War, I would have "been strapped into the first available plane and sent to Vietnam."

President John F. Kennedy was assassinated while I was at Thunderbird; I remember my friend Richard Aguirre (who had introduced me to Cummins and whom I would later see in South Africa) pulling over in his car to tell me the news of the president's death, as I was walking from class.

I was in shock! At the Virginia Tech fraternity house, I had often observed Kennedy's televised press conferences admiring his wit and charm. I was particularly struck by his oft-repeated inaugural call to action: "Ask not what your country can do for you—ask what you can do for your country."

After spending those long days watching the assassination events unfold on network TV, I vowed that someday I would most certainly find a way to do what I could for our country in either the military, the government, or politics.

Years later, when I was in the Reagan Administration, I attended an oil-industry symposium in Houston, where I sat on the speaker's dais next to former Texas Governor John Connally, who had been in the car with President Kennedy that fateful Friday, November 22, 1963. I couldn't help but look at his hand knowing that a bullet had shattered his wrist that day.

My father had been an Eisenhower supporter, and most likely a Nixon supporter, but I admired Kennedy, his wit, and his grasp of issues. That fateful weekend at Thunderbird I began to think that somehow, some day, I would enter politics.

GREENVILLE, PA, DETROIT AND CHICAGO 1964–1965, CB&I TRAINEE

Following my graduation from Thunderbird in June 1964, Chicago Bridge assigned me to the Greenville, Pennsylvania, facility south of Erie. CB&I fabricated steel there for water towers, large oil-storage tanks, nuclear containment vessels, and submarine hulls. My task in the engineering department was to learn the codes and principles governing the erection of oil-storage tanks and water towers. During my Greenville assignment, I was assigned to work in the field, New Jersey, on a water tower, the kind that looks like a golf ball on a tee. I enjoyed the week with one of the best teams erecting the steel shell 125 feet to the top and found that work in the field was far more engaging than work in the engineering department, something that would play to my benefit a year or so later.

In another field assignment, I and a fellow trainee were tasked to observe an oil-storage-tank project in Louisiana. My colleague's name was Olatunji, Tunji for short. He was from Nigeria and had graduated from Rensselaer Polytechnical University (RPI). He had one of those smiles that lit the whole room. In America, in the mid-'60s, civil rights demonstrators were seeking to end segregation, which was then prevalent throughout the South. Not all such demonstrations were peaceful and as we approached Louisiana, I began to see the usual one-finger salute confirming that people in other cars were not happy to see us. For safety's sake, I found a payphone and called the home office, which instructed us to turn around and head to another project, this time in Detroit.

To my surprise, the welcome we received in Detroit was not much better. It wasn't until I asked Tunji to stay in the car that I was able to get a room in a motel near our worksite. As I was checking us in, the manager invited us to have a drink in the bar, where he said they had booked a band. I asked if he minded that my colleague was black, and he assured me, "Absolutely not!"

That evening, I received word that my uncle and godfather in Pittsburgh, Rogers Flannery, had died suddenly, so I hastily made plans to fly there. He was fifty-one and seemingly in good health but, like so many others in those days, was a heavy smoker and probably didn't turn down too many martinis.

Coming so soon after my father's death, this was a shock to me and a huge blow to my cousin Roger who, just out of Yale, would become head of Flannery and Associates, a significant Pittsburgh company. Uncle Rogers was a model of success within our extended Irish families and his early death was a surprise to us all. For me it brought back all the emotions I had experienced a few years before on my father's death.

After several days of the funeral and aftermath, I returned to Detroit, to our project, and to the motel. Arriving late in the evening, I found a crowd in the bar. They had come to hear Tunji play the drums, something he had been doing each night I had been away, and word of his skill had spread.

The crowds overflowed, a fair dividend to the motel owner who had so graciously given us a room when others had not. Whether Tunji was or was not related to the famous Nigerian drummer and recording star Olatunji, I never knew. Years later, while in the Reagan Administration, I visited Lagos and was hosted by the Supreme Court chief justice, who arranged a brief phone call with Tunji, during which I learned that he was chief of his tribe in a distant region of the country.

My Grandmother Kelly died a short time after my uncle's death and as had occurred with my father and uncle, the funeral took place at the Flannery house on Indian Hill Road in Fox Chapel. My Aunt Sarah's experience was like my mother's, losing her husband and then, in her case, her mother shortly after. For me, it was another shock and a return trip to Pittsburgh. Grandmother Kelly had been over ninety, so we invoked more Irish humor than grief. Knowing she had liked golf in her youth, a group of us placed a putter in the casket.

Some of us, all cousins, were playing with a football on the front lawn when a limousine with Pittsburgh Mayor Joseph Barr and another individual came up the drive. They stepped out of the limo and asked us to throw them the ball. My Aunt Pat English later told me that the fellow with the mayor was Harry Stuhldreher, one of the legendary Notre Dame football Four Horsemen.

In early 1965, I was transferred by Chicago Bridge to their Chicago headquarters and assigned to the sales department. After a few very cold months there, I was dispatched to the London engineering department to prepare for a job in the European sales group.

II. TRAINEE TO MANAGER

LONDON 1965, A BRIEF STOP IN SALES

My flight to London departed from the modern JFK TWA terminal that today has become an upscale hotel. The plane was a four-engine Boeing 707, the international workhorse of the airline industry that would be replaced five years later by the much larger two-aisle, four-engine 747.

After my six months in Greenville, Pennsylvania, doing both engineering and field work, and a few months in Chicago as sales support, I was headed to Chicago Bridge and Iron's European headquarters in London. It was expected I would join the sales department after spending a few months in the engineering department familiarizing myself with our European projects.

I found an apartment in West London in Chiswick, not far from the Chiswick Park tube (underground) station; the office was about a half an hour's drive to the north. This was just short of twenty years after the end of WWII, so there were still open spaces between buildings and houses, evidence of what London had suffered during the WWII German bombing known as the Blitz.

This was my first international posting, and it was rare for people my age—I was twenty-four—so I began to think more highly of myself than I should have. I was also spending more time with my English colleagues than with my few fellow American employees. Neither action was appreciated by the modest American head of the engineering department, who let the managing director know I was "too big for my britches."

Because of my bad attitude, I was given the choice of returning to the States or accepting an assignment as a field engineer on a construction project in Francophone Gabon, West Africa. The field engineer, responsible for reviewing construction drawings and making sure of field measurements, was the lowest position on the trainee totem pole. To say I was humiliated would be an understatement. I took from the experience two important lessons. First, I began to internalize that I wasn't as smart as I thought I was, and second, I took closer notice of how people reacted to me.

Rather than return to the U.S. to a difficult-to-explain new job search, I got the point, vowed to do better, and accepted the Africa assignment. Before my departure, I received notice that I had to report for a physical for military service. In those days, American men were required to notify our draft board of address changes, so I had kept my Kentucky draft board up to date. They knew where to find me.

The notice required me to report to the nearest U.S. facility and that turned out to be the U.S. Air Force Ruislip Airbase, not far from London. During my interview at the base, it was noted that I had had shoulder surgery, that I had been in Air Force ROTC, and finally, that I spoke French. I was deemed not eligible for service, but I was asked to become an "operational contact" for the American intelligence community, during my international assignments, something I readily agreed to do (and continued to do during much of my international career). It was the first way I had found to honor Kennedy's words and "do something for my country."

Shortly after, and for reasons I'm not sure of, CB&I changed my assignment from Gabon to Algeria.

Algeria had become independent from France in 1962 after a horrific eight-year war of independence. With a population of 12.5 million in 1965 and approximately 45 million today, Algeria is the largest country by area on the African continent and stretches south from Mediterranean coastal towns through much of the Sahara Desert. By the time of my assignment in 1965, and because of the French discovery of high-quality oil, newly independent Algeria was seeking to join other global oil and gas producers. Chicago Bridge was contracted by the state-owned oil company Sonatrach to build oil storage tanks used to collect, store, and discharge production to nearby offshore ships.

ALGERIA 1965–1966, CB&I AND A LIFE-CHANGING SIX MONTHS

In late 1965, I flew from London to Paris, where I stayed overnight, before taking a twin-engine propeller Algerian military night flight to Oran, a large city on the Mediterranean in Northwestern Algeria. For some strange reason, the aircraft was filled with small caged birds and armed men, all of us seated on the floor of what appeared to be a cargo plane with a few seats. The armed men I could understand, but the birds?

Another group of armed men met me on the tarmac and escorted me to a hotel in town overseeing the Mers El Kabir port, where the WWII British Navy had destroyed the French Vichy Navy in 1940. The Vichy Navy had refused to change sides in the face of the impending North African invasion that would center on nearby Arzew, where I was to work.

I knew next to nothing about Algeria—other than its location—when I had received the assignment. I initially assumed that if the project foreman gave me clear instructions as to what to do, my brief field experience in the States would suffice. But such an attitude was shortsighted, and I quickly realized that it was for that arrogance that I was being booted out of London, so I did my homework before departure.

The history of Algeria and its war for independence is little known outside France and Algeria, but what happened there likely resulted in the election of Charles de Gaulle and in many ways dramatically changed France and her relations with the rest of the world. My encounters with Algeria from 1965 to 1988 were foundational to my international perspective and were threads through my engineering, management, and government experience.

Algeria initially came to the attention of the United States in the late seventeen- and early eighteen-hundreds, when its fleet of corsairs captured multiple American merchant ships along the Portuguese and Moroccan coasts and in the Western Mediterranean. Often the crews were held for ransom or sold into North African or Middle Eastern slavery.

Lacking any protection from the English or French navies, who were engaged in a war of their own, presidents Washington, Adams, Jefferson, and Madison built and deployed frigates that included the *Constitution*, known as "Old Ironsides." The desire was not only to protect American ships, but also to destroy the Algerian Corsairs. The action resulted in the First and Second Barbary wars against Tunis, Tripoli, and Algiers. (The conflict was also known as the U.S. Algerian War.) Ultimately, the Treaty of Algiers was signed in 1815, which granted the United States unfettered, full shipping rights in the Mediterranean Sea.

The Treaty of Algiers did not, however, resolve the situation for the European powers who were no longer at war with each other. Ultimately, after various provocations, France grew tired of the game and in 1830 invaded Algeria. This action by the French initiated its colonization of North Africa, which would ultimately include the countries of Morocco and Tunisia. Throughout the remainder of the century, France expended significant military resources taming the indigenous Algerian population, while more than fifty thousand French citizens, and those of other European descent, settled there. These settlers became known, for unclear reasons, as Pieds Noirs (Black Feet).

By the time of the First World War, a variety of Europeans constituted one-fifth of the Algerian population and they, along with Algeria's indigenous people, participated in both world wars, the indigenous people often suffering severe casualties because of poor training and frequent assignment to the front lines as, some people would claim, cannon fodder. In fact, an elite Algerian Battalion continued to fight alongside the French in Vietnam and was overrun at the 1954 fall of Dien Bien Phu. The loss of the garrison at Dien Bien Phu marked not only the end of the French in Vietnam, but also the beginning of the end of the French in Algeria. By that time, the eleven million people in Algeria included 1.2 million Europeans, most of whom had been born in Algeria.

It was not lost on the indigenous Algerians, and perhaps even the Pieds Noirs, that if Vietnam could become independent from France, so could Algeria. First notice of this sentiment had been given at the end of WWII. On May 8, 1945, in the small town of Sétif with a gendarmerie of only twenty, eight thousand Muslims appeared with seditious banners and killed over a hundred Europeans, badly mutilating their corpses. This set the stage for repression and retribution, killing upwards of thirty thousand indigenous Algerians in the Sétif region and beginning a nine-year period of schizophrenic attempts by the French to repress dissent or encourage French nationalism, all for naught.

All Saints' Day, November 1, 1954, known as "Toussaint Rouge," brought seventy planned, violent, and bloody attacks across Algeria by members of the Algerian Liberation Front, and marked the beginning of the Algerian War of independence. Among the worst of the attacks, often referred to as the first shots of the war, were the machine gunning of a local official and the shooting of two young French national teachers after their bus had been stopped near Biskra, where I would undertake another assignment in 1977.

The war subsequently spawned a widely read textbook by Alistair Horne, *A Savage War of Peace, Algeria 1954-1962*, published in 1976. In the book, Horne details the various groups that took part in the war, including the National Liberation Front (FLN) and its various factions; the French Army and its opposition splinter group, the Secret Army Organization (OAS); the multiple para-military groups of European Pieds Noirs; and the indigenous groups loyal to France (Harkis, Bedouin, etc.).

Horne goes to great length to describe the brutality of the war's numerous instances of cold-blooded murder and mutilation perpetrated by all sides one against the others. Many people familiar with the "Battle of Algiers," which occurred from January to March 1957, have little idea that the war dragged on for five additional years, during which the use of plastique (small malleable explosives) became prevalent. Although the use of plastique created a memory of its own, it was really the barbarism, the cold-blooded killing of people in a crowd, the mutilation of corpses, and the use of torture by all sides that momentarily caught the attention of the world.

Historians like Horne agreed on two fundamental elements of torture in the Algerian War: Tortured individuals only gave information, mostly incorrect, they thought their captors expected them to give (little was truly current or useful); and the process scarred the people (and their superiors) doing the torturing as much as the individuals being tortured. This was a lesson about torture never understood later in Vietnam, Iraq, South Africa, Northern Ireland, or perhaps even by Russia in Ukraine today.

As late as March 2021, French President Emmanuel Macron apologized on behalf of France to the family of an Algerian lawyer who, during the war, had been thrown from a fourth-floor window to hide the scars of his death by torture. Previously the family had been told the individual jumped trying to escape.

France was attached to the Algerian territory for reasons beyond just the French and European population; she would test atomic weapons in the deep Sahara and discover petroleum in the interior. Furthermore, the French military, many based in Algeria, having lost Vietnam in 1954, were not about to lose Algeria. This attitude by the military created a conflict between the French civilian government, who had grown weary of war, and the military, keen to prevail. Ultimately, it was this internal conflict that brought down the government in France.

In 1958, as the Fourth Republic struggled, the National Assembly asked the one individual trusted by all sides, Charles de Gaulle, to become the provisional head of government and to rewrite the French Constitution, which he accomplished in short order. As a true politician, he agreed with all sides in the war and was elected president of the ensuing 5th Republic, ultimately setting the stage for negotiations and the signing of a peace agreement in 1962 at the town of Evian, near the Swiss border.

After the Evian Agreement, the choice for the Europeans became "the suitcase or the coffin"; all but a few took the suitcase and everything else they could carry with them. De Gaulle went on to withdraw from NATO as he focused on "restoring France."

The war had ended barely two years before I arrived, and there were still hard feelings between the Algerians and the few remaining French Pieds Noirs. Since I was obviously not Arab-Berber, many assumed I was French. I was quick to say I was American, as the Algerians had a high regard for Americans. President Kennedy was among the first to recognize the new country and had extended an invitation to visit the White House to the young country's first president, Ahmed Ben Bella.

At the time, so soon after the Algerian War, there were no Americans in Oran, not to mention nearby Arzew, site of the 1942 WWII invasion. My assignment was to work in Arzew as a field engineer for the construction of three 500,000-barrel crude-oil storage tanks (202' diameter x 56' high) for the Algerian National Oil Company, Sonatrach. They were described as "floating-roof tanks" because of a thin layer of steel on the oil surface supported at the edge by a ring of pontoons to reduce evaporation as the tank filled and emptied; every precious drop represented Algeria's primary source of foreign exchange and each full tank had the capacity at the time to fill one ship.

I rented an apartment in nearby Oran and learned that it had been owned by a prominent French official. While standing in the bedroom, he had been shot from another building. The bullet had penetrated him and passed through the closet, the wall, and the kitchen cupboard and left three-inch holes in each, physical evidence of what had transpired.

After settling in, I learned from our French administrative assistant that the project foreman was sick and would not arrive from Libya for a week or two. He eventually did arrive but was seldom well enough to stay at the jobsite, so I found myself as both field engineer and onsite project foreman. Fortunately, I was able to visit the foreman's apartment in Oran from time to time, where he reviewed my progress and gave me helpful guidance.

By pure career luck, I ended up running the project for most of its six-month life. I had ten expatriate employees, "expats" (from France, Greece, Egypt, Italy, and elsewhere), and approximately fifty Algerians, most of whom understood French. The job was a crash course in leadership and managing people; every day I learned how to see things from other peoples' diverse cultural points of view. It was my first leadership position.

Diversity is a subject touted today in most companies and studied at universities, but I didn't have the benefit of that training then. At age twenty-four, I learned on the fly how to work with a large mix of nationalities in a harsh environment. Fortunately, I had learned important project functions, including welding, during my brief assignments in the States, and was able to lead by example, such as welding the interior of a steel pontoon, where the temperature usually exceeded 130°F, to show how it could be done safely.

In need of an assistant, called a pusher in those days, I got permission from the company to hire from outside the firm, and sent a telex invitation to a Canadian friend whom I had met in a London pub. Patrick Bentley was my age and travelling through Europe taking on odd jobs. I suggested he contact our London office, get an Algerian visa, and come over and give me a hand. He did within a matter of days.

Patrick was able to smuggle a bottle of Scotch whiskey into Algeria that I later used for pain relief when I injured my foot. For six months, we basically had no medicine because what was sent to us by the company, purposely hidden in the welding machines, was stolen in port. We also didn't have sunscreen, if it even existed at the time, something I would regret later in life as the dermatologists worked me over. The biggest problem we expats had was constant dysentery.

With my boss in absentia, my first major task was to receive the project's steel, which had been imported from Italy, at the port. Because of a workers' strike, the ship was not able to offload most of the steel onto the pier. And since the ship was scheduled to sail soon after arriving, the ship's officer made the decision to dump our steel over the waterside of the boat…and leave.

My leadership baptism was to determine where in the waters of the harbor the steel had come to rest and arrange for it to be retrieved. I spoke with various port officials and learned that the water in the harbor was about twenty-five feet deep, and that there was a group of French divers in the port. I provided the divers with automatic clamps, more than a handful of money, and instructions to raise the steel onto the trucks we had hired. Using a port crane, they soon had the steel out of the water and on the trucks. Alas, we eventually found that the circumferential plates of the tank had been cut inches too short and we had to undertake some engineering wizardry before beginning construction. In hindsight, I suppose my first lesson of leadership had been learning the art of improvisation.

The divers I hired had initially come to Algeria to cut chevrons on the sea floor to hold the anchors of the tanker ships, which were there to transport the oil from the Arzew fields. From them, I learned how to dive and was able to observe the remains of a Roman city, which had slid into the sea along the Arzew coast; the archeological remains were littered with debris left over from the WWII invasion.

Our days were routine: I had a Land Rover truck and each morning Patrick and I would drive through Oran, pick up the expat crew, and drive them to the jobsite in Arzew, about half an hour away. Oran was one of the places that had been populated early on by Spanish Pieds Noirs, and the city and its architecture resembled a moderate-sized Spanish metropolis. Now, though, its population had been reduced from four hundred thousand European Pieds Noirs to three hundred thousand native Algerians.

Nearly all of Oran's Pieds Noirs who had emigrated from Algeria at the end of the war were determined to leave nothing behind. They stripped their apartments and houses of everything they could and destroyed what they couldn't: windows, mirrors, doors, elevators, wiring, switches, metal pipes, etc. The houses and apartments were then occupied by Arabs who had travelled in from the countryside and who seemed to have little interest in restoring them. In fact, it was not unusual to see cows and chickens peering from apartment window ledges, even on the upper floors of apartment buildings. Rolling gray smoke often belched forth from windows, presumably from wood cooking fires laid on tile floors or in kitchen sinks.

Patrick and I eventually rented a large house in Arzew and moved there with the other expats and lived dormitory style. There were no showers, only bathtubs, so we installed wall unit "instant" showers in the basement to wash off the sand and dust after work.

The house had a tennis court (without a net), but we were advised not to think about using it: The previous owner had been killed in the war and was buried somewhere under the court. Anyway, tennis was the last thing on our minds; most of our days, we worked twelve hours straight, from 6 A.M. to 6 P.M., then went home for dinner and bed.

While stationed in Algeria, I travelled a few times to the U.S. Embassy in Algiers to give my intelligence report and to inform them of what I was seeing. Four items were of interest to the embassy personnel: what the quality of the oil was; who my contacts were with Sonatrach personnel; who my contacts were within the Algerian government; and what were the names of my incidental contacts with those Russians straying from Algeria's Annaba Naval Base, along with where and when they docked.

I once met the designated Algerian Minister of Commerce, who was about my age and who had earned his senior position within the party by successfully chucking grenades at French Army vehicles. It was my first meeting with a foreign government official and I was immensely impressed by his title. Little did I know it would be the first of many such meetings over the years, with a multitude of foreign government officials, including a president of Algeria.

In June 1965, while I was in Arzew, then-President Ahmed Ben Bella was deposed and jailed in Algiers by his own FLN (National Liberation Front) regime, though he subsequently escaped. Although Oran and Arzew were relatively far from Algiers, our local officials apparently thought he might be in the area. One evening, as I was taking our elderly French cook home, the Land Rover was stopped and I was taken into custody, suspected of participating in Ben Bella's escape.

It didn't help that on that day I had decided to send our principal welder—who was losing his eyesight—home to Egypt for medical attention as soon as possible. At dinner, he decided he didn't want to go and jumped over the table with a knife to send *me* home. It took all ten expats, me, and Patrick to subdue him, but in the process, we were plastered with spaghetti sauce that looked like blood.

It was determined, after a night in a not-so-pleasant jail, that I had had nothing to do with Ben Bella's escape, but that did not free me from surveillance, and I would be taken into police custody on another charge not long after. Notified by a company telex of my cousin Sherry English's death in an Erie, Pennsylvania, auto accident, I had attempted to leave for the funeral and was being assisted by Air France at the Oran Airport. However, I did not have time to get the requisite exit visa. Once again, I was stopped and taken into custody. This time, I was released in short order when I told the police that, having missed the flight, I wouldn't be able to make the funeral anyway.

It was not until near the end of the project that I left Algeria for Paris among a group of Algerians given French residency for having fought for France in the revolution. Unfortunately, upon our completion of the project, most of us expatriates took home a good case of dysentery, some even required hospitalization upon their return, due to the food and lack of medicine during the six-month life of the project. There was little we could do to escape it; even the supposedly pasteurized beer brought it on, and the nearest jobsite john was a hole in the sand off to the side.

After a stop in Marseilles, I arrived in Paris with a few Algerian dinars and little more than my passport and the clothes on my back. My bank was the Pittsburgh National Bank (now PNC), which had an office at the Place de La Concorde. I went there by taxi to withdraw French francs to pay the taxi and buy a plane ticket for London, where I had kept my apartment. Unfortunately, that was easier said than done. In those days the cashier had to send a telex to my Sewickley branch and wait for a response.

The bank's international vice president, who was an American and who had just arrived in Paris from the States, fortunately walked into the branch at the Place de La Concorde, where I was standing. Seeing me, he stopped and asked where I was from. I told him Sewickley, Pennsylvania, and that my mother, Marnie Schuette, lived there. He said he had just left his dog at her kennel before departing. He then authorized my withdrawal request, and when he got home and picked up his dog, he told my mother I seriously needed a haircut.

True! In our "dormitory," we cut each other's hair, but not very often.

Arzew, Algeria, just before departure. Two of the three floating roof oil tanks in the background.

The Algerian assignment was my first real-life opportunity to lead with real-life consequences. As a young project engineer thrust into covering for the foreman, I improvised when necessary, which was often, and made lemonade from lemons. I grabbed opportunities when they presented themselves, and I led an exceptionally diverse team by listening to and respecting the cultures and languages all.

For me, Algeria was a lifechanging assignment. It was the first time I had been given responsibility for an arduous task under physically difficult circumstances. I had to re-engineer and build three large steel structures with the help of sixty people of various nationalities and languages in a desert environment with most of us suffering acute dysentery. It was a maturation process during which I grew ten years in six months. As difficult as it was, I am, to this day, thankful for it.

Though I was given little choice in accepting my Algerian assignment—it was that or go home—I soon began to see it for what it was: a fabulous opportunity. In the end, I came away with a greater sense of humility than I had before leaving London. It was my first effort at leadership; I practiced much of what I had read about or observed around my father: Treat everybody with respect, listen carefully, and lead by example.

LA CORUÑA, SPAIN 1967, CB&I AND BREAKFAST WITH A KING

After a brief respite in my London apartment, I was assigned to the Astano Shipyard between Pontedeume and La Coruña, cities in the northwest corner of Spain. My job was to manage the part of a shipbuilding project charged with specifying, allocating, and cutting aluminum-rolled plates for four Liquid Natural Gas (LNG) tanks, which were going to be placed in the interior of an innovative 750-foot ESSO LNG carrier.

This ship was one of four to be used in transporting LNG from Libya to Europe. The other three ships were under construction in Genoa, Italy, where I spent a few days observing their construction with Sam Johnson, the construction manager who had recruited me from Thunderbird. Although Sam didn't say so, he gave me the impression that my future was in project management and that I likely got the position in Spain because of the job I had done in Algeria. It now appeared, at least for the time being, that a sales career path was on the backburner.

Before I landed in La Coruña in 1967, I again knew very little about where I was going and did my host-country-history homework—something I highly recommend today for individuals tackling a foreign assignment. I knew of the Spanish Civil War, perhaps as awful as the Algerian Revolution, and that Francisco Franco had served as head of state for some time since.

Franco was a dictator who adopted many of the Fascist trappings of Hitler and Mussolini; however, contrary to them, his rise to power came via his successful military career. In 1926, at the age of thirty-three, he became the youngest general in the Spanish Army and two years later commanded the General Military Academy in Zaragoza, from where he had graduated.

As a conservative and a monarchist, Franco did not favor the end of the monarchy or the 1931 establishment of the Second Spanish Republic, although he served it as chief of army staff for a brief period. After a leftist government was elected in 1932, and Franco was assigned to the Canary Islands, he joined the 1936 military coup that sparked the Spanish Civil War. In the initial phase of the war, he served in Africa but ultimately became Generalissimo and head of state upon the death of the Nationalist leader Emilio Mola. He served in that position throughout the war and from its end in 1939 to his death in 1975.

Upon my arrival, I moved into a motel near Pontedeume for a short time, and then rented a quay-side apartment in nearby La Coruña, the northwestern summer home of the Spanish government. When Franco was on his boat in the water below my apartment, the building entrance was guarded by a well-uniformed member of the Guardia Civil wearing the traditional three-corner hat. The town hall and main square was close by, and on Sundays we witnessed military parades that, remarkably, resembled those of WWII Germany. No swastikas, but similar large flags, German-style uniforms and helmets, trumpets, and fascist salutes. I made friends with a young lieutenant who was later to play an important role in my life.

I had rented the apartment with a fellow engineer from France, and we rode together to the Pontedeume shipyard office. Eight young well-to-do graduate engineers from different parts of Spain were assigned to me, obviously a step apart from the expat workers I had managed in Algeria. As I only spoke English and French, I told the team it was their added duty to be sure I learned Castilian Spanish. We had roughly 1,200 Spanish workers on the project, so it was essential that I learn not only Castilian Spanish, but also some of the local dialogue, Gallego, a mixture of Spanish and Portuguese.

My responsibility required a disciplined organizational ability more than an Engineering degree. My role was to interpret the drawings of the four large aluminum tanks inside the ship and assign each engineer a section for which he would prescribe the dimensions and patterns to be used in the field, where a piece would be cut from a larger plate. Aside from giving exacting measurements, an important objective was to provide a layout that maximized the use of the expensive aluminum and minimized scrap. It was a tedious job that a modern computer could do in seconds, and the important part for me in managing it was to create an enjoyable atmosphere for my team that was doing some not-so-enjoyable work. I found the same tool my father had used in Alaska: personality! We got the job done as it should have been, and I think in the end the engineers enjoyed both the work and me.

I sometimes went hunting with the local laborers who had learned of my interest in shooting clay pigeons, something I had often done with my father and uncle in Pittsburgh. Somehow or another they found the plans for a mechanical clay pigeon thrower and managed to make one from spare aluminum. One day, while I was walking through the shipyard, something dark whizzed across my vision. It took a few seconds, but I realized it was a clay pigeon; the workers had made a thrower and came up with the clays, which became one of our pleasures on days off.

Spanish gun laws were such that I was required to register my shotgun with the local constabulary, though my Spanish hunting friends did not want to register theirs, for a variety of reasons. Many of the guns the men shot with were very old—over a hundred years! One, made of forged steel wire, had a hole in the side of the barrel. I stayed far away from him.

Pontedeume was about twenty miles from La Coruña and halfway to El Ferrol, Franco's hometown, where his sister still lived. It was sometimes referred to as El Ferrol del Caudillo, El Ferrol of the Leader, Franco's chosen title. I bought a Montesa motorcycle to get to work and sometimes saw Spanish soldiers along my route between the apartment and the Astano Shipyard, one stationed every couple of hundred yards. I learned they were there whenever Franco left his summer residence or boat in La Coruña to visit his sister.

Dinner in Spain was customarily quite late, around 10 or 11 P.M. And so, after work, people met up in the town and along the docks, often stopping for tapas. I often carried an American football as a conversation piece; most thought it was a rugby ball.

DON JUAN, THE EXILED KING OF SPAIN

One evening a gentleman standing alone on the deck of one of the sailboats asked me to throw it to him, which I did. He invited me aboard, offered me a drink, and we got into conversation. Chicago Bridge was one of the largest employers in the region, so he was interested in hearing all about my work and as a follow-up invited me to come back for breakfast. The next morning, as he fixed us a light breakfast, I asked him, "What do you do?" and he responded with a smile, "Well, I'm Don Juan, the exiled King of Spain!" (I later learned that his preferred title was Count of Barcelona.)

He explained that his deceased father had been the previous king and further that Franco permitted him to dock his boat in Spain so long as he did not leave it. My thought was that he probably met there with Franco who, years later, designated this man's son, Juan Carlos, his successor as the head of government and King of Spain. (Juan Carlos, too, would follow his father into exile [in Saudi Arabia], but for reasons of corruption. He left *his* son on the throne.) Meeting the former King of Spain was another of the more interesting experiences of my life.

My staff was as intensely interested in bullfighting as we are of American football today. One of them convinced me that the study of bullfighting was essential to the study of Spain itself, so I became interested in bullfighting. I learned the history and vocabulary of the bullring and watched matadors El Cordobés, in La Coruña, and Paco Camino and El Viti, in Madrid. In a café there, one of my engineers arranged for me to meet Dominguin, known for having been in the ring the day the great Manolete was killed. Dominguin was also the subject of Hemingway's book *The Dangerous Summer.*

III. ELECTIVE POLITICS

PITTSBURGH 1968, SEGUE TO POLITICS

I hadn't been in the States since my 1965 departure but was able to leave the Spanish ship project over Christmas 1967. I returned home with Jeanne Cooley, a young British woman whom I was dating at the time. We had met in the London CB&I office between my Algeria and Spain assignments, and she had subsequently taken a secretarial position with a member of the British House of Commons.

She visited me in Spain, and we vacationed in Portugal. As our relationship grew and we began to write each other about the future, I thought it would be a good idea for her to come to the States, meet my family, and see what life in America might be like.

In Algeria, I had no access to news of current events. I don't recall seeing a television and can remember only one radio in a bar where everybody hovered listening to 1966 World Cup soccer competition (England and the famous Charlton brothers won). A stray French newspaper came our way every so often, but didn't have much to say about the United States or Vietnam, from which the French had withdrawn in 1954. Staying up with international news in Spain wasn't any easier, even though the Spanish government summered in La Coruña. When we arrived in the States, I had little idea of either the depth of America's involvement in Vietnam or the volatile temperament of the country as it moved toward the upcoming 1968 U.S. presidential election. Learning of the foment in America was to cause me to sharply pivot within my professional life.

Our first stop was snowy Augusta, Maine, to visit my father's closest cousin, Fred O'Connell. Aside from wanting to introduce Jeanne to one of my favorite relatives, I had it in mind that his being the son of a Boston congressman (my

Grandmother Kelly's brother, Joseph O'Connell, the 10th Massachusetts Congressional District later represented by John F. Kennedy), and having run for the governorship of Maine, he could give me a contemporary view of U.S. events. I was loosely beginning to think about some form of government service, continuing the thought process begun in my public administration coursework in undergrad and at Thunderbird, following the death of President John Kennedy. These thoughts, however, would coalesce quickly after I became aware of the difficulties being faced by the country in the late 1960s.

Fred introduced me to his friend Chauncey Robbins, who had been the executive director of the Republican National Committee, a deputy assistant secretary of defense in the Eisenhower Administration, and the director of the Republican Congressional Campaign Committee. I peppered him with questions, and he briefed me on the politics of the day surrounding President Johnson and Vietnam. Because he had been intimately involved in recruiting people for Republican congressional campaigns, he suggested I give thought to coming back to work in a 1968 campaign. He promised to introduce me to some key players in Washington, and I promised him I would consider it. In fact, his words lit a fire.

Jeanne and I next went to Pittsburgh and stayed with my mom and stepfather in Sewickley. Mom had been invited to a Christmas party in the city near where we had lived on Wightman Street. Knowing of my protean interest in the political situation, Mom suggested Jeanne and I go with her and meet Elsie Hillman.

ELSIE HILLMAN, ALLEGHENY COUNTY REPUBLICAN PARTY CHAIR

Elsie Hillman was married to Henry Hillman, one of the wealthiest businessmen and philanthropists in America. Elsie was a philanthropist in her own right, and a civic leader and active proponent of civil and women's rights. Over time, she and Henry were to provide for the building of the University of Pittsburgh Hillman Library and the UPMC Hillman Cancer Canter, among their many other contributions to Pittsburgh.

When I met Elsie, she had just become head of the Republican Party of Allegheny County, the county that surrounds and includes Pittsburgh. Then, the population of the county was roughly 1.6 million, about four hundred thousand more than today due largely to the decline of the steel industry and the graying of the citizenry. Then as now, approximately 60% of the county's voters were registered as Democrats while 30% were registered as Republicans. The remainder were independents or members of splinter parties.

Previously, Elsie had been a volunteer for President Dwight Eisenhower and then active in Pennsylvania Governor William Scranton's 1962 successful gubernatorial candidacy and his halfhearted presidential run against Arizona U.S. Senator Barry Goldwater. Goldwater eventually lost to President Lyndon Johnson in 1964. Elsie was a "moderate Republican," more common then, and worked closely with Pittsburgh Tuskegee Airman Wendell Freeland in support not only of civil rights but also in the recruitment of black support for politicians like Pennsylvania U.S. Senator Hugh Scott of Philadelphia, Governor Scranton, and New York Governor Nelson Rockefeller.

Over the years, Elsie formed a close friendship with Senator Hugh Scott, and it was Scott who had been most influential in convincing her to become chairperson of the Allegheny County Republicans. In 1967, when she was elected chairperson, the county Republican Party apparatus had all but disappeared because of the Great Depression, Roosevelt's election victories, and the rise of labor unions in industrial Pittsburgh. Elsie's task was to rebuild the organization and recruit candidates, which she was doing with her usual high energy.

At the Christmas party, the first thing I noticed about Elsie was that she had an enormous smile coupled with a hearty laugh. We had met some time previously in Pittsburgh, so we were not total strangers. When I approached her that evening, she asked where I had been and then what I was doing in Spain. As we talked, I told her of my discussion with Chauncey Robbins and of my family's history in Illinois and Massachusetts politics and asked whether it might be a good time to think about becoming politically involved in Pittsburgh or Pennsylvania. She said something to the effect of "Why give up what you are doing in Spain?"

I told her that in view of what I was learning about the issues swirling around the upcoming 1968 elections and Vietnam, I felt I should perhaps consider returning home to find a way to participate and contribute. Looking back, I see it as a rather bold statement for a guy living in Spain with a good job. She responded that there were no guarantees, but *if* I did come back, I should consider working in a local Republican campaign and that she would be happy to support my efforts however she could. It would be a lifechanging and inviting response from someone I intuitively understood to mean what she said.

I talked all this over with Jeanne in London after we returned in January. A few days after that, I went on to Spain. On the one hand, my CB&I work was interesting, and it did pay well. Over the space of nearly four years, I felt I had gained humility and, with it, far greater self-confidence. I'd worked in three foreign countries while progressing from trainee to project executive and likely had a bright future ahead. On the other hand, serving my country in some way, somehow, had been a goal in the back of my mind since my years at Virginia Tech, and Kennedy's assassination while I was at Thunderbird. The possibility of entering government at the campaign level as described by Chauncey and suggested by Elsie seemed an exciting way in for me, a way I figured that might even lead to a meaningful staff position.

After several days back in Spain, thinking all this through, I concluded there would probably never be a better time, nor a better entrée. Furthermore, I was twenty-six at the time and realized that were I eventually able to secure a congressional staff position, it could lead to elective politics or at least expose me to more senior-level U.S. and international business executives. The more I thought it through, the more excited I got. It was certainly a risk, but the prospect of playing a role on our national stage was far more appealing than what I was doing in Spain!

I decided to give CB&I my resignation, leaving what most contemporaries considered the start of a budding career for an uncertain one; it was an important decision and one as consequential as the decision to go to Thunderbird. I resigned with the expectation that I would be better for it in the long run.

Things immediately got complicated. I learned from my Spanish Army friend who was passing through London that Jeanne had just been diagnosed with tuberculosis, having most likely contracted it during the earlier visit with me in Spain. I immediately flew to London to spend time with her at the hospital and with her family. While I was there, we decided to get married and return to the States together.

This was not a simple decision for Jeanne. Her family was conservative and had spent little time outside London, much less England. Oddly, her father, an insurance salesman, had served in Algeria in the Royal Air Force

(RAF) during WWII, so he had some understanding of where I had been and what I had gone through. But still, she was one of two daughters and would be moving to the United States which, in those days, was not an easy or inexpensive phone call away (calls were $55/three minutes, $570 today, and had to be scheduled). Furthermore, she would be giving up her job in Parliament and going with a husband who might be unemployed for some time.

The decision on my side for the two of us was almost as complex. I was giving up a good job and a promising career with CB&I, leaving the company and the project unexpectedly after they had heavily invested in me. I remember thinking that a future reference would probably be difficult. I had saved some money, but for two people it wouldn't last more than a few months, and congressional campaign staffers weren't known to receive hefty salaries. Finally, we would be returning to an unknown future in my country, which in 1968 was in turmoil over Vietnam and the upcoming presidential election. As many expat Americans will testify, returning to the States after an extended stay abroad is often more difficult than leaving.

Nevertheless, call it what you like, a shot in the dark or the road less taken, we both somehow saw it as the chance of a lifetime.

I packed out of Spain in February, and we were soon married in London and happily honeymooned in Majorca. After a short time in London with Jeanne's family, we flew to Pittsburgh in mid-March and stayed with my mother, hoping at some point to locate to Washington on the congressional or campaign staff of a Pennsylvania congressman.

My first call in Pittsburgh was to Elsie, now my political godmother, to let her know what we had done and ask for her help. I began making the rounds, meeting with Republican congressional staffs in Pittsburgh and then Washington, and I attended a Republican Campaign School in St. Louis suggested by Chauncey Robbins. Most of what I heard there was common sense, but all of us attending were young compared to the congressional speakers, and were energized by Michigan Congressman, later Senator, Don Riegle, who was only three years older than I. While we were there, President Johnson announced he would not seek reelection, an event we assumed would inure to the Republican Party's benefit, and therefore ours.

Jeanne and I then went to Washington together just in time to experience the riots that followed the assassination of Martin Luther King. Jeanne must certainly have wondered what she had gotten into. Because everything in Washington was shut down due to the riots, we decided to visit my former Canadian colleague from my days in Algeria, Patrick Bentley, so we drove my mother's car across the border to see him. On our return, we spent a few hours at the crossing sorting out an immigration issue related to Jeanne's history of tuberculosis, and then it was back to the job search.

WASHINGTON 1968–1970, WITH PA SENATOR RICHARD S. SCHWEIKER

It wasn't until years later that I was able to fully recognize how pivotal and difficult a year 1968 had been for the United States. The top of the list included the assassination of Martin Luther King (I had seen him speak in Chicago in 1965) and the ensuing riots, and the assassination of Robert Kennedy in California, two months later, as he campaigned for the presidency. Also tumultuous was the end of the Johnson Administration and the election of Nixon. The war in Vietnam, which saw shocking American losses during the Tet Offensive, reached its nadir and eventually became the source of Johnson's basement ratings and the violent riots at the Democrat Chicago Convention in August.

It was at some point in April of that year, while I was in Pittsburgh, that Elsie asked me to pick up the Pennsylvania Republican Senate candidate, Congressman Richard (Dick) Schweiker, at the Greater Pittsburgh Airport. Schweiker was coming from Eastern Pennsylvania and had no one on his staff on the ground in Western Pennsylvania to meet him. Elsie had suggested I might be a good addition to the campaign staff and offered my services to take him around. I didn't yet have a car, so I told a local dealer that if he'd loan me a used car, and things worked out with the congressman, I'd buy it.

CONGRESSMAN RICHARD S. SCHWEIKER

Schweiker was a four-term Congressman from Montgomery County (near Philadelphia). In 1968, he was running for the U.S. Senate against two-term Democratic incumbent Senator Joe Clark, the former reform mayor of Philadelphia. Although Clark was known to be cantankerous, he had been mayor of Philadelphia and in the Senate long enough to be well recognized across the state. His liberal record was solidly in line with the preferences of Pennsylvania's ubiquitous unions. He was an important member of the Senate Foreign Relations Committee and opposed the Vietnam War even though he had supported the 1964 Gulf of Tonkin resolution further extending American involvement.

Schweiker had served in the Navy in WWII before attending Slippery Rock University and graduating from Penn State in 1950. He entered the family business, American Olean Tile Company, where he became president. He ran for and won a seat in Congress in 1960, the same year as fellow Pennsylvania Republican congressman, future governor, and presidential candidate, Bill Scranton. Schweiker was best known in Philadelphia and in his Montgomery County-based district that covered conservative Philadelphia bedroom communities, and was thought of there as right of center and fiscally responsible. As a member of the Armed Services and Government Operations Committees, he had successfully sponsored legislation rewarding military personnel for cost-cutting ideas. However, because of his plan to end the Vietnam War and his support for the Civil Rights acts of 1964 and 1968, plus the creation of Medicare, he was sometimes considered a progressive. In other words, he was really a centrist.

Pennsylvania at that time was neither strong Republican nor strong Democrat. The two Senate seats were split, and the governorship was Republican. At the time I picked Schweiker up at the airport, Pennsylvania political pundits were betting on the Democrat top of the ticket to win, Hubert Humphrey and Joe Clark.

Most people interviewing for campaign positions at the time were just out of college, or were about to be, and there weren't many young executives in the hunt. The people who interviewed me, including Schweiker and his senior staff, recognized my experience and expressed surprise I had left my assignment in Spain. In the end, it was my Pittsburgh background and my connection with Elsie Hillman that got Schweiker's attention.

For my part, I was certainly more interested in participating in a statewide Senate campaign than in a congressional campaign. Furthermore, I was impressed that Schweiker, as a member of the House Armed Services Committee, had expressed support for what I thought were realistic ways to wind down the Vietnam War. In his congressional district, he was viewed as a conservative, but early opinions of his positions in the Senate race pegged him as a moderate. I liked the guy and his views and was convinced he could win.

Schweiker invited me to meet key members of the Washington staff: Administrative Assistant Dave Newhall, a young former Philadelphia newspaper editor; Dick Siegel, a legislative assistant and Harvard Law grad; and Steve Blakeslee, once an aide to former Governor Scranton, also an experienced legislative assistant.

Subsequently, Newhall contacted me and offered me the position of special assistant, with the responsibility of traveling with the congressman wherever he went—even to the extent of sharing hotel rooms with him to better filter visitors and phone calls. Newhall warned me that the position would not be a walk in the park; I was told outright that Schweiker was very demanding. My responsibilities were later detailed in a widely circulated *Philadelphia Magazine* article by Greg Walter:

"It is the red-headed Kelly who holds open car doors, lugs briefcases, supervises local campaign workers, makes the occasional drink on a private plane, handles travel plans and makes suggestions as to approaches.

"It is exhausting, often nerve-wracking, sometimes rewarding job that Kelly does with no little aplomb. The Schweiker day on the road can begin at 4 a.m., up in time to appear at the gate of some huge steel mill to shake the workers' hands. It can last far past midnight with fund-raising discussions in a Pittsburgh hotel room."

Not mentioned were my other responsibilities. Those were: to liaise with the Harrisburg campaign office and Washington congressional staff, dictate follow-up and thank-you notes, supervise the five advance men and, finally, do whatever the congressman directed.

Although the job would involve a great deal of travelling in the state, and the outcome of the election was obviously not certain, Jeanne and I leased an apartment in Springfield, Virginia, about half an hour from the Capitol. Jeanne quickly found a position with Congressman Sam Devine of Ohio, who appreciated her experience in the British Parliament.

On my way to what was to be my first trip with the congressman, fittingly to Pittsburgh, I got stuck behind a traffic accident, and missed the early morning flight. I was mortified. Lesson learned; it became the only flight I ever missed in my life!

Fortunately, I made another flight a few minutes later and was able to join the congressman in the first meeting of the day. The meeting was with Allegheny County Controller Bob Friend, the famous former Pirates pitcher. I recall staring at his hands, thinking those were the ones that pitched against the Yankees in the 1960 World Series won by Pittsburgh.

After that meeting, we were invited by Allegheny County District Attorney Robert Duggan to fly to Harrisburg with Republican financier Richard Mellon Scaife on his plane. At the time, Duggan was the top Republican in the county. Here's where it gets complicated: Acting as Duggan's campaign finance chairman, Scaife would eventually fall out with Duggan over questions pertaining to Duggan's undocumented campaign contributions. But during it all, Duggan married Scaife's sister, Cordelia.

Duggan allegedly committed suicide (there was dissent as to who pulled the trigger) to avoid prosecution under an indictment for undocumented sources of income and relations with criminal elements. The charges were brought by the IRS and U.S. Attorney Dick Thornburgh. Thornburgh would later become a Pennsylvania governor and a United States attorney general.

Dick Schweiker was a good man, a good politician, and a good boss. Perhaps because of his strict German Schwenkfelder sect upbringing, he did not, however, generate what today we call "warm fuzzies"—he was all family and politics, in that order. If anything interfered with family plans, it didn't happen. It was always frustrating for staff when he nixed major events, including White House dinners, because he and his wife Claire had planned something else.

Initially, he and I spent time discussing his position on issues: I learned where he stood and incorporated his positions into my work for him. He was smart and straightforward; you always knew where you stood. And he didn't tolerate fools.

As a wet-behind-the-ears, lowest-guy-on-the-professional-ladder, I loved the campaign. It seemed a natural for me, though some of the roles I had to play, especially in the beginning, make me laugh even today. One of my responsibilities was the requirement that I carry the congressman's hat whenever we were outside and there was the possibility of a breeze—or, worse, if we were on an airport tarmac near a potential airplane prop wash. The congressman had a most unusual way of arranging his hair (they call them combovers today), and if he got caught in the wind my job was to quickly come up with the hat before the hairdo required a redo; he didn't want people thinking he was wearing a toupee!

Once, it was suggested by campaign chairman Drew Lewis (more about him in a minute), Schweiker's best friend, that when Schweiker next visited his favorite tailor, I pick a couple of suits that didn't "glow in the dark" like his others. When he received the suits, I nearly got fired, but Drew stepped in and saved me.

Because of the size of Pennsylvania, we leased a campaign plane with two engines and two pilots that seated six people. Dick's wife, Claire, was a strong presence in the campaign and on the plane when she traveled with us. Prior to leaving the Philadelphia area for Washington, she was Miss Claire on her well-known TV program *Romper Room*, sharing an office with Dick Clark of *American Bandstand* fame. When she traveled with us, she and the congressman sat across from each other and usually I sat next to her, so in rough weather I did the hand-holding.

Much of our work was done on that plane as we moved between airports, but flying also gave us time to relax, often with other high-ranking politicians who endorsed and campaigned with Schweiker. Many of the relationships I formed on the campaign plane proved helpful after the election.

On one occasion, it was decided I would debate one of Senator Clark's staffers in Greenville, Pennsylvania, where I had worked at CB&I. The campaign rented a small single-engine plane (no two engines for staff, but at least two pilots) to get me there.

Shortly after departure from Washington, I looked over the pilot's shoulder and noticed we were heading south, toward the wrong Greenville! We quickly turned around and went north. After the debate, the weather was such that the pilots made the decision to stay overnight, but they forgot to cancel the flight plan and during the night while we were sleeping, we were reported missing. The next morning when I called the office, Jeanne and my mother were relieved to hear I was still in Greenville.

DREW LEWIS, CAMPAIGN CHAIRMAN

Through Schweiker, I met Drew Lewis, who was the campaign chairman and principal fundraiser for Schweiker. Drew and Dick had grown up together as members of the small Schwenkfelder religious sect in Lansdale, Pennsylvania, and had worked together at American Olean Tile, the Schweiker family company. My work with Drew on the campaign began a lasting personal relationship I maintained for the rest of my life.

Drew was one of the closest people to the congressman, so whenever I had a difficult situation, I would go to him for help or advice. He eventually became my model and principal mentor for much of the campaign and the rest of my career; there were things about him I tried to emulate. He had an intense focus and avoided clutter and distraction. He had a clean desk when I visited him years later at Time Warner Cable, where he was CEO; there were only three or four papers he was working on, not just on his desk, but in his entire office. He was also crystal clear about his duty and where he stood on anything, and he never equivocated.

Drew's role in the 1981 Air Traffic Controller (ATC) strike provides an excellent example of his clear, honest, and straightforward thinking. Named secretary of transportation in 1981 by President Reagan, he favored a revised contract he had negotiated with ATC union leaders to avoid a strike, but the rank and file refused to ratify it. After being briefed, President Reagan gave union members forty-eight hours to return or face termination. About 1,300 of the nearly thirteen thousand controllers came back—and Drew fired the rest. Many considered it the first major test of Reagan Administration resolve.

In 1986, Drew was to receive an honorary degree from his alma mater, Haverford College, when some faculty and students protested because of his role in ending the strike. Recognizing the school's Quaker roots and the Quaker tradition of composing differences rather than displaying them, Drew declined the degree and said, "I believe in consensus. There is no consensus on this degree when one-third of your faculty objects. With great respect for the college, I return the degree." The *Washington Post* lauded Drew's position, saying he had decided, then honored his decision, taking responsibility for it. Presumably, he could have passed the buck to the president, but chose not to. The *Post* also gave examples of two other politicians who had made similar difficult decisions, then walked away from them.

As the campaign gathered steam, and money, Schweiker brought on Howard (Howie) Phillips as campaign manager. This was a surprising addition to the team. Howie came from New England, not Pennsylvania, and had graduated from Harvard (not in Pennsylvania), where he headed the Young Republicans. He had little, if any, Pennsylvania experience. He also espoused the most conservative views in the Republican Party, which were at some distance from Schweiker's moderate campaign positions that were perceived as being more aligned with Pennsylvania's voters' views. I never understood why Schweiker chose someone with limited campaign management experience and little knowledge of Pennsylvania politics or issues, and I was not alone.

Within weeks, the wheels started to come off Howie's campaign direction for several reasons, one soon after his appointment.

Our opponent, Senator Clark, called for the registration and licensing of *all* firearms as a means of preventing gun violence. In those days gun violence meant inner-city gang warfare or robbery at gunpoint, primarily with pistols; this was well before mass shootings involving military-style weapons and large clips.

Whatever your position is on gun control today, Senator Clark's position was not a popular stance in Pennsylvania in a time and place where more than a million hunting licenses were issued annually to those hunters using deer rifles and shotguns. Both Howie and Dave Newhall advised the congressman to "cozy up" to Clark's position and call for a more limited form of registration and licensing that they never defined.

Coming from Western Pennsylvania, I knew how important the few days off work for deer season were to our steel workers and I knew how opposed they were to registering their deer rifles after having just paid for a hunting license. I urged the congressman to tack in the opposite direction. I wrote out a statement for him that stated that he would oppose registration and licensing. I recommended that instead, he propose a mandatory twenty-five-year prison sentence for those committing a felony with a firearm.

Newhall was persuaded to my view, while Howie stuck to the idea of a statement not far from Clark's that we never released. Within hours of releasing the statement, we were in Pittsburgh, where I arranged to give Schweiker a skeet-shooting lesson at a Sewickley gun club. One of our local backers active in a major sportsman's club then arranged for us to meet conservation and outdoors groups, and within days hundreds of billboards appeared around the state claiming that more than one million licensed hunters backed Schweiker.

We cemented our relationship with the steelworkers in a two-hour mill-gate handshaking morning. Many political analysts later cited Schweiker's position on gun control as the key issue of the campaign and the beginning of the end of Joe Clark's Senate career. Unfortunately, or perhaps fortunately, it was also the end of Howie's active management of the campaign. Although Howie remained in the position through election day, Newhall, Press Secre-

Outside Pittsburgh steel mill with Congressman Richard Schweiker in his successful Senate campaign.

tary Jack Conmy, and I collaborated closely, working with the congressman on the strategic aspects of the campaign. Years later Howie would run for president, not once but three times under a conservative banner.

Other key members of the campaign were Elsie May, Schweiker's assistant, and Tony Scirica, who managed scheduling. Later he and I would serve together in the Pennsylvania House of Representatives and Tony would be appointed to the Philadelphia Federal District Court and eventually the Third Circuit Court of Appeals, where he served as chief judge. He was always my personal choice for a Supreme Court appointment.

RICHARD M. NIXON, PRESIDENTIAL CANDIDATE

Perhaps one of the most memorable experiences of the campaign occurred in Philadelphia at the City Line Motel when, after a parade, five of us stood in a circle discussing the campaigns: me, Senator Scott, Congressman Schweiker, Presidential Candidate Richard Nixon, and Philadelphia Judge Arlin Adams. Adams, a pillar of the Philadelphia Jewish Community and a Republican, would later be appointed by Nixon to the 3rd Circuit Court of Appeals and considered for the Supreme Court by President Ford. Although I had been "around" Nixon at various campaign events, this was the first time I was engaged in a conversation with him, and frankly, I was embarrassed. I recall carefully studying my shoelaces as Nixon, true to form, used awful, but unfortunately common, epithets for Jews and Italians as we discussed Philadelphia voters.

During the campaign, Schweiker seldom mentioned Nixon because none of us ever thought Nixon could carry the state, and we did not want to go down with the ship. Throughout our campaign, there had been increasing pressure from the Nixon campaign for Schweiker to talk up Nixon, to the point that the *Philadelphia Inquirer* ran an editorial critical of Schweiker for not supporting the ticket. We knew this had been the work of Walter Annenberg, the paper's owner, a top Nixon supporter, and later Nixon's ambassador to the United Kingdom, and we did our best to ignore it. Senator Scott stepped up on Schweiker's behalf and mildly assured everybody that indeed Schweiker supported the ticket.

While the campaign wound down it remained clear in what polling we did that Schweiker's differentiation from Clark had largely been due to their respective positions on gun legislation. It was also clear that except for Schweiker, the Democrats would take the top of the statewide ticket: Hubert Humphrey for President and Bob Casey for Pennsylvania Auditor General. Casey would in a subsequent election become governor, and it is his son of the same name, who is today Pennsylvania's senior U.S. senator. That name would later pose a problem for me.

As the campaign came to an end, we spent election night at the Philadelphia Bellevue-Stratford Hotel (now the Bellevue). Around midnight, it became clear that Schweiker would win the election, so I started to hammer out notes for an acceptance speech, names to thank, etc., on my traveling typewriter. Before I could polish or even finish the notes, Schweiker said, "Let's go, Chief [my most common title]!" We headed for the elevator with *Philadelphia Magazine*'s Greg Walter. Most of the staff were on the ground floor with the Philadelphia volunteers.

We got on the elevator, and I gave Schweiker the notes to read as we passed several floors. He stopped the elevator saying that he needed time to make some edits, so we got off and found a space where he spent a few minutes adding his own spin. As we got up and headed for the elevator, he asked, "What's next, Chief?" to which I responded, "In six years you'll probably run against [future mayor] Pete Flaherty from Pittsburgh." That was, in fact, what happened.

When all the votes were counted, Schweiker was the only statewide Republican candidate to win election and it was one of the few times Pennsylvania did not go with the winning presidential candidate. In a state of roughly 11.7 million people with approximately 4.7 million voters, Schweiker's total votes exceeded Richard Nixon's by 309,745 and Democrat presidential candidate Senator Hubert Humphrey's by 140,347. Humphrey had defeated Nixon in Pennsylvania by 169,388 votes while Schweiker defeated Senator Clark by 282,100. It was considered a significant victory for Schweiker.

Schweiker said he wanted to work something out with me after election day but couldn't until after he determined how to handle Howie Phillips. Howie had kept the title of campaign manager and remained in our Harrisburg headquarters throughout the campaign with, I suspect, the expectation of being added to the new senator's staff.

A freshman senator moving from the House had few additional personnel slots to fill, so I sensed it was either me or Howie. I knew I had a leg up: I was intensely loyal, close to and trusted by the other staffers, and obviously close to the senator, with whom I had practically lived for seven months. He trusted me and usually listened carefully to my youthful advice, not always following it, but always telling me why he did or didn't. Finally, I had the institutional memory of what had been learned and who had done what in the campaign.

I was in New York visiting my college friend Jim Grossmann and interviewing for an assistant's job with the head of a cosmetics company (the whys and wherefores of that, I don't recall) when the senator-elect reached me and asked me to join his staff as special assistant, handling political and international matters for a whopping salary of $11,000/year ($95,000 today), well below my CB&I earnings in Spain. I gladly accepted.

My first assignment was to go to the Senate side of the Capitol with the senator to pick out an office in the New Senate Office Building (today the Dirksen Senate Office Building). As we rummaged around one office vacated by a well-known retiring Florida senator, we came across a mailbag and wondered why it had been left behind. In checking the contents, we found letters from women who had had amorous liaisons with the previous occupant. This was not an issue we had to worry about with Schweiker, whose life revolved around Claire and their five children.

While other staffers handled administrative and legislative matters, my primary responsibility was to deal with the political side of the office. I maintained contact with Republican county chairmen and Pennsylvania politicians of both parties while working various political events and traveling with the senator. I handled follow-up, and maintained his calendar with his long-time assistant, Elsie May. Because of my international experience, I was sometimes brought in on international legislative issues.

One such issue I worked on was continuing Federal funding for the SST (Supersonic Transport) Airliner. Because of my interest in airplanes, I told Senator Schweiker and Senator Scott why I thought this was an important area for America to establish a leadership position. Unfortunately, the Senate didn't see it that way. The funding did not pass, the program was eventually cancelled, and France and the United Kingdom proceeded to build their version of the SST, the *Concorde*. During that debate, I sat next to Minority Leader

Hugh Scott on the Senate floor, one of the first staffers to be given access, a memory that is often stirred when I see TV clips of the Senate.

Our son, Jimmy, was born at Columbia Hospital in Washington, D.C., on August 1, 1969, nine months after the election. Jeanne had been working for Ohio Congressman Devine since our arrival in Washington and on her last day in the office, a photo of her with the congressman was taken as she threw her steno pad in the air. Jimmy was born a few hours later and the picture of her, the congressman, and the flying notebook appeared in the *Washington Post*.

For us, this was an exciting time, settling into the Washington hubbub, such as it was in those days. There were only a few good restaurants, the modern development of K Street and the city itself had just begun, the Shirley Highway was only two lanes (now it's eighteen), and the Beltway was a faraway, sparsely traveled interstate highway. Although it was the senator who had won the election, those of us on staff felt that we had too; we were proud and stood just a bit taller. The election and my participation in it validated my return from Spain and the faith that people like Elsie Hillman, then Congressman Schweiker, and Drew Lewis had put in me. For Jeanne, Jimmy's birth was a real joy and we had more free time to kibitz with neighbors and other parents as we rolled through the events of 1969, including the first manned moon landing.

For those of us working directly with the senator, as opposed to the committee staffers, the days were seldom our own. We generally started very early in the morning and went home in time for a late dinner, assuming we could avoid attending some function or another for the senator. There were frequent staff meetings in which four or five of us would kick around a variety of national and local issues with the senator and then handle any follow-up. Lunches were usually spent with visiting constituents or the ever-present lobbyists. Most of my time at my desk was spent writing to, or on the phone with, party and government officials, Republicans and Democrats alike, in the state. If the senator met with them in his office, I attended. When the senator traveled, so did I. Every minute there was something new and there were many memorable events, a few of which illustrate what made the job so interesting and exciting.

VICE PRESIDENT SPIRO AGNEW
GOVERNOR THOMAS DEWEY
SENATE MINORITY LEADER HUGH SCOTT

I once traveled on Air Force Two with Vice President Spiro Agnew (who later resigned after a corruption investigation) to and from the Harrisburg State Farm Show, where I met Thomas Dewey, the 1944 and 1948 unsuccessful Republican presidential candidate. Returning to Washington that evening with the vice president and Senator Scott, who rode back with us, they asked me about the political situation in Virginia, something I knew little about even though I had gone to school there. I was amazed that these national figures wanted my opinion about anything.

ADMIRAL HYMAN RICKOVER, FATHER OF THE NUCLEAR NAVY

Schweiker asked me one afternoon as we were walking in the Russell Senate Office Building whether I had any idea who could take his place for a speech at the Union League in Philadelphia. Seeing Admiral Hyman Rickover approaching, I suggested the senator ask him. Known as the Father of our Nuclear Navy, Rickover, true to form, responded, "Senator, do you want me to make speeches or submarines?"

CHARLES DE GAULLE, PRÉSIDENT OF FRANCE

As a Pennsylvania Republican, Schweiker had often conferred with former President Eisenhower, who died March 28, 1969, and was laid in state in the Capitol Rotunda on March 30. I accompanied the senator that day to a small room where dignitaries waited to individually pass by the bier. French President Charles De Gaulle stepped into the room, practically right next to me. By that time, I had become accustomed to political celebrities, but this was a jaw-dropping moment. I quietly addressed the general in my exuberant French and he gave me his full attention while I took a minute to describe my Algeria experience. It was an unforgettable experience for me. De Gaulle would die the following year.

Some of us once had lunch on the House side of the Capitol with Evelyn Lincoln, President John Kennedy's secretary, and she told us stories of the Kennedy White House. Insisting that the president couldn't spell, she and Attorney General Robert Kennedy put a Justice Department report on his desk showing that a common denominator among psychotic killers was they couldn't spell.

The two years spent with Schweiker turned out to be more beneficial than anything I had expected on my return from Spain. Foremost, while in the Senate office I learned from Schweiker and Newhall how to write succinctly and convincingly, whether letters or briefs. Initially, Newhall reviewed and heavily marked up all my drafts. After a month or two they went directly to Schweiker, and the process of a heavy markup started all over again. Eventually I got the hang of their effective and businesslike style, and my submissions went directly to signature.

Although the comments were not attributed to me, Greg Walter in the previously referenced *Philadelphia Magazine* story quoted me as follows:

"The Schweiker method for testing employees may be effective, but it is not always comfortable. 'Once you're hired,' says one staffer, 'he'll stay on your back incessantly for two or three weeks. Every decision must be referred to him. Then all of a sudden one day—boom—you never see him. He is satisfied you know his philosophy toward things. He leaves you alone.'"

But it was not Schweiker who would, in the end, take me under his wing. My working with Drew Lewis created a bond that influenced not only my work with Schweiker in the campaign and Senate, but the rest of my career. Drew Lewis' mentorship led to my eventual assignment in the second Reagan Administration. When I started my software companies, Drew was a patient mentor, perhaps what I would have wanted most from my father.

Working in the Senate with Schweiker (who was later to be Reagan's choice for vice president in 1976 and became Secretary of Health and Human Services in 1981) and other national government figures added not only to my knowledge of the Federal Government, but also gave me a higher level of confidence and humility I probably would not have found in engineering. This paid off well throughout the rest of my career. Working in the Senate was an opportunity with instant feedback every long day. It required me to think, speak, and present quickly and clearly to my colleagues and other important (and impatient) people. Most importantly, it prepared me for the next phase of my career.

PITTSBURGH & HARRISBURG 1970–1976, PA HOUSE OF REPRESENTATIVES

In 1970, two years after going to the Senate with Schweiker, I made another career move: I decided to take a risk again, put myself out there, and return to Pittsburgh to run for the Pennsylvania House of Representatives. It was once more a question of where I was and where I wanted to go.

I was ambitious and I didn't see myself working behind the scenes in a staff position much longer. If I were to go into politics myself, returning to Pittsburgh was an obvious first move. Pittsburghers today remark on how many other Pittsburghers are "returnees"; for me, it was a question of what I might be able to do for the city where I grew up, using what I had learned in Washington.

I reviewed the economic and political situation in Pittsburgh and Pennsylvania and found that their respective finances were so bad that both were on the verge of bankruptcy (ultimately achieved by the city, but not the state). I did a scan of the State budget, certainly less convoluted than the Federal budget, and found a multitude of questionable items. Without Google in those days, it took some telephone "legwork" to determine that many items had been inserted by various interest groups long ago and never challenged, and that other items that should have been in the budget weren't.

It was clear to me that by properly handling the economic issues, taxes, and spending, I could contribute to getting the region back on track. Obviously, I would need to be elected first and that would require the support of Republican committeepersons and friends in the party like Elsie Hillman, Governor Scranton, and senators Scott and Schweiker. I would also need the support of the Pittsburgh business community that was pointedly concerned about the State's deteriorating finances, high business taxes, and various antiquated laws, which prohibited one activity or another, like the Sunday blue laws prohibiting the sale of alcohol on Sundays, or the law prohibiting statewide branch banking. I was confident I could properly frame the issues and gain the needed support.

A three-term lowkey Republican with a reputation for not having done much held the 28th Legislative District that covered the northwest corner of Allegheny County and included my Pennsylvania address where I voted. This was still my mother and stepfather's home in Sewickley Hills Borough. It was considered a safe Republican seat, one of the few in the county, which explained why the incumbent had had little previous opposition.

I took the essential and customary exploratory steps before deciding to run. With my mother I met with Republican committee members from Sewickley and then on my own with those of the neighboring communities. All expressed openness to my candidacy. I cold-called Attorney Evans Rose of Sewickley to be my finance chairman. I had seen him from our window the summer before my college sophomore year while recovering from shoulder surgery and remembered my mother saying he was one of the best lawyers in Pittsburgh from one of the most prestigious firms. He accepted what was to be his first campaign finance role that eventually led to his doing the same for President Reagan.

I talked it over with Schweiker and although he didn't like my leaving, he agreed to support me. I met with Elsie Hillman and secured her backing. Even though I would be running against a Republican incumbent, she strongly encouraged me to get in the race. I met with Bailey Deardorff, a Washington consulting firm used by the Schweiker campaign. They agreed to develop a campaign plan for my legislative race, although I would be somewhat below their usual national-level clientele. Shady Side classmates Bruce Hill and Jay Carson agreed to serve as campaign manager and press secretary respectively and Governor Scranton committed not only to support me, but also to campaign with me. As word filtered out in the Pittsburgh business community that I was considering running, I received encouraging phone calls from several corporate leaders. All these steps made a "go" decision all the easier.

Jeanne and I found a duplex home in the center and most populous township of the legislative district, and I sent out the press release announcing my candidacy. In short order five other Republicans entered the race, all for different reasons, but all also figuring the incumbent was vulnerable and that I was a carpetbagger. One of them decided to petition the court to remove me from the ballot claiming that since I was not living in the district and had not paid taxes in Pennsylvania, I was ineligible to hold office if elected.

A court date was expeditiously set and a partner of Ev Rose's, Harold Schmidt, was engaged to represent me. Harold was recognized as an outstanding trial attorney and for advising LTV (Jim Ling's then-well-known conglomerate, Ling-Temco-Vought) on the acquisition of a large Pittsburgh-based steel-making company.

On the residency charge, I was not concerned. I had maintained my Pennsylvania address at my mother's Sewickley home since our return from Kentucky in 1959, during college, during my time in Europe and Africa, and while living in Virginia. Mom and I went together to Harrisburg (Dauphin County 12th Judicial District Court), where election cases were adjudicated, and Ev Rose and Harold Schmidt joined us. We rented a suite in the Holiday Inn, where we went over all the evidence with my mother about what dates and why I had been home, and which of my personal effects had remained there.

Dave Newhall, Senator Schweiker's administrative assistant, came to Harrisburg and testified that like other Pennsylvania members of the staff I had always been considered a Pennsylvania resident. He also testified that he had advised me, and other staffers, to pay taxes owed where we lived, for me, Virginia.

The case was decided in my favor, partly on the basis I never owed taxes in Pennsylvania. The judge also referred to our decision, when Jeanne had come to the States in 1968, to select a Pittsburgh doctor to review and report her health every six months to immigration health authorities who required follow-up evaluations because she had had tuberculosis. Jeanne's having named a Pittsburgh doctor was considered evidence of our intent to remain Pennsylvania residents even though we planned to live in Virginia while I was working for the senator.

Of course, there were many other factors, including my mother's well-delivered and effective testimony, and the Sewickley address on my Pennsylvania driver's license. I had a Pittsburgh bank account, and oddly, the judge mentioned I left a tennis racquet, at my mother's house. At the end of the day, the case added precedent to Pennsylvania's legal distinction between residence and domicile.

FORMER PENNSYLVANIA GOVERNOR, WILLIAM SCRANTON

With my participation in the campaign cleared, Former Governor Bill Scranton came to Pittsburgh and campaigned with me. We designed a mailing with a letter from Scranton and a joint photo, which we sent out in the final weeks, along with a replica telegram giving reasons for people to vote for me.

Campaigning with former Pennsylvania Governor Bill Scranton.

I found myself speaking publicly almost every day to small coffee klatches, student classrooms, committee meetings, and larger groups of interested voters. Despite my avid interest and participation in my high school Debate Club, you could count on one hand the number of speeches I had given since then, so it was time for a tune-up.

I remembered what I learned in Debate and followed these rules:

- An hour of preparation for a minute of speech.
- Mind the rule of three: Focus on the three things you want people to remember.
- Tell the audience what you will tell them; tell them; tell them what you told them.
- Make the complex simple.
- Avoid staring at notes; look people in the eye; be positive and courteous.
- Stand up straight and button my jacket (we wore suits and ties when campaigning then!).
- Identify the source of any statistics or outside opinions.
- Open the floor to comments/questions and listen carefully; use humor where appropriate.

I learned to project two traits that served me well: honesty and confidence. Years later, a headhunter told me she thought I was an effective speaker and would be a good poker player. I asked her to tell me why. She said, "You mastered speaking by using a conversational tone and faithfully and fairly addressing different sides of the issue." She went on to tell me I subtly projected confidence, something I had often heard about my father.

Ev Rose did a great job in the fundraising department and while tapping contributors introduced me to Parkman Clancy, a former senior vice president of Gulf Oil and founder of Citizen's Energy, a nonprofit run by the sons of Robert F. Kennedy. Over time, Parkman became a close friend and another important mentor on personal and business issues. All in all, everything worked, and I became the Republican nominee with a significant majority.

Because the 28th District was a safe Republican seat, there was little meaningful opposition from the Democrats. In fact, I have no recollection of my opponent.

Even son Jim got into my successful legislative campaign.

Jeanne and I used the time between the May primary and the general election to settle in, get to know our new neighbors, and fix up the house. Because I was in those days considered young for the office, I received a lot of media attention and frequently appeared on radio talk shows. In November, I was elected to the Pennsylvania House of Representatives.

Entering the House in January 1971, as one of 203 members, I had three hills to climb:

- At twenty-nine I was the youngest and, by the way, one of the few with any engineering experience.
- Not that it mattered much to me, but I had no seniority.
- I was in the minority party; that did matter.

State Government departments, in general, are a step behind Federal Government agencies when it comes to getting things done and I found them not as responsive as Federal agencies had been to requests and queriers from Schweiker. I resolved that if I were to get anything done, I had to develop a plan, so I did.

First, I personally showed up at various agencies to listen and learn and let them know who I was and what I thought my district might need. This was particularly effective with the department of transportation, which was always struggling with highway engineering problems and pothole reports. Second, I presented myself with less importance than some of my colleagues. Third, I developed friends on the other side of the aisle and organized a group of younger legislators from both sides that met now and then, shared apartments, and often ate together.

We thought of ourselves as a state version of Congress's Wednesday Group, what was then a version of today's Problem Solvers Caucus. I have already mentioned one member of the group, Tony Scirica, whom I knew from the Schweiker campaign. Jay Haskell, Governor Raymond Shaffer's former assistant secretary for legislation, was another whom I met in the Schweiker campaign; he and I looked so much alike the speaker often recognized one of us as the other. A third member was Democrat Joe Rhodes, a black legislator from Homewood. A remarkable guy, Joe's education included the California Institute of Technology and Harvard. I had a small sailboat at the time and remember Joe stashing himself in the forward V berth and writing his thesis on racism in Victorian England as we circumnavigated Lake Erie. On certain occasions, young Jimmy was able to join me on the House floor and he often snuck over to Joe's desk to play tic-tac-toe.

Democrats were in the majority in the House, and the state was at an economic inflection point: We were running out of money. The legislature was under the gun to develop a fiscal program with the newly elected governor, Milton Shapp. I had studied the budget in detail throughout the campaign and appeared in the media suggesting a variety of solutions. Because of my interest, I requested an appointment to the Ways and Means Committee that oversaw revenue-raising measures.

Since the Pittsburgh business community had solidly backed me, the leadership in the House honored my request to be appointed to the Ways and Means Committee, unusual then for a freshman legislator. Within days of beginning the legislative session I, along with several other legislators, was invited to the governor's mansion for dinner, during which the governor asked my opinion about what should be done. I was surprised to be asked; I had expected the governor to present his own plan at the dinner.

I set out to work with other freshmen legislators following that evening meeting to see if we couldn't come up with something to present to the House. As it turned out, some of our ideas were adopted by the Republican Caucus, and some of them were not, at which point the two parties entered floor debate, the Democrats proposing a personal income tax, and the Republicans opposing it. Usually when facing budget shortfalls, Democrats would turn to increasing taxes on businesses, but at the time, business taxes were already bumping against the ceiling, and everybody recognized that the state's competitive position was eroding. Higher business taxes were not the answer.

The debate went on for days and nights with neither party willing to budge. At some point, the idea of instituting a state income tax was raised (up until then, there was not a Pennsylvania income tax). As the Democrats did not have sufficient votes to pass the new income tax, it seemed we were at a stalemate. Although the parties in those days were much closer to each other than today, it was clear that the stalemate could continue ad infinitum. Putting responsibility ahead of ideology, a group of twelve of us Republicans, mostly freshmen, decided to vote in favor of the new tax, albeit with a variety of conditions, and so informed the leadership.

The committee had cut the appropriation bill to the bare minimum and ratcheted up a variety of existing minor taxes, but there was no way out of the state's economic quagmire without an income tax. Our votes in favor brought the debate to a conclusion, resulted in the enactment of the tax, and set the state on a sound financial footing. My vote was not looked on favorably by the Republican leadership, but I viewed it as the most important of my six years in the House.

I have always felt that my vote on the income tax represented me to a "T." I am pro-business, and generally anti-tax. But mostly, I feel I was fiscally responsible. Sometimes the right decision is a hard one. Getting Pennsylvania back on a solid economic footing was essential for business—and for the entire state. In the end, it seemed the smart, responsible act to take. Another similar situation raised its head that same year—and caused a remarkable bruhaha!

In 1971, Pennsylvania still had many blue laws on the books, including a law that prohibited the sale of alcohol on Sundays (the laws were enacted to ensure that the Lord's Day remained reserved for prayer and rest). The Poconos resort hotels for years had been calling for the end of these Sunday "blue" laws so that they could entice their guests, many from New York City, to stay for brunch…and a Bloody Mary, and perhaps some local shopping. When legislators from the area called up the bill, I was in the cloakroom on the phone. Someone interrupted my call, telling me that I needed to return to the floor to vote. I quickly went to my desk and flipped the switch to "Aye." Though I knew the topic of the vote, I did not bother to check the tote board to see how close it was. As it turned out, the sides were evenly divided, and my vote, appearing last, became the deciding one. Immediately, the opponents said I was on the payroll of the Poconos hotels and merchants. I was sensitive about the attack on my reputation, but in the end figured most of my constituents supported Sunday sales.

Along that vein I, like many other legislators before and after, persistently opposed the state's exclusive sale of liquor, expressing the view that the employees of the state stores had little knowledge of, or interest in, what they were doing. Furthermore, the state should not be in the business of selling booze. Because it makes money for the state and has been unionized, few legislators were willing to call the system up for a vote, even though all the governors in modern times have made a campaign pledge to do away with it. Yep, it's still there.

We frequently heard pledges made in hard-fought elections that many of us supported but were never allowed by leadership on both sides of the aisle to vote on. The best example was a constitutional amendment to reduce the size of the legislature by downsizing the 203-member House, the second largest in the country behind, oddly, New Hampshire, with four hundred.

There were several votes I made that perhaps surprised a few constituents. One of these was about the creation of the State Lottery: I opposed it, and pointed out that nearly all the revenue would come from people who could hardly afford daily or weekly tickets, and I felt the state should not be in the business of running it. Nevertheless, it passed and was followed on several occasions by convictions for rigging the results, and by unsuccessful calls to privatize it.

A moderate position at odds with the greater Republican Party was my take on the death penalty. I spoke at length on the House floor against it because, as we found out later using DNA, the wrong person might be executed. Although not used recently, it still exists in Pennsylvania.

My position as a moderate can be seen as well in my votes on social welfare issues. During my service with Senator Schweiker, he had made a point of revealing on national television the horrible state of those facilities that housed retarded children (the term used then). Firmly sharing Schweiker's concerns, I made it a point as a member of the Education Committee to work with the welfare secretary to close outmoded facilities and provide for disadvantaged children in different, and better, ways.

Responsible, commonsense legislating should not be a thing of the past. And yet compromises on gun control seem not only right; they seem essential. After a woman was fatally shot by a security guard in a grocery store, I chaired a select committee, held hearings, and successfully sponsored legislation requiring state police training and licensing of security guards who carry guns (subject of the book *On Guard* by Milton Lipson). Were I in the legislature today, having been a shooter (birds and clay pigeons) all my life, I would vote to inhibit the spread of military-style weapons, clips, and ammunition that have no place in modern life.

Abortion was as much an issue then as today and views on it were just as heated. I could count on it coming up in coffee klatches and town hall meetings. My position was and is that abortion is a subject for the woman to decide within a reasonable time limit.

I was interested in the state prison system and was the only non-lawyer appointed to the Judiciary Committee, Corrections Subcommittee, responsible for reviewing conditions in the state prisons and formulating legislation aimed at reducing recidivism. That appointment led to my brief career in the music business and my friendship with the rock musician Alice Cooper. Even more meaningfully, it led to my friendship with Shep Gordon, the well-known talent manager who worked with a stable of music groups (as seen in the film *Supermensch: The Legend of Shep Gordon*). It is a stranger-than-fiction story that bears repeating.

ALICE COOPER & SHEP GORDON

I cannot claim much knowledge of the music scene in Pittsburgh in the 1970s, which is not to say that I didn't like music; I did. We lived next door to Bob Harper, station manager of radio station KQV-AM, which in those days was the biggest, loudest rock station in Pittsburgh. Bob often gave me 45rpm records he received from promoters and once or twice I suggested records I thought he should air. One time he did, and because his was the first station to promote the record, and the record achieved prominence on the charts, he received a gold facsimile in recognition.

Most of the well-known rock groups that came to Pittsburgh stopped by KQV for an interview or, as in Alice Cooper's case, to promote their concert by reading the weather. These more famous groups usually played the Civic Arena, which looked like an observatory with a retractable roof and seated about sixteen thousand with a few more thousand standing; it has since been torn down. Bob, who generally went to all the concerts, invited me to attend an Alice Cooper concert on a Friday evening on my return from Harrisburg. Having never heard of Alice Cooper, and knowing nothing about the music business, I had not thought of anything beyond attending this one concert; I had no idea of the long-term, fun relationship I was getting myself into. I agreed to meet Bob before the concert in the rock group's dressing room by using Bob's name at the stage entrance.

Being known to the Pittsburgh Police helped get me backstage, without their needing to summon Bob. There I met this weird guy in the hallway who was wearing knee-high leopard-skin boots, long hair, and wacky makeup—sure enough, it was Alice Cooper. He took me into the dressing room, which was stacked with Budweiser Beer, and introduced me to Shep Gordon, his manager. Shep and Alice travelled together when Alice was on tour. I immediately fell in with Shep Gordon. It was the business side of concerts that fascinated me: how everyone traveled, how many trucks they had, how much money they were making on tour. Though that's not to say that I didn't like the music.

Alice was born in Detroit as Vincent Fornier and moved to Phoenix, where he attended high school. At the time of our meeting, he was about twenty-five years old, and his act featured unusual props like fake dead chickens and reptiles, and electric chairs and guillotines. He was on the top of the charts with songs like "School's Out" and "I'm Eighteen." This was 1974, and the world, particularly Great Britain and the U.S., were witnessing Alice's "shock rock."

Alice invited me to observe the concert from backstage, and Shep invited me to their nearby hotel suite for the after-show party, where we sat on the floor and discussed politics and what it was like to go through elections (the subject of Alice's 1972 hit song "Elected") until early in the morning.

A short time later, as a member of the Corrections Subcommittee, I toured Graterford Prison in Montgomery County near Philadelphia. There I observed a group of musicians making impressive music. I asked them whether they had ever recorded anything. Some of the nine members of the group were lifers, so of course there was no way they had been together in a recording studio, and most likely never individually either.

I suspected that most rock musicians had warehouses full of used instruments, so I called Shep and asked whether he could help the Graterford musicians with some instruments. I knew he had studied sociology at the State University of New York at Buffalo and that his first, very brief job had been in the California Corrections System (he left the job only a few hours after starting it). Shep agreed not only to help with instruments; he also suggested a producer, Stan Vincent, to help the inmates make a record. Stan had written and produced "O-o-h Child," a popular song recorded in 1970 by the Stair Steps (and used in various 2020 campaigns because of the lines "Things are gonna get easier...Things'll get brighter").

With support from Shep and Stan, I managed to schedule time in the famous Philadelphia Sigma Sound Studio with the idea that our prisons contained many talented people who perhaps deserved another chance. And then with help from the farsighted Lieutenant Governor Ernie Kline, I was able to spring the men for recording sessions while accompanying guards looked on. I spent several nights in the studio, a couple of times sleeping in the car at turnpike rest stops on my way back to the House.

We named the group "The Power of Attorney" and spent a month recording an album entitled *From the Inside*. It was released on the Polydor label with the last tracks recorded in a New York City studio. Taking the men to New York on a bus, I arranged the cooperation of Pennsylvania, New Jersey, and New York police and several prison guards. During that trip Stan made a short documentary that received limited distribution.

The album, which featured liner notes by James Brown and the Lieutenant Governor, did reasonably well, but the improbability of a tour and a host of other factors meant it would be a one-off, useful only to demonstrate there were a lot of talented people behind bars.

In 1976, during the presidential campaign, a *People Magazine* reporter in Boston asked Alice where he got the "WIN" button he was wearing. It was a staple of the Ford presidential campaign standing for "Whip Inflation Now." Alice said he got it from me and that was what the magazine reported in the caption below his photograph. Why he said that, I'll never know, perhaps Shep said it. I never asked him, but the result was that I received a ton of mail, and a couple of Pittsburgh-area bands contacted me and with my newfound knowledge I helped them briefly reach the bottom of the charts.

At one point, the Pittsburgh Penguins hockey team, which was not doing well, was up for sale. Shep called me to ask if I would investigate what it would take for Alice to buy it, so I contacted the Penguin's CEO Paul Martha, a former Shady Side classmate and Steelers star, who indicated there were several potential buyers already and that the number being kicked around was $64 million, a lot less than the recent reputed $900-million sale. I don't remember why, but at some point, Shep and Alice lost interest.

A short time later, early 1977, while I was in New York City on business, Bob invited me to attend the Eagles' *Hotel California* album-opening concert, where I briefly met Paul Simon in the next box, and Linda Ronstadt in the Eagles' dressing room. I asked her who I had been talking to while taking his picture and she told me it was Mick Jagger. I was amazed by how "normal" everybody was off stage. That party was my last hurrah in the music business, though much later, in 2014, a Philadelphia newspaper contacted me wanting to retell the story of the Graterford prisoner album. One of the prisoners was due for parole and, in an interview, referred to the group's composition during his time at Graterford. The papers interviewed Shep, who accurately referred to me as "a strait-laced and buttoned-up Pennsylvania Representative who found his way into the music business," and then they interviewed me and rehashed the story.

Cover of the album by the Power of Attorney

Alice Cooper and I at the Warhol Museum in Pittsburgh

Even later, in 2017, after I had moved back to Pittsburgh, a story hit the global press that Alice found he had a painting in storage: *The Little Electric Chair, Red*, by Andy Warhol, with whom he had been close in the '70s and '80s. There was a connection between the image and the prop Alice used in his show. Although in his autobiography, *They Call Me Supermensch*, Shep said Andy had given it to Alice, he told me later that Alice's then-girlfriend and Revlon model, Cindy Lang, had bought it from Warhol for $2,500 as a gift for Alice. I suggested to Shep that Alice hang the painting at the Pittsburgh Warhol Museum, so Shep arranged for Alice and his wife Sharon to join me and my wife Janet on a private late-night tour of the museum with its management.

During several hours together at the museum, Alice talked about his relationship with Andy and looked over the artifacts Andy had collected, including Alice's Christmas cards. Before the evening ended, he told us some crazy stories about Elvis, Fats Domino, and other rock-and-roll legends he had met along the way.

Shep had suggested that hanging the painting in the Pittsburgh Warhol would be a great venue to celebrate the close relationship between Alice and Andy. Unfortunately, museum management didn't take to the idea because, like many other Warhol originals, Alice's was unsigned, and so the museum missed an opportunity to generate patrons and contributions.

During the lead up to the 1974 election for what would be my third term, I met with my mentors, Elsie Hillman, who was still the County Republican chairman, and Drew Lewis, who was now the State Republican chairman, and who had announced his candidacy for governor. I had the idea I might run for lieutenant governor and with my Kelly name perhaps even draw some support from Philadelphia Democrats as John Kelly, brother of the movie star and princess Grace Kelly, was on the City Council. Over the years John's father and my Grandfather Kelly had been business associates. However, it soon became clear that I would be running against House Speaker Ken Lee, and it would be highly unlikely for me to be nominated because Lee would have the support of most House Republicans and state committee members. As it happened, because the election was held on the heels of the Watergate fiasco, many Republicans, including Drew Lewis and Ken Lee, were defeated (I considered myself lucky to have been reelected to the House).

By early 1976, I was beginning to think, again, about the next stage of my life. Perhaps brought on by a recent near-death experience with appendicitis, but more likely the terrible state of my marriage, I began to think that going further in elective politics was not in my future.

I was in an awful frame of mind as my marriage to Jeanne was coming apart. My self-imposed requirement of being a twenty-four-by-seven Representative, even in a parttime legislature, didn't leave much of me to my family, other than on summer weekends. And when Jeanne brought it forcefully to my attention, I frankly didn't have the relationship maturity to take corrective steps. In very short order, Jeanne and Jimmy left Pittsburgh and moved to New York. After several months, they returned to Pittsburgh before Jeanne decided to return to England, taking Jimmy with her.

When it came time for me to register for the May 1976 primary and the possibility of a fourth term in the legislature, I let the leadership know I would not run again and issued a press release to that effect.

VALERY GISCARD D'ESTANG, PRESIDENT OF FRANCE

It may have been a consolation prize, or because I spoke French, that the Democrat speaker, Herb Fineman, asked me to represent the legislature in welcoming French President Valery Giscard d'Estaing to the July 4, 1976, Philadelphia Bicentennial Celebration. As a meaningful final goodbye to the legislature, this was also my second conversation with a French president.

As for the future: I hoped to return to international business and resume a career I had thought of as starting successfully after a major London speedbump. At heart it was the international scene I was looking to return to, and perhaps even an opportunity to make some money. During my six years in the legislature, I had had extensive exposure to the Pittsburgh business community, which had many large international companies. I figured it wouldn't be too difficult to find something. Much like what my father expressed about his WWII Army service, I had come to feel about my time in the world of politics: I had done my duty.

PITTSBURGH 1976, A RUN FOR CONGRESS, THE GENERAL AND THE IMPOSTER

Just as I announced my decision not to run again, U.S. Senate Minority Leader Hugh Scott (R-PA) said he would not seek a fourth term. U.S. Congressman John Heinz quickly announced that he would run for Scott's senate seat and *not* run simultaneously in his 18th Congressional District, in which my legislative district was located. Suddenly, I was hearing from people encouraging me to run for Heinz' congressional seat. I had name recognition, so the pressure to enter the May primary quickly ratcheted up. Elsie Hillman encouraged me to run, even though Heinz would not endorse anyone because two of his staff (one who had previously worked for me) were primed to enter the race.

Ev Rose, my finance guy, said he thought he could raise the campaign finances, and Bailey Deardorff again agreed to handle strategy. In making the decision to run, the most convincing advice came from my cousin Roger, who said, "If you don't do it, you'll never know whether you should have." So with some trepidation, I threw my hat in the ring. This time, I was not as convinced of a favorable outcome as I had been in my earlier races for the legislature.

GENERAL MATHEW B. RIDGWAY

While I was putting my new campaign together, I received an important endorsement of someone I had come to know during my time in the legislature. With my interest in military history, I had become friends with General Mathew B. Ridgway, who was well known as the commander of the 82nd Airborne Division that spearheaded the WWII Normandy invasion, and as commander of UN forces during the Korean War. General Ridgway had retired as Army chief of staff and come to Pittsburgh in the mid-'50s, as head of the Mellon Institute, later the Mellon part of Carnegie Mellon University.

He lived in the Fox Chapel area of Pittsburgh in a relatively small house with a porch, where he and I sometimes got together to discuss world events, but more often interesting people he had gotten to know. Among his coterie of friends and associates were Eisenhower, Churchill, and General Bernard Montgomery. About Eisenhower, he said, "Ike was a great politician!" He liked Churchill a great deal, and Montgomery not at all. Our conversations were often interrupted by calls from senior military or political leaders seeking his advice. One afternoon, when I was at his house, Georgia Governor Jimmy Carter called looking to see whether a thought had merit for his presidential campaign. Spending time with General Ridgway was always a learning experience and I found his stories fascinating.

Recognizing my friendship with the general, the Pittsburgh West Point Society asked me for an idea of what they might present to General Ridgway for speaking to their chapter. I suggested a flag from the 82nd Army Airborne Division because he had shown me in the entrance hall of his house the flags of all his commands and noted that the 82nd Airborne's standard was the one flag he didn't have.

After a call to Senator Schweiker, and a return call from Secretary of Defense Harold Brown's aide, the flag was delivered to General Ridgway by the 82nd Airborne color sergeant in full-dress uniform immediately after his speech. I have a great photo of him and the sergeant embracing around the flag. Following Ridgeway's death, the flag was placed in the Soldiers and Sailors Memorial Hall in Pittsburgh with details of why and how he received it.

As for the May primary, all was for naught when three disadvantages occurred simultaneously: Eight other candidates entered after me and stayed to split the vote; a terrible machine ballot position was drawn for me—the lowest rung, below eye level, about three feet from the bottom of the analog machine—and Robert Casey drew ballot position one on the left of the top eye-level row. For me, it was just not meant to be.

Whatever Casey was, he was not the well-known Democrat Pennsylvania auditor general of the same name. However, many people thought he was, and since he drew position one on the ballot, they also assumed he was the endorsed Republican candidate. The local newspapers, saying it was not their practice at the time to cover primary elections as they considered them political intra-party affairs, were reluctant to point out that Casey was not the Pennsylvania auditor general, and he won the primary election.

Subsequently, the newspapers *did* point out he was not the auditor general and so he lost the general election to Democrat Doug Walgren. John Heinz was elected to the Senate, but Elsie was furious with him for having refused to endorse a Republican for his former congressional seat.

In a "what-comes-around-goes-around" way, Walgren lost the seat after three terms to Republican Rick Santorum, who served two terms in the House.

Santorum then defeated Harris Wofford, who had been appointed by Governor Robert Casey, the former auditor general, to fill John Heinz' Senate seat after his death in 1991. After two terms in the Senate, Santorum then lost to current Senator Robert Casey, the son of the auditor general and governor, Robert Casey.

Pennsylvania politics are always fascinating, always frustrating, and always exhilarating. I was glad for my time in the legislature, but I thought my time in elective politics was finally over (again!). Having lost the primary, I turned back to figuring out what I would do after my third term ended December 31, 1976. I called several people in business and politics, including Governor Scranton, who was serving as U.S. Ambassador to the United Nations. Scranton said he had an idea he would appreciate my following up on and asked that I call him back in a week or so. I was pleased with the prospect of being able to return his favor in my first legislative campaign and of doing something for him. When the time and opportunity came to call him, I did so from a yacht club in Buffalo, a stop in a Lake Erie sailboat race I was crewing.

When I got through to Scranton, he asked me to come to New York to meet with him at the U.N. Fortunately, I had a suit with me, so not wasting any time, I arranged to fly from Buffalo to LaGuardia early the next morning. At the airport I decided to get a shoeshine. Unfortunately, the shoeshine guy was drunk and plastered polish over my shoes and socks. I decided it was too much to ask him in his state to clean up his mess, so I waited until I arrived at LaGuardia and got the shoeshine folks there to help clean up the mess. At that point, I thought I was in good shape, but then my foreign cabdriver got lost on our way to the U.N. (No digital driver assistance then!)

After arriving in a frantic state, I was ushered into the ambassador's office. After small talk, he asked me to go to Washington and get a feel for what was going on in Ford's White House. Perhaps I could help the Ford campaign in Pennsylvania. Scranton set up a meeting for me at the White House with his former long-time assistant, Bill Kiesling, who at that time was deputy to Ford's chief of staff, Dick Cheney.

Scranton himself had been an on-again, off-again candidate for president in the 1964 presidential campaign runup to Goldwater's nomination as the Republican candidate opposing Lyndon Johnson. When I got to the White House, I was not oblivious to the thought that Scranton was perhaps being considered for Ford's vice president, although he had not mentioned that to me.

What I remember from my conversations with Kiesling was that Ford's choice for vice president was William Ruckelshaus, former deputy attorney general who was known for resigning rather than executing President Nixon's order to fire Watergate Special Prosecutor Archibald Cox. I didn't understand that choice because both men were Midwesterners and, other than the fact that he had resigned in the "Saturday Night Massacre," I didn't see Ruckelshaus bringing an accretive constituency.

My take on the visit, which I reported to Ambassador Scranton, was that first, I was not able to identify a way I could help the Ford campaign, and second, that if he had any interest in the vice presidency, he was not being considered. In the end, Ford chose another Midwesterner, Senator Bob Dole. fter the election, I looked at the numbers: Had he chosen Scranton for his VP, Ford certainly would have carried Pennsylvania and thereby won the election. As it was, he lost Pennsylvania and the election to Georgia Governor Jimmy Carter.

I came away from my eight years in the political world with the strong sense that I had indeed done my duty. It began with the election of Senator Schweiker, who would go on to make major contributions in the Senate and as President Reagan's Secretary of Health and Welfare. In my own right, I had played a key role in reestablishing sound fiscal policy in my state while working to improve the lives of disadvantaged children. Finally, I had responded effectively to thousands of constituent requests for assistance with one or another Pennsylvania department or institution.

Most importantly, I had created meaningful relationships, with Senator Scott, Elsie Hillman, and Drew Lewis, who would later power important shifts in my international life. Although I didn't know it at the time, my relationships with them and my experiences in the Schweiker campaign and in the Pennsylvania Legislature would come back into play in the future, but for the moment it was the international business world that beckoned.

As the youngest member of the legislature I enjoyed speaking to students at all levels.

IV. THE INTERNATIONALIST

PITTSBURGH 1977–1980, ALGERIA (AGAIN), THE MIDDLE EAST, AND CHINA

After the November election of President Jimmy Carter, and with my legislative career coming to an end, I began my job search in earnest. I focused on the Pittsburgh corporate-headquarters community, much larger then, contacting people I knew to express interest in an international position in marketing or project management. It was my hope to build on my CB&I experience and my resume focused on that as opposed to my service with Schweiker and in the legislature.

By then, the terms of my divorce had been decided. I was thirty-five and living in a one-bedroom apartment, about thirty-five minutes from Downtown Pittsburgh, not far from where Jeanne, Jimmy, and I had lived. I had begun a year-long series of counseling sessions in what I today believe was a successful effort to increase my emotional intelligence and derive a deeper understanding of what had happened to my marriage. When I could afford it, every couple of months or so, I arranged for Jimmy to come first from Albany, and then after he left Pittsburgh, from London, to spend time with me.

Most corporate career opportunities then and perhaps even now tend to come by word of mouth, so I systematically dialed my business community friends. The initial reaction was usually an assumption I was interested in government relations, but by letter I reinforced my international and language experience, albeit in three countries only, and stated a clear preference for finding a position in international marketing or operations, which were most often conducted by a separate international department.

After a couple of dead ends, I was fortunate to secure an interview with Pittsburgh's diversified Dravo Corporation. The part of the company that interested me, in many ways like CB&I, was a growing engineering services business supporting the steel, petrochemical, chemical, and mining industries. It also had constructed river locks and dams long ago, then acquired a river barge line, and built barges and towboats. That part of the business didn't interest me; in six months, though, it would get my full attention. Wanting to enter global markets, Dravo's CEO had recently established an international division and hired Bill Thorbecke to be its first president.

Bill was an intense, intriguing guy with multiple international bona fides. He had been born in Paris to a Dutch diplomat (later Ambassador to China in the mid-1930s) and was the great-grandson of the three-time prime minister and author of the Dutch constitution. In WWII, he enlisted at age eighteen in the Dutch Army by way of South Africa. He would go on to serve in the British RAF as a Lancaster bomber pilot, completing thirty missions over Germany. He earned the Distinguished Flying Cross for managing to bring his severely damaged bomber home on two of four engines and for his crew having shot down a German ME262, the first operational fighter jet.

After the war, Bill married Sonya Stokowski, the daughter of the famous conductor Leopold Stokowski, and then graduated from MIT. He joined Royal Dutch Shell and served in a variety of international management positions in several large companies in the petrochemical industry before joining Dravo in late 1975. Because of recommendations from mutual contacts, and because of Dravo's industrial construction activities in Algeria, Bill was keen to interview me and invited me to the Downtown Pittsburgh headquarters as soon as I could get there.

Since Bill was a relatively recent arrival in Pittsburgh and with no internet at the time, research on him with my contacts was thin and revealed only his Dutch background, MIT engineering and management degrees, and his history in the international petrochemical construction industry after the war. I would not know about Sonya or his war service until much later. He was not much for small talk and got right to the point: "Tell me about your experience in Algeria."

In describing my involvement in the project there, and in Spain, I said I had not been at CB&I long enough to have firmly established a career track, but that I felt I could add to his new organization in project management or marketing. By that time, Bill explained, Dravo had established a subsidiary in Spain and acquired two relatively small companies, one in Holland and another in Italy. He had hired only a vice president as his assistant and was contemplating the addition of others overseas. From all that, I surmised that he probably needed additional backup in the home office. As the conversation evolved, I could tell that Bill was focused on my Algeria experience; he kept coming back to it, so I figured there must be an immediate need for someone who had more than a passing knowledge of the country.

Although I was hesitant to think of a return to Algeria, the fact was, I needed a job, and Dravo apparently needed Algeria expertise. So I played my Algeria card, but proposed that I be given a regional role. Shortly after that, I received an offer from Bill, a salary four times my miserly legislative salary, and a title, Director of Middle East Marketing (although Algeria is not in the Middle East). I accepted with a start date immediately after the end of my third legislative term.

I reported for work January 3rd, 1977, and was given the nominal responsibility for marketing in the seventeen countries traditionally known as the Middle East, but with an initial focus on Algeria. A couple of the engineering managers had made contacts in Saudi Arabia and Egypt that I was told would eventually come under my wing—after Algeria.

More than in our interview, I gave Bill a detailed description of the difficulties I experienced in Algeria while at CB&I, especially the pervasive dysentery, but he was uninterested in all that, and in no time I was Algeria-bound for the second time!

Although I was apprehensive about returning, I was in fact interested to see whether the country had made any progress since I had left more than ten years before. I was also excited to be back in the greater world. During my time in Washington and the Pennsylvania Legislature, I had made only one international trip and that was to visit Jeanne's family in the UK.

Dravo, through its Italian subsidiary, had contracted for the design and construction of a $25-million salt-purification plant at El Outaya near Biskra, 250 miles southeast of Algiers in the desert. The rather large (for Algeria) city was formerly home of the 2nd Foreign Cavalry Regiment of the French Foreign Legion. In essence, the project was to build a plant to convert a naturally occurring mountain of salt, which was 97% pure to 99.85% pure, to meet European, particularly French, retail standards. The project was behind schedule and over budget, and I was told to go with the newly hired American project manager to Algiers and Biskra to get it back on track. It was clearly more of an operating role than it was marketing.

We arrived in Algiers and first met with our government-sponsored joint-venture partner, who described what I knew to be the usual set of problems: Equipment and material were not clearing the port fast enough, government construction permits were being held up, there were issues with transports to Biskra, and there were the usual workforce issues. I took the front seat for the Algiers issues as we first met with the responsible government officials, apologizing profusely for the state of the project, but then asking the officials to take responsibility for helping us resolve them. Indeed, my government experience was helpful in fashioning my approach. There was always a little chatter about extraordinary payments to various officials, but we managed with the help of our attorney to avoid them, and then to resolve the various local issues, one by one.

Our lawyer was Ms. Marie-Claude Radziewski, and without her we might still be there. Her story began with the French incarceration of the Algerian National Liberation Front (FLN) leader and future Algerian president, Ahmed Ben Bella.

During the Algerian War, 1956, Ben Bella had been captured when his Air Atlas flight from Morocco to Tunisia was diverted to Algiers and he was seized. He was incarcerated for the rest of the war. The Evian Agreement, which brought peace between France and Algeria, was signed in 1962 by the French and FLN representatives. It had been largely written by the young Polish French attorney Radziewski, who represented the Algerian FLN. The Evian Agreement ended the war and set Ben Bella free.

Receiving much publicity, including having her picture run on the cover of major French publications like *Paris Match*, Radziewski moved to Algiers, where Ben Bella gave her a villa in a private section of town. It was there that she and I would have informal dinners and conversations about the history of the new country and how Ms. Radziewski, at a very young age, played such an important role in its founding. She spoke of her Polish family background and how remarkable it was that she had come to play such an important part helping to end a devastating war and found a new country.

After several weeks bouncing around government offices and drinking tons of coffee, the project manager and I set out for Biskra, where he took the front seat reviewing the construction plans and negotiating the various workforce issues. All in all, I remember us shuttling back and forth between Algiers and Biskra, making sure everybody was doing what they promised before we could report the project as on track and I was able to leave. The project manager stayed on site to complete the project.

Following Algeria and a brief return to the States, Bill sent me to Jeddah, then the capital of Saudi Arabia on its west coast, to meet the Alirezas, the family of the former Saudi ambassador to the United States and founders of the oldest organized commercial enterprise in the Kingdom. The family included four brothers, who created the Xenel Group, with which Thorbecke established a joint venture to represent us in bidding engineering projects in-country. My assignment this time was a clear traditional marketing role: Apprise Xenel of Dravo capabilities, jointly identify and pursue Saudi opportunities, and support in country the company unit responsible for winning the bid and executing the contract.

The toughest issue I had to work through was the Arab boycott of Israel, specifically the secondary boycott that prohibited Arab trade with companies doing business in Israel. The secondary boycott was the reason behind Coke in Israel and Pepsi in Saudi Arabia, Ford in Saudi Arabia, but not in Israel. An attestation to the effect we were not trading with Israel was required with any project bid. Although we had no business in Israel at the time, the Carter Administration had just approved legislation prohibiting American companies and their subsidiaries from making such an attestation. After much back-and-forth with lawyers on both sides, we came up with what I call a positive-negative, i.e., we certified that we were doing business only in certain countries (which did not include Israel). That, or something close, was acceptable to both governments. For many reasons, Israel was not a prospective market for us.

We won a major project: the construction of a gas-oil separation plant for Aramco in Safaniya in the northeast corner of the Kingdom on the Kuwaiti border. The price tag was two hundred million dollars (one billion today). The project was run by our most senior engineer, a Brit, and was staffed by Philippine workers who lived on a multi-tiered houseboat off the beach, where they raced small sailboats we provided.

To create a local presence in an urban area closer to the jobsite than Jeddah, we rented a house in Al Khobar, on the east coast of Saudi Arabia, overlooking the Persian Gulf. The house was staffed by two distant cousins, one an American of Lebanese descent, the other from Lebanon itself. Being as there was not much to do in the Kingdom, we usually ended up at the house in the evening when I was there. I never asked how the cousins did it, but we seemed to have a stash of quality Scotch that fueled parties for Americans and Saudis alike even though drinking was prohibited in the Kingdom. I once got lost driving to my hotel and stopped at a store for directions because I couldn't read the Arab signs. Afterward it occurred to me that had the religious police been in the store and come close enough to smell my breath, there is no telling how long I would have spent in jail. From then on, I either used one of our drivers, or I didn't go to the house.

My time in the Kingdom turned out to be a useful learning opportunity. Working in the Saudi culture with the Alireza family gave me an inside look at how the family-centric Saudi commercial world operated. I was fortunate to be invited by several family business leaders, some of whom had gone to school in the States, to Iftar, the meal following the day of Ramadan fasting, which spawned informative conversation well into the night. These experiences gave me friendships that would prove helpful during my later time with SAIC, in the Reagan Administration, and in evaluating more recent events in the Kingdom.

CHINA 1977–1980, A PIONEER

In mid-1977, after my trips to Algeria and Saudi Arabia, I found myself back in my Pittsburgh Dravo office looking at a large spread-out map of the world. I had not thought much about the People's Republic of China (PRC) previously, but that morning, looking at the map, I noticed how large it was. My immediate thought was that it would make an interesting—and possibly enormous—market for any number of our engineering services, so long as we got there first.

United States relations with China had taken a turn for the worse in 1949, when Mao Zedong and the Chinese Communist Party (CCP) created the PRC and subsequently opposed the United Nations and America in North Korea. The Republic of China (ROC), which had ended the Qing Dynasty in 1911 and reconstituted itself on the Island of Taiwan, remained a United States ally and held one of the five permanent United Nations Security Council seats until 1971, when the United Nations passed Albania's resolution recognizing the PRC as the sole representative of China.

Diplomatic relations between the United States and the PRC naturally halted during the Korean War, but a warming began in 1971 following two visits by Secretary of State Henry Kissinger to China to meet Premier Zhou Enlai to set the stage for a visit by President Richard Nixon in February 1972. Although minimal liaison offices were established in 1973, the full normalization of relations would not occur until 1979 under President Jimmy Carter and Communist Party Chairman Deng Xiaoping, who had been rehabilitated following Zhou's and Mao's deaths and the end of the Gang of Four after the Cultural Revolution in 1976.

In late 1977, with no official relations with the PRC, there were few Americans giving thought to doing business there. I saw this as an advantage and approached Thorbecke with the idea we should at least investigate the possibilities. Bill's father had been ambassador to the ROC before Japan's invasion of mainland China preceding World War II, so he had many memories there and contacts in Taiwan. He was more than enthusiastic.

FORMER PENNSYLVANIA SENATOR HUGH SCOTT
DEPUTY CHIEF LIAISON HAN XU, LATER AMBASSADOR

I reached out to a known sinologist, my friend from my days in Washington, retired Pennsylvania Senator Hugh Scott, who easily secured a meeting for the two of us with Han Xu. Han Xu, a former English professor who was said to have been Premier Zhou Enlai's secretary, had been sent to Washington as China's Deputy Chief Liaison while future President George H. W. Bush headed America's early mission in Beijing. Han was later named the vice minister of foreign affairs and then ambassador to the United States during the Reagan Administration.

Not having been a student of Chinese history and thinking through what I knew of the reign of Mao and the Cultural Revolution, I was surprised when, at our meeting, Han said, "Communism is the bump on the log of Chinese history." I wasn't sure what he meant, but I took it as a signal of China's interest in doing business with us. Today, I wonder whether he would make the same remark in view of Xi Jinping's efforts to strengthen the Communist Party.

In the meeting, I described various Dravo capabilities, focusing on what I thought might be of most interest to the Chinese government: steelmaking, petrochemical and chemical facilities engineering, and mining. He suggested that Senator Scott and I go to China, meet with engineers and officials there, and see whether they would have interest in working with Dravo. With Thorbecke's encouragement, Sen. Scott and I headed for Beijing. "Director, Asia Marketing" was added to my title.

We arrived in Beijing in the dead of night on an Iran Air flight, which offered the best connection available, through Tokyo, in the days before the Shaw's overthrow. The Beijing airport was about the size of an American regional airport and consisted of five or six dimly lit, small, single-story buildings. We were directed by soldiers of the People's Liberation Army in green uniforms with a red star on their cap to the airport medical office in one of the buildings where, after a review of our International Vaccination Certificates, we were given an additional immunization shot. I had seen the movie *The Manchurian Candidate* and wondered whether it was some form of psychological drug but figured they had better things to do with us.

I left Senator Scott in Beijing to call on foreign ministry officials while I spent the week with commerce ministry guides and a translator visiting steel mills, traveling the northeast of the country, Manchuria, by steam engine train and gray Soviet ZiL cars that resembled 1949 Fords. There were just a few hundred government cars in the entire country, but thousands of bicycles, each costing more than a year's salary. While congratulating myself on being one of the first foreigners in country, I was surprised to find Japanese engineers playing baseball outside a steel mill. That made it clear to me that we had some catching up to do.

Senator Scott and I returned to the States, and I reported to Thorbecke that the Chinese seemed interested in our steelmaking engineering capabilities. In fact, they had asked about nothing else, even though I had submitted reports covering *all* Dravo capabilities. Within short order, the Chinese asked me to return as soon as possible to further discuss steelmaking, and Thorbecke authorized my taking a delegation of five or six of our top engineers.

Travelling with that delegation, I quickly surmised that the Chinese were endeavoring to obtain as much "free" information as we would provide. I noted that they would ask a question of our engineers and after the answer would say nothing. The engineer, assuming he had not given an adequate answer, would carry on with what other information he knew to be pertinent. After a couple of go-rounds like that I realized most Americans couldn't handle silence, so I asked for a break and met privately with the delegation, telling them to keep their answers brief, and to wait quietly for the next question. Sometimes we had ten minutes' silence between questions, but our engineers learned a lesson and stopped giving out proprietary information.

After the delegation and I returned to the States, I was asked to bring a delegation of mining experts. Following a day or two in our Denver office for mutual briefings, I again headed to Beijing, this time with a delegation of five or six mining engineers. We visited several laboratories and above-ground facilities, but never ventured below. After that delegation, I decided to stay in Beijing to make the rounds of the commerce ministry and get a better handle on where we stood. Ministry officials sometimes introduced me to "experts" who took me on trips to various facilities they felt would interest our engineers.

Usually, I was one of only twenty Americans at the Beijing Hotel. Not deterred by the early morning smog, I would go for a run around Tiananmen Square collecting at least a thousand followers by the time I got back to the hotel, all wanting to see the American with blue eyes.

My ministry hosts took me one afternoon to visit Mao's Mausoleum on Tiananmen Square and I expressed embarrassment at our cutting in front of the line of thousands, ten wide and a mile long, waiting to see Mao's body lying in state and pay their respects. From my perspective, I was glad to see Mao where he was. Often when I traveled outside Beijing, people would stop me on the street or lean out of trolley cars wanting to shake hands. In the evenings, we foreigners attracted crowds as we walked to the central Post Telephone and Telegraph Office to print (punch tape) and telex our reports to the home office.

Flying in country was always a novel experience. Some of the smaller planes were biplanes with single engines throwing sparks and fireballs with a huge bang. Once we used a painter's ladder to climb into the cabin of an old Boeing 727, one of the earliest narrow-body jets acquired by the Chinese—obviously without stairways.

On one occasion I was asked by a Boeing representative to join the first 707 flight to and back from Japan. The Chinese crew was wearing t-shirts and flip-flops, which didn't inspire confidence, nor did the memento of the flight, a feather pressed in plastic to be used as a bookmark. We landed at over 180 knots, fifty more than usual, because of the pilots' experience in Russian aircraft, which require higher landing speeds. The Boeing rep told us the Russian planes in China burned out engines while the American planes in China burned out tires.

Travelling by train was not as exciting. I usually worked and met officials during the day and traveled at night by crowded, smoke-belching steam-engine-drawn passenger trains with the windows wide open. By morning my face was covered in black soot. During one memorable stop I heard there had been a nearby deep-coalmine disaster and was able to determine from local officials and reports that twenty-five thousand miners had died while official Chinese channels confirmed only a few hundred, something to remember today when reading Chinese press reports.

Out of the blue, my commerce ministry minders reading our annual report expressed interest in Dravo's history of building locks and dams on America's rivers, and in the towboats and barges we manufactured in Pittsburgh. I didn't get the entire picture, but I was hearing enough about a very large "Three Gorges Dam" to substantiate their interest in a dam on the Yangtze River and a need for boats and barges. For bulk carriers, the Chinese were using American LSTs that had been captured during the Korean War and understandably wanted an upgrade.

I returned to Pittsburgh with what I knew and the belief that the Chinese would be more apt to entertain discussions about the Yangtse River than they would about steel or mining. Thorbecke and I kicked this thought around with Dravo senior corporate officers who expressed skepticism after having funded two expensive, non-productive delegations, but agreed to one more go-around.

Dravo certainly knew how to make boats and barges and had some time ago built locks and dams on the Ohio River and its tributaries but never a super-huge dam like what the Three Gorges Dam was imagined to be. The company's senior leadership therefore formed a partnership with the U.S. Army Corps of Engineers and a Chicago design firm, Harza Engineers, which had relevant dam construction experience, though again not for anything that big. A delegation was formed that included the chief of the Army Corps of Engineers, Harza executives, our Mechling barge line executives, and various Dravo engineers. My job was to coordinate all the moving parts and supply "local knowledge," i.e. the way of doing business in China, for which I now knew more than most after several months in country.

We ended up as a delegation of ten or twelve headed first to Beijing and from there along the Yangtse River from Wuhan to Shanghai. Although

Taking a break near the future site of China's Three Gorges Dam on a boat assigned us as working space to develop a plan for the Yangtze River.

Wuhan has recently been tied to the Coronavirus, it has a long history of water transportation study and is known as the home of the Wuhan Water Research University, where we began our meetings. Our objective was to define all the parameters of the project, including the dam construction and the provision of boats and barges. We usually worked while travelling on a large crowded tour boat. We lived on an upper deck and used the top enclosed deck as an engineering studio. We were accompanied by two very interesting and special people I remember well.

The first was our excellent translator, Mrs. Zhou Ju Mei, whom I recall sitting in a chair on the upper deck outside knitting and kibitzing while we worked. She had learned English alongside her father, Zhou Peiyuan, a noted physicist who obtained his doctorate from the California Institute of Technology and studied at Princeton under Albert Einstein and subsequently in Europe. He and his family returned to China shortly before the Communist takeover.

As I got to know Mrs. Zhou, she told me her family story. They had been arrested early in the Cultural Revolution by hooligans energized by Chairman Mao. Mrs. Zhou's sentence was to work as a bricklayer and she said she had "built the best walls in China, almost as good as the Great Wall." Her doctor husband, later head of the Beijing Hospital, was sentenced to farm fields, where he learned to practice homeopathic medicine.

Her brilliant father was sentenced to house arrest, where he continued studies that eventually led to his appointment as president of Peking (Beijing) University. Although Mrs. Zhou, her husband, and her father survived the revolution intact, her sons were separated from them and trained as welders, which left them outside the elite cultural society of their parents and grandparents.

The second person was Ye Fe, Vice Minister of Communications (which included overseeing transportation on the Yangtze River), who had long been associated with Mao, having participated in his famous Long March of 1934-'5 as the Communists evaded Chiang Kai-shek's Kuomintang Army. Many evenings, we sat on the outside upper deck observing the shoreline and discussing how the People's Republic of China had evolved.

At the time, I was reading Theodore White's book, *In Search of History* (the 1976 history of modern Communist China during and after WWII).

Thankfully, because of my reading, I was able to have reasonably intelligent conversations with Minister Ye and Mrs. Zhou. Because we all used the same bathrooms in our living quarters on the boat (with the appropriate stalls), I usually found myself shaving and brushing my teeth in the morning between the two of them.

Although we had a permanent American representative in the Philippines, Thorbecke decided we needed one for China. After a substantive search, he hired Mel Searles in Hong Kong, which was then a British Colony on a ninety-nine-year lease from the People's Republic of China. Mel spoke fluent Mandarin Chinese and worked for Esso (Standard Oil) and was also head of the Hong Kong American Chamber of Commerce.

After Mel joined the company, Thorbecke decided to hire a Chinese national representative to work for Dravo in China proper. Around that time, the *Wall Street Journal* ran a story about a Chinese man who had been a fighter pilot during WWII. After the war, this man had joined the Chinese merchant marine and defected in Baltimore Harbor only to return to China after détente to represent American companies. He had an agriculture degree and for some reason, having to do with his management of a chicken farm, was known as "Dr. Chicken." I don't remember what qualified him to represent an engineering firm, but he was hired.

After Dr. Chicken signed on, he invited me and Mel to fly from Hong Kong to Guangzhou. It was easier to fly the short distance and enter China through an airport than to undertake a time-consuming drive and border crossing from Hong Kong with hundreds of others. When we arrived, Dr. Chicken invited us to dinner at a famous local restaurant known for serving live monkey brains. I won't describe the details but will say I didn't partake. I did, however, agree to a bowl of snake soup specially made for us. I shouldn't have.

I told Mel on the flight that I seldom got sick, so I was much surprised the next morning to wake up nearly paralyzed. I crawled to the bathroom hoping a hot bath would help. I didn't make it to breakfast and when Mel came to my room, I explained that this was a first, and I didn't understand why. Later we found out the soup, usually served in winter, was made from snakes and purposely contained a few drops of venom to "warm you up," which affected my nervous system and scared the hell out of me. From then on, I didn't experiment with food in China unless I knew exactly what it was.

We didn't make the cut for design of the Three Georges Dam; it went to others, notably including the much larger Bechtel, helmed by future Secretary of State George Schultz. However, we did agree to negotiate transportation solutions for the Yangtze River, downstream from the dam. After several return trips, we presented our final price. I was stationed alone in the Beijing Hotel to wait for a decision. After a couple of days of silence, I decided I couldn't wait any longer and booked my flight.

I told a ministry official what my new plans were, and he asked me to extend for further negotiations. I told him we had given our best terms and that I had booked my flight, packed, and checked out. As I waited for the car to the airport, a fellow stepped from behind a lobby pillar and handed me an envelope, saying, "I trust this will be sufficient to start." It was a letter of credit for the requested down payment.

There was a lesson in this: Never let your host know your schedule beyond your meeting. If you do, they'll push final negotiations to just before your desired departure, forcing you to give in or change your schedule, which may not be so easy. If you have truly given your final price, don't hang around. From then on, my answer to the question of when I would leave was always "When we've finished."

The ultimate contracts for the Yangtse transportation solutions included the provision of two huge 5,000-horsepower river towboats and two hundred large river barges. At that time, and at $200 million ($900 million in today's dollars), it was a premier American contract in China. We later invited our Chinese customers to study Houston's port operations and while there, they were invited by the former American Representative in China, George H. W. Bush, to dinner at his house.

Throughout the period 1977 to mid-1980, I was the Dravo marketing director for both the Middle East and Asia, serving as the principal corporate contact for our representatives in Al Khobar, Hong Kong, and Manilla. Although I was nominally responsible for a long list of countries, and actively pursued opportunities in many of them, I was most active in Algeria, Saudi Arabia, and China. Much of my deskwork was done on an airplane and personal contact with the representatives was by phone, usually at hours inconvenient for them. Since I was single, I didn't really try to understand; years later, I did.

Obviously, my big win was the $200-million China contract, unusual for a small Pittsburgh engineering company with sales of roughly $850 million then compared to Bechtel's $3.5 billion. I credit much of my success to Bill Thorbecke who, after my having spent eight years away from the international scene, gave me autonomy and stepped in only when he felt he could help, a process I replicated in the future. It was the one opportunity I had both identified and landed. More important were the key things I learned in both regions during those years:

- Foreign governments play a bigger role in their business communities than ours does.
- Knowledge of the history and culture of a host country is essential.
- Respected local partners are a necessity.
- Ignorance of the Foreign Corrupt Practices Act (FCPA) is no excuse.

PITTSBURGH 1980, A BRUSH WITH PRESIDENTIAL POLITICS

Nineteen-eighty was a presidential election year and with all my travel, I hadn't really paid much attention. Having concluded one of the first major contracts in China, I was invited early in the year to the White House to brief Professor Michael Oxenberg, President Jimmy Carter's National Security Council China adviser. Headlines at the time were about 14% inflation and American Embassy personnel being held hostage in Iran. California Governor Ronald Reagan and George Bush were neck-and-neck in a horserace for the Republican nomination.

Early in the year, Bill Thorbecke told me the company was looking to station someone in Europe, most likely in Holland or Italy, and I told him I would like to be considered. He had already given me a raise and a surprise case of Lanson Champagne for our success, but as a further reward he promised to consider me for, as it turned out, Milan, Italy.

It was at about the same time that Elsie Hillman called and asked me to run as a delegate to the 1980 Republican Convention committed to her close friend

GEORGE BUSH

710 NORTH POST OAK ROAD

SUITE 208

HOUSTON, TEXAS 77024

(713) 457 1900

February 5, 1979

Mr. James B. Kelly
Dravo Corporation
One Oliver Plaza
Pittsburgh, PA 15222

Dear Jim,

I got your letter of January 23 and I would like very much to follow up with Ev Rose. I am on the road every minute now. In fact, I am dictating this from snow covered Massachusetts.

From all you tell me, I'd love to have Rose involved. Inasmuch as I won't be in Pittsburgh soon, should I write him a letter or should I give him a call? You tell him that we want him involved as fully as he would care to be in whatever we do in Pennsylvania.

Since I last saw you, I am more confident than ever that I can get this nomination. We need people of excellence like him (and you too, darn it) involved. Thanks for the lead. Tell me what is the best approach.

Sincerely,

George Bush

Bringing together a couple of friends. Ev Rose subsequently worked on the Reagan Campaign and George Bush's 1988 Presidential Campaign.

George H. W. Bush. I, of course, agreed to do it, even though I was living in the city and would not have the name recognition I enjoyed in the North Hills. I mentioned this to Bill, and he expressed concern that I might return to politics.

An unexpected phone call helped convince him I was serious about staying with Dravo. As we were in my office discussing the company's situation in Europe, our assistant leaned in to say that Jim Baker was on the phone. Jim Baker, the future secretary of state, was managing Bush's presidential campaign against Reagan and was asking if I could play a role in Pennsylvania. In front of Bill, I said that since I might be transferred to Italy, I couldn't be of help, thus confirming my commitment to the company and the potential transfer. As it turned out, I was out of the country by the July Republican Convention.

The years between 1976 to 1980 were a difficult time for two of my mentors. In 1976, as chairman of the Pennsylvania Republican Delegation, Drew Lewis polled the delegation and committed it to President Ford. Shortly thereafter, Governor Reagan, in hopes of swinging the Pennsylvania delegation, and Drew Lewis, to his side, named Senator Richard Schweiker as his running mate. Lewis, sticking to his word, said that he and the delegation had already committed to Ford and would not change course.

Four years later, in 1980, Lewis solidly backed Reagan, who said he had admired Lewis in 1976 for keeping his word with President Ford. After the 1980 election, Schweiker was appointed Secretary of Health and Human Services while Lewis was appointed Secretary of Transportation, where he became known for firing the striking air-traffic controllers. It was unusual for Pennsylvania to have two cabinet secretaries, especially two from the small Pennsylvania Schwenkfelder religious sect, who had come up through state politics together.

Schweiker never accepted Lewis supporting Ford instead of the Reagan-Schweiker ticket in 1976, and Lewis never accepted that Schweiker couldn't understand his position as the already committed delegation chairman. Neither Lewis nor Schweiker ever said anything to me, but eventually I learned not to talk about one in the presence of the other. It was a sad outcome that years later I discussed with Claire Schweiker, who just shook her head.

For me it was clear example of Lewis honoring his word, an example I have always endeavored to follow.

MILAN, ITALY 1980–1983, DRAVO ENGINEERS

By 1980, Dravo had three successful operations in Europe. The Dutch acquisition focused on architecture projects, while the Spanish subsidiary engineered conventional and nuclear electric power plants. The Italian operation consisted of two parts: One provided small plant construction service (like in Algeria) and the other executed high-voltage electrical transmission projects and provided associated heavy-duty components.

Home office professional engineers in the power sector had been assigned to the Spanish subsidiary, but there were no other Americans in any of the units. Dravo management therefore decided it was time to align these subsidiaries more closely with each other, and with headquarters, while giving them more marketing support.

This was the point at which senior management decided to assign me to Italy as Director of European Marketing with three responsibilities, in this order, that would require every bit of my political skills:

- Market Dravo home-office capabilities in Europe.
- Support the marketing and sales activities of the Italian construction company Dravo Costruttori and engage home-office engineers when helpful.
- Coordinate relations among the subsidiaries and with the home office.

My Italian adventure began with my arrival at my apartment on Via Melzie D'Eril, Milan. I arrived midweek, found my office in our space above L'Assassino Ristorante, and went to a lunch there welcoming me to Milan. Unfortunately, another adventure was to interrupt my celebratory arrival.

During lunch, we had an overabundance of wine and, whether related or not, I began to feel a terrible pain in my backside. Meanwhile, one of my new colleagues, Stan Caracciolo, invited me to his summer apartment in Comogli, not far from Portofino, which was three hours by car from Milan, and I readily agreed to go, even though the pain in my backside was intensifying.

The uncomfortable situation got so bad over the weekend that I could hardly walk, so Stan called a friend of his, a general surgeon, and asked him to see me first thing Monday morning. We returned to Milan, and I went to the doctor's office. Although my Italian was limited, I was able to understand him when he made a phone call to see if an operating room were available immediately. I said that if I understood him correctly, he was reserving an operating room, but that I could not go because I had my first Dravo Europe meeting that afternoon and absolutely had to be there.

The doctor picked up the phone and called my colleague and future close friend Alberto Gnesutta, President of Dravo Costruttori, and informed him I would not be at the meeting. So that was the way they do things in Italy! Off to the hospital and the surgery I went. As I was recovering from the removal of an abscess, I was placed in a large double room with an opera singer whose girlfriend was a dancer, so for a couple of days I was gloriously entertained with classical opera and ballet, a real Italian welcome.

The doctor showed me a drawing of the modest castle the King of France had given *his* doctor for performing a similar surgery. I explained to the doctor that I was just a poor American not capable of providing my good doctor with an estate! We had a laugh, and I went to Portofino and Alberto's house in Paraggi for a week of recovery.

I spent some of the best time of my life in Italy. My apartment was a penthouse from which I could see many of the famous structures in the city center, including the Duomo, the Galleria Vittorio Emanuele II, and the Castello Sforzesco. Frequently, I walked to work. In doing so, I passed Casa Verdi, the musicians' retirement house founded by Verdi, where sounds of various instruments played by the sixty retirees reached the street via open windows. Further on, I would often stop to investigate Mrs. Pinin Brambilla's progress restoring Leonardo da Vinci's *Last Supper* in the Santa Maria delle Grazie Church and Convent, a task that only ended in 1999, nearly twenty years later. After seeing me often, she once invited me to sit with her on the scaffold. Today's tourists should be so lucky.

I generally spent my time off with Paola and Alberto Gnesutta at their houses either in Paraggi on the Mediterranean, or Macugnaga at the base of Monte Rosa in the Alps, where we often skied. My closest friends included Alberto's cousin as well as a young MBA student and his girlfriend, soon to be his wife, who was a model from Australia. They were such good friends that my twelve-year-old son, Jim, and I went with them on their honeymoon to Elba Island in the Mediterranean.

Speaking of Jim, when traveling through London I would spend an extra day or two with him, or he would visit Milan when not in school. We would go skiing or visit sites around Milan, Venice, Florence, Naples, and Rome. We once celebrated New Year's in Florence with pizza and a bottle of champagne. Later that year, we made a trip to Venice, where I had an important late-night meeting.

The two of us ate an early dinner at the famous Harry's Bar, where Jim had lobster thermidor (he'll never forget), after which he got violently ill—food poisoning. We returned to our room in the Danieli Hotel, where the staff found a doctor and a staffer to look over Jim while I went to the previously scheduled, very important meeting. My need to leave Jim alone was hard to explain to the doctor, who assumed I was off for a night on the town.

Back at work after my arrival and recovery from the surgery, I briefly visited Algeria and Saudi Arabia to review the progress of Dravo Costruttori's contribution to the corporate projects there. I also made a quick trip to Sri Lanka in pursuit of a World Bank irrigation project. The smothering bureaucratic oversight associated with that project was such that I left it behind (it wasn't completed until decades later), a lesson in international development bureaucracy I would take with me to the Reagan Administration. My principal activity, however, soon became marketing a feasibility study by our Denver mining engineers to Bulgaria authorities.

BULGARIA

In 1980, Communist Bulgaria was dependent on parts of the Soviet Union for coal and gas for heating and electricity generation, not unlike today's Bulgaria and Russia. To reduce that dependence, the Bulgarian deputy prime minister began a search for technology that would enable mining of their known-to-exist, ultra-deep deposits of coal. He had in his office a gadfly he often authorized to travel outside the country to resource luxury goods for senior party members. The gadfly spoke Italian, so he spent most of his time partying in Milan and shopping on the famed Via Monte Napoleone. In this case, the gadfly was instructed to use his Italian contacts to find suitable technology to mine their coal.

In a contract with the Canadian International Nickel Company (INCO Nickel), Dravo's Denver mining division engineered what was known as the

"Frozen Hole" concept: Mine shafts in Canada, up to a mile deep, were dug; collars were placed where there were water aquifers; low-temperature freon was pumped through the collar; and the aquifer water was frozen before it could enter the shaft up which the nickel was brought to the surface.

I'm not sure how he did so without the internet, but the Bulgarian gadfly learned of Dravo's "Frozen Hole" concept and approached Dravo Costruttori. He asked whether it could be applied in Bulgaria's eastern region, where it was known that deep, multiple strata of coal existed separated by aquifers. After a day or two of discussion, we agreed to a Dravo Costruttori contract, supported by Dravo Denver, to determine whether a comprehensive feasibility study would be worthwhile.

Over the period 1980-'82, Alberto and I, or I alone, frequently spent weeks at a time traveling to Sofia and from there driving or flying to Varna on the Black Sea coast, not far from the site of the coal deposits. We did so usually as the guest of the deputy prime minister. Our objective was to gather geologic data for our Denver engineers, and to review their return questions with the Bulgarian mine engineers and energy officials, returning the responses to Denver. Mostly, we worked with a team under the direction of the energy minister, who oversaw our project. Eventually we traveled with him and members of his staff to our Denver office, introducing the two teams, and back through Washington, where we arranged a tour of the White House for his delegation.

Aside from the technical back-and-forth, my experience in Bulgaria gave me a bird's-eye view of the Communist world prior to the fall of the Berlin Wall in 1989 and the collapse of the Soviet Union two years later. Much of what I saw or heard I reported to my contact in our Rome embassy, who happened to be from Pittsburgh and whom I stayed with when in Rome. After my first few months in Italy, he and his family moved to Milan and then, shortly before I left Italy, they moved to, of all places, Bulgaria.

My contact was most interested in what I knew about the people I met and the state of the relationship between the Bulgarians and the Russians. From my vantage point, the relationship wasn't always amicable, mostly because of Bulgaria's state of dependence. I usually tried to figure out who was the obligatory Communist Party observer, or sometimes even a Moscow overseer, in my meetings that were conducted in a combination of Italian, English,

Driving from Sofia to Varna, Bulgaria. Vice Minister Kanev, second from left.

and French. I spoke no Bulgarian or Russian, both Cyrillic languages with similar sounds I couldn't tell apart. Usually I was able to identify the party official or a Russian "minder" from the body language and the deference paid him.

One important friendship was with a Bulgarian, Andrey Lukanov, whom I recall being in the Economics or Trade Ministry at the time; he had been born and educated in Moscow, some said by the KGB, and spoke American English. I would meet him again during my Reagan years, when he was Bulgaria's minister of economic affairs. He served briefly as Communist Bulgaria's last prime minister in 1990, and was assassinated by a lone, unidentified gunman in 1996, when no longer in government.

I sometimes hobnobbed after work and late into the night with Communist Party and government officials like Andrey at their private clubs in Sofia and Varna. It may have been a club to them, but to me it looked like a Depression-era dance hall serving cheap vodka. When in Varna, I sometimes went to the nearby beach on the Black Sea, where the sharp stones made walking along the waterline painful, but the Bulgarians didn't seem to mind.

When I was in Sofia, the capital, I stayed directly across from parliament in the Grand Hotel Sofia, which wasn't so grand and where I assumed everybody participated in keeping track of me. When Alberto was there, we knew that both our rooms were bugged, and as we decided on various approaches, we masked our language, once playing with the Chinese I Ching coins while discussing the probabilities of one strategy or another. I would have liked to know what our minders were thinking.

One late evening while in Sofia, I sent a barely encrypted report to our Denver office by telex, a direct connection using a networked typewriter located in the Bulgarian Post, Telephone and Telegraph Office, which was empty at the time. As I was pondering my next line, the machine abruptly came to life and the message read: "Are you finished, Mr. Kelly?"

Not only were they reading my messages but, out of sight, they let me know they knew when I was there and at which machine and, obviously, what I was sending.

It took us more than a year to finish the preliminary, deep-mine study and conclude with our Bulgarian colleagues that with their resources the project was not viable and would therefore not warrant a full feasibility study. The coal was of lowest quality and the cost of extracting it, even with the most modern technology, was unreasonably high, even if it were the only alternative to Russian energy.

Dravo's chairman and CEO retired near the end of my second year in Italy, after naming the CFO as his successor. The CFO, a Harvard MBA, had previously been CFO of F&M Schaefer Brewing in New York and before that with consulting and manufacturing companies; some of the engineers were critical of him for having limited experience in their world. At the time of his appointment, some of the major projects, like those in Saudi Arabia and China, were coming to an end, and project engineering manhours were falling rapidly. The company was also completing an extravagant headquarters building; today, that building is the BNY Mellon fifty-five-story skyscraper in Downtown Pittsburgh. It seemed to many that these were signs of impending doom.

And they were right. All the signs foretold the eminent demise of Dravo and just as the situation neared the tipping point, a headhunter contacted me for an international marketing position with the Cleveland-based McKee Division of the English firm Davy McKee, Ltd., a 1,400-person engineering subsidiary pursuing oil refinery and petrochemical projects around the world.

I decided to accept the Davy McKee offer because it represented a step up from world-regional marketing to global marketing and it included a salary uptick. The decision was made all the easier because the corporate headquarters were in London and Jimmy lived in Reading, a short train ride away.

Dravo leadership, including the new CEO and Bill Thorbecke, did their best to keep me on board, but the writing was on the wall, and I was reading it. It wasn't long after that that Dravo Engineers collapsed and was liquidated piece by piece; the final small piece being sold in 2019.

CLEVELAND AND HOUSTON 1983–1984, DAVY MCKEE

Davy McKee had purchased the Cleveland firm Arthur G. McKee in 1978. By 1983, manhours sold were descending there too and it badly needed marketing help. I was to take on the international marketing role that included identifying projects requiring services for petroleum facilities design, engineering, procurement, and construction management outside the United States.

I had hoped first to spend time at company headquarters and with Jimmy in the UK and was not aware that Davy McKee Cleveland was only a few downward steps behind Dravo and needed immediate help. I was asked to go directly from Milan to Cleveland. For me, there was no turning back.

It was summer 1983 when I reported to Cleveland. I was barely able to rent an apartment before I was asked to travel to Korea to scout an oil-refining project. I had been to Korea several times with Dravo simply to familiarize myself with the market and evaluate partners for engineering services, but I had never pursued a specific opportunity there. In this case I made several trips followed by Korean client visits to Cleveland. Throughout the process I sought the advice of the retired head of a Korean engineering firm who had been introduced to me by Parkman Clancy, my Pittsburgh mentor retired from Gulf Oil.

Concurrently, I identified and pursued a chemical-plant engineering assignment with Michelin, making several trips to their headquarters in Clermont-Ferrand, France. The most enjoyable part of that work was making friends with one of the senior executives, who introduced me to a couple of Michelin-rated restaurants.

Because of Cleveland's proximity to Pittsburgh, I was able to spend a few weekends with family and friends in Pittsburgh, including attending my brother's wedding. As time went by, it was unfortunately becoming more apparent that Davy McKee was not going to make it in Cleveland.

From 1980 to 1983, the United States had been in the most severe recession since WWII; for Davy McKee, change was in the wind. After six months, London decided to close the Cleveland facility and transfer many, including me and the two projects I had initiated in Korea and France, to Davy McKee's relatively new Houston office that had been established to pursue oil and gas projects in the Southern United States.

Unfortunately, Houston's economy was not much better than Cleveland's. For me, this was a very difficult time of adjustment, having left my friends in Milan, and then my family in Pittsburgh. I arrived in Houston knowing only two people there, and they were both overseas.

In the face of outside concern over the future of Davy McKee in the United States, I was fortunately able to continue the relationship established with senior Michelin staff and they approved transferring the work to the

Houston office. My work representing Davy McKee in Korea also continued, but due to the worsening atmosphere in the company, and in the city of Houston caught in the recession, I began to reconsider staying either with Davy McKee or in Houston. More and more, I felt that I should be looking for another assignment before I had to.

I began to think about options. In my spare time, I escaped the office by renting planes and flying to places like Galveston, Austin, College Station, and Corpus Christi. On several occasions, I found wide-open, abandoned runways where WWII pilots and planes had been trained and tested. Once, when Jimmy came to visit me in Houston, he joined me on a flight and as we ascended, we had an incredible sighting—a hot-air balloon rising through the clouds.

I thought that might interest him in aviation, but it didn't take.

WASHINGTON 1984–1988, REAGAN ADMINISTRATION

Over the years, from time to time, I would speak with my Virginia Tech swim-team buddy, Jim Grossmann who, after serving in the Army in Vietnam, had followed me a few years later to Thunderbird and subsequently developed a New York banking career before joining the United States Agency for International Development (USAID).

He served in Asia, Africa, and Central America before being assigned to Washington, where he became aware of a high-level vacancy in the Department of Commerce's International Trade Administration (ITA). He thought it had something to do with U.S. economic policy in Asia and in view of my China experience suggested I investigate it. As I have often said to students and friends seeking career changes, personal contacts are key.

I vaguely knew about these positions from my time with Senator Schweiker and thought that if it was truly at a senior level, it would be worth pursuing as it would give me entrée to a whole new level of international business contacts. I also knew it would take some maneuvering to land it.

I had not spoken for some time with Drew Lewis, who was now chairman and CEO of Warner Amex Cable after serving as Reagan's transportation secretary. I gave him a call to see if he could help me evaluate the ITA opportunity Jim had mentioned.

Drew was close friends with Commerce Secretary Malcolm Baldrige and gave him a call. He said that Baldrige told him he had several openings and asked to meet me.

MALCOM BALDRIGE, SECRETARY OF COMMERCE

I flew to Washington over the 1984 July 4th weekend, stayed with Jim Grossmann, and met with Secretary Baldrige in the Commerce Department after the holiday. At the time of its construction, the Commerce Building was the largest building in the world and the secretary of commerce's office was, and still is, the largest in Washington, likely because Herbert Hoover was secretary of commerce when the building was begun in 1927; the building was renamed after him in 1982. It was intimidating to cross the threshold of a room the size of a five-lane bowling alley and meet not only the secretary of commerce, but the undersecretary of the International Trade Administration, Lionel Olmer.

Malcolm Baldrige was the quintessential Marlboro Man. In fact, he looked so much like the classic cowboy that Philip Morris & Company, the manufacturer of Marlboro cigarettes, had once approached him to be the model. At the time I was to meet him, he was sixty-two years old and known to be colorful. He was well liked. He had a slight stoop and a slow speech that belied the successful Connecticut-New York businessman who previously headed Scovill, Inc., a diversified manufacturer. He in fact did smoke Marlboros and wore a huge cowboy belt buckle awarded to him as the 1981 Rodeo Man of the Year. In the corner of the office was a cowboy hat and a coiled rope he used to give lessons to visitors from around the world. Known to prefer plain English, he peppered his speech with Western witticisms like "Well, I always thought he was one taco short of a combination plate."

Lionel Olmer, on the other hand, was quick to the point. He had been a Navy captain on the staff of the chief of naval operations, responsible for intelligence. After that he had worked for Motorola, successfully introducing their electronic products in Japan. He began our meeting with a blizzard of acronyms describing two openings to me: Deputy Assistant Secretary (DAS) of International Economic Policy (IEP) for East Asia (EA), and DAS for Africa, the Near East and South Asia (ANESA). Undersecretary Olmer asked about my time in China and then whether I spoke Japanese (they were also looking to replace their Japan specialist). I told him I did not, so he turned to Secretary Baldrige and suggested that I be vetted for the ANESA position.

Secretary Baldrige asked me to work with his chief of staff and the department's White House liaison to schedule an interview at the White House. His chief of staff had come to Washington from Connecticut with the secretary and through her I learned that she and the secretary were close friends with Elsie Hillman, my political mentor in Pittsburgh.

In short order I was asked to meet with the deputy White House personnel secretary. After a brief interview during which it became clear I had not worked in the first Reagan presidential campaign and was not active in the second that was underway at the time of our meeting, I was told, "You'll need to be a legend in your own time to get this job." Furthermore, he assumed that living in Italy I had not voted in the president's first election, a firm requirement. In fact, I had been traveling to Dravo's Denver mining office on election day and stopped in Pittsburgh to see my mother—and vote. That didn't seem to make any difference.

Having been referred to the White House by a member of the president's cabinet, I assumed the White House interview was just a formality. I was thoroughly confused as I left the White House, but as I thought it through, I came to the realization that in the end, the White House would have the final say, no matter how much Baldrige wanted me, and their primary consideration would be my political backing, not my international experience. I had my work cut out for me!

Before returning to Houston, I stopped in to see my old boss, former senator and cabinet member, Dick Schweiker, who was now head of the American Council of Life Insurance. When I explained what I was doing in Washington, he offered his support. I also managed to schedule a private meeting with Pennsylvania Senator John Heinz, who didn't tell me, but I knew from quick calls to mutual contacts, he had already pledged support to a member of his staff, a Democrat (who hadn't worked in the president's campaign either) seeking the same position. I did not have a close enough relationship with Pennsylvania's other Republican senator, Arlen Specter, to get on his calendar while I was there.

As soon as I got back to Houston, I made follow-up calls to Elsie Hillman, Secretary Baldrige's chief of staff and, of course, Drew Lewis, telling them of my experience at the White House personnel office. For a job where political backing was more important than international experience, I now had support from one current cabinet member, Malcomb Baldrige; two former cabinet members, Drew Lewis and Dick Schweiker; and a Republican National Committee woman, Elsie Hillman.

In early August, I got a call from Drew saying he had spoken with Reagan's first White House personnel secretary (in office when Drew was appointed), who cleared my appointment with the current White House personnel office while setting aside Heinz' Democrat candidate. I "had become a legend" and should report as soon as possible after the November '84 election, assuming Reagan's victory.

Believing that Reagan would defeat former Vice President Walter Mondale, and rather than hang around Houston in an uncomfortable job, I resigned my position at Davy McKee, packed out, and headed to Washington, where I rented a room in a Georgetown house owned by a friend of Jim Grossmann's.

Although the staff would be surprised by the speed of my security clearance, there was a fair amount of additional paperwork associated with the appointment, just not enough to keep me busy for the three months between my resignation and the election. At one point I joined some friends from Pittsburgh, Milan, and Saudi Arabia at a New York dinner party, where I met Janet Bennett. She subsequently asked for my help interviewing a Venetian mask maker in Italian, but when I couldn't make it happen, I asked her out for dinner on my next visit to New York, which I quickly scheduled.

We had dinner at Il Continori Restaurant in New York and spent hours on the phone many evenings after that. By that time, I was forty-three years old; I had been married for seven years and single the following nine. I began to think this might get serious, and it did. I found Janet to be just incredibly nice and easy to be with. Except for flying and sports, we shared similar levels of curiosity. Following numerous back-and-forth trips on both our parts, Janet came to live with me in Washington in 1985.

I was officially appointed Deputy Assistant Secretary of Commerce in the International Trade Administration (ITA) by Secretary Baldrige November 18, 1984, with my start day to be November 26. At the time, ITA was divided into four parts: the U.S. and Foreign Commercial Service, Trade Promotion, Trade Enforcement and Compliance, and Economic Policy. There were four regions within Economic Policy and my assignment was for the largest, Africa; the

Near East; and South Asia, seventy-two countries that included Algeria, Saudi Arabia, and Egypt, where I had previously worked.

The president and the administration were strongly committed to the principle of free and open trade with a notable difference between then and now: Then we were focused on competition with Japan; today it is China. My primary responsibility was to provide American companies with up-to-date business and economic intelligence for the broad range of countries in my region. Beyond that, I was to spotlight and seek to change unfavorable business conditions while assisting American firms in the event of a dispute with a host partner or government.

From my previous experience, I realized that foreign businesses related to their government as a partner in world markets; in America, government was usually viewed as the enemy, or just not very helpful. I set out to change that. When traveling abroad I often found that by simply appearing with American businessmen, or mentioning the name of their company, I increased the awareness and importance of the company locally.

On the home front, my team at first resisted helping Company A because they would then feel compelled to help Company B, A's competitor. I changed that practice, telling my staff they should help whoever asks them. If Company B asks, support them too; if they don't, too bad.

In a position such as I had, there is not much you can do by yourself. You have little sway over foreign governments, and you cannot handle seventy-two countries alone. Both require skills I alluded to previously: bringing people together, listening carefully, and leading by example. In the vignettes below you'll see the variety of issues my team and I faced (Saudi Arabia and Nigeria, for example). Often, there was not an issue to be resolved, just an impression to be made or taken (Zimbabwe and Mozambique).

My team included a secretary and administrative assistant, and the three area directors for Africa, the Near East, and South Asia, to whom the desk officers covering the seventy-two countries reported. I also shared responsibility for rating American embassy commercial officers in my region with their ambassadors and the head of the Foreign Commercial Service.

MOHAMED SAHNOUN, ALGERIAN AMBASSADOR

I went to my designated Commerce Department office early my first day with little idea what to expect, hoping to get ahead of things. My administrative as-

My new Algerian friend, Ambassador Mohamed Sahnoun

Introducing Janet to Iraqi Ambassador Nizar Hamdoon. We were to work closely over my four years in the administration, and for a short time after I left when he was Deputy Foreign Minister.

sistant greeted me with an invitation from Algerian Ambassador Mohamed Sahnoun, who had learned I had worked in Algeria and invited me to breakfast at the ambassador's residence, formerly Vice President Lyndon Johnson's house and before that Perle Mesta's, the wealthy widow of the founder of Mesta Machine in Pittsburgh. Small world.

That breakfast in the formal dining room began an enjoyable four-year association with the ambassador, during which I and Middle East hands, including former CIA directors Helms, Schlesinger, and Colby, and Ambassador (to Algeria and Syria) Chris Ross, came to the residence with our wives for dinner and discussion.

After breakfast, a former U.S. ambassador to Saudi Arabia called to ask if I would like to attend an evening reception with him at the Iraqi residence celebrating the restoration that day of diplomatic ties, broken since 1967. I supposed the ambassador called because he knew I had spent time in the region, although not in Iraq.

The breakfast and reception were a stunning change of pace. I had suddenly gone from an unhappy, slow-moving assignment in a place where I was not comfortable to a fast-paced, high-level position in a place that I both knew and liked.

TARIQ AZIZ, IRAQ FOREIGN MINISTER, DEPUTY PRIME MINISTER
NIZAR HAMDOON, IRAQ AMBASSADOR TO THE U.S AND U.N., LATER DEPUTY FOREIGN MINISTER
GEORGE SCHULTZ, U.S. SECRETARY OF STATE

The former U.S. ambassador to Saudi Arabia and I were greeted at the front door of the Iraqi ambassadorial residence by Chargé Nizar Hamdoon (he had not yet presented his ambassadorial credentials). Hamdoon and I had met briefly at a conference in Colorado, and I recall being surprised by how much his English had improved. As we were exchanging pleasantries, Iraq's foreign minister, Tariq Aziz, joined us. He was to become infamous later as President Saddam Hussain's righthand man before and during the Gulf War in 1990 and the Iraq War of 2003- 2011.

Secretary of State George Schultz arrived, and after introductions, Minister Aziz asked what could be done to recognize the new amity between our countries. Secretary Schultz turned to me and, as if we had been working together for years, asked whether I could lead a commercial delegation to Iraq. I hid my surprise as best I could and said I would raise the subject with Secretary Baldrige when next I saw him. I had no idea whether this was within my paygrade or even when I would next see Baldrige.

A day or two after the Iraqi reception, Baldrige's assistant called me to the secretary's fifth-floor office. He welcomed me on board and said he had heard from Secretary Schultz that my leading a commercial delegation to Iraq would be helpful to our new relationship and that I should start on it as soon as possible.

He also said that in view of the recent (October 31, 1984) assassination of Indian Prime Minister Indira Gandhi, President Reagan had asked him to scope out her son, the new prime minister, Rajiv Gandhi, and invite him to the White House. The secretary asked that I alert my team to prepare for him to visit Gandhi in New Delhi and also to prepare for the expected Gandhi follow-up visit to Washington. Any high-level business meetings I had previously participated in would be nothing compared to what it would take to choreograph these meetings.

The two assignments, Iraq and India, would absorb much of my time through June of 1985. They would also elevate recognition of my team (soon to be known as Kelly's Fighter Pilots) to a level they had not previously experienced. I did not know it at the time, but Commerce officials did not usually appear this high on the diplomatic totem pole.

IRAQ

Territorial Iraq has been around a long time, but its modern-day version was formed after World War I in 1921 as the Hashemite Kingdom of Iraq. It was governed by Faisal I under British authority granted by the League of Nations. In 1932, Iraq achieved independence from Great Britain. In 1958, the monarchy of Faisal II was overthrown in the 14 July Revolution and the Iraq Republic was created.

The Arab Socialist Ba'ath Party took over the country in 1968, naming Ahmed Hassan Al-Bakr as president. However, the Ba'ath Party gradually came to be controlled by Saddam Hussain. In 1979, he was named head of the Revolutionary Command Council and President of Iraq. In September 1980, following the Iranian Revolution, Saddam initiated war with Iran, which brought him favorable reviews in the United States since Iran still held American diplomats detained at the time of the revolution.

As for United States relations with Iraq, we first formally recognized it in 1930 and established a legation there in 1931, which was elevated to an embassy in 1946. Diplomatic relations were severed during the 1967 Arab-Israeli War but reestablished by the agreement signed by President Reagan and Minister Tariq Aziz. Iraq, Saddam, and Aziz were unknown to most of the world at that moment, something that would change dramatically just six years later.

It was at the November 26, 1984, celebration of the signing of that agreement at the Iraqi Residence, my first day on the job, that Secretary Schultz suggested to Minister Aziz that I lead a commercial delegation to Iraq as a sign of the renewed relations. I had not yet begun my detailed security briefings, but I understood that Iraq's war with Iran could turn against Iraq, and there was fear it would spread throughout the region, thus the enemy of our enemy became our friend.

In early 1985, I led a U.S. delegation to Iraq with the support of our ambassador to Iraq, David Newton, and Jim Placke, former deputy ambassador to both Iraq and Saudi Arabia, and at the time deputy assistant secretary of state for the Near East. Jim would become a lifelong friend.

The primary objective of our delegation was the negotiation of a trade agreement with the Iraqi Trade Ministry to remove trade barriers and encourage and protect U.S. investment in various sectors of the Iraq economy, notably agriculture and oil. The usual path for bilateral trade agreements was through the United States Trade Representative (USTR—a cabinet position), but in this case, in planning for the mission with the State Department and USTR, I was assigned the responsibility, again unusual for my Commerce Department position.

The final negotiation and the signing of the agreement were televised, which undoubtedly was the reason for the young deputy trade minister's heavy perspiration—President Saddam was likely watching.

Since this was the first visit of a senior U.S. official to Iraq in nearly twenty years, there were many ceremonies and meetings held that were unrelated to the agreement. These were intended to introduce us to key Iraqi decisionmakers. When our delegation first arrived in Iraq, we were met at the airport by a sizable delegation that included individuals from the Ministry of Trade and the Ministry of Foreign Affairs.

One of the first things I was asked to do was lay a wreath at the Tomb of the Unknown Soldier. I agreed to do so and was accompanied by a young English-educated captain who was quick to explain there really was a body in the tomb. I was also taken to the front lines, where soldiers strapped coffins of artillery casualties onto the roofs of beat-up taxies for delivery to the families. Few people in Washington realized the extent of suffering that war caused over the course of its eight years. In 1988, at the war's conclusion, over five hundred thousand Iraqi and Iranian soldiers had been killed.

Also on the trip, our delegation met with the Iraqi Ambassador to the United States, Nizar Hamdoon, who was in-country, and with Hussein Kamel, Commander of the Republican Guards, President Saddam Hussein's elite troops. Kamel was married to Saddam's daughter but later defected to Jordan before the Second Iraq War. Shortly thereafter he petitioned his father-in-law to be allowed to return to Iraq. Saddam approved Kamel's return saying he would be treated like any other returning prodigal Iraqi. He returned, was ordered to divorce his wife, and was assassinated by his father-in-law. His family received the coffin along with an invoice for the bullets.

For the remainder of my service in the administration, I would lead the interagency process overseeing commercial relations with Iraq. This entailed participation in decision-making as to whether to license sophisticated technology or equipment to Iraq. Doing so often brought me into the orbit of Assistant Defense Secretary Richard Pearl, an architect of the Second Iraq War and the man often referred to as the Prince of Darkness. On almost every occasion, Pearl refused to license anything to a country he considered a threat to Israel.

INDIA

Behind Iraq came India, my second important early responsibility. My staff and I were to liaise with Prime Minister Rajiv Gandhi's staff in preparation for Secretary Baldrige to visit India in May and for a June return visit by Prime Minister Gandhi to the United States. Prime Minister Indira Gandhi had been assassinated by her Sikh bodyguards immediately preceding Reagan's reelection because she had directed a military action to remove Sikh pilgrims from the Harmandir Sahib Temple in Amritsar, which resulted in many Sikh casualties. Her son Rajiv was appointed to the position the same day of her assassination. A somewhat apolitical individual and Indian Airlines pilot, he had become politically active four years earlier after assuming his older brother Sanjay's parliamentary seat following Sanjay's death in an acrobatic plane crash.

We had several issues with India that we wanted to spotlight at the time, notably the theft of U.S. intellectual property like movies and drug patents that were widely copied. On the other hand, India was one of our largest markets for commercial aircraft and engines and we had a tenuous hold on part of its defense market. Of most importance within administration policy was recognition of India as a regional democracy; anything that could be done to distance India from the Soviet Union would be on the table.

After the initial staff work laying the groundwork for Baldrige's visit to India, I accompanied him first to China (where I suggested he recruit my former Dravo colleague and current commercial counselor in Beijing, Mel Searls, to the East Asia equivalent of my position) and then to India on one of the Air Force Boeing 707s. Before departing, I had expected to brief Baldrige on the India aspect of the trip, and probably go there on my own ahead of him, but that did not happen. Instead, a series of unexpected events rerouted my travels.

Because I was new to the job, I had asked the secretary's assistant if I could attend the China briefing, which was to be held the day before the India briefing, to see how it was conducted. Permission was given, and I showed up the next day ready to take notes on protocols, the methods of briefing, the level of formality, etc.

The secretary's office, as large as it is, accommodated as many as twelve to fifteen department briefers at a large conference table. The various agency observers and contributors, usually thirty or more, sat in folding chairs off to one side of the table. That morning, after everyone assembled, Secretary Baldrige turned to the acting deputy assistant secretary, who was covering China, and asked him to begin the briefing.

He stood up, as if to turn to the easel, and instead excused himself saying that he had to leave for his previously scheduled commercial flight to China to be there to arrange for the secretary's arrival in Beijing. He apologized and said that his boss, the Assistant Secretary (AS) of Economic Policy, would continue the briefing.

Caught totally off guard, the assistant secretary was obviously unprepared. With no briefings on China, Baldrige adjourned the meeting and asked that the India briefing be ready to go first the next day, after which he would give the assistant secretary another shot to redeem himself. Not wanting to endure the same fate as the assistant secretary, and not knowing anything more about how these briefings were conducted, I spent all night with my knowledgeable career staff preparing what I assumed should be the India briefing. Happily, I delivered it first thing the next morning and was pleased to hear the undersecretary comment that it had been one of the best briefings he had seen.

Perhaps because of my China experience, perhaps because of my briefing, and certainly because of my India responsibilities, instead of my travelling directly to New Delhi, Secretary Baldrige invited me to travel with him from Washington to Beijing and Beijing to New Delhi.

A few days later, we took off from Andrews Air Force Base, refueled in Alaska and Japan, and landed in Beijing, where we spent several days before heading to India. Since I had already spent so much time in Beijing and didn't really have any responsibility for that part of the trip, Baldrige's chief of staff asked me to take her to where they sold antiques, Liulichang Street. In the end, she didn't buy anything, saying that if she had to dust it, she didn't buy it. Memorable!

There were numerous logistics problems in Beijing—a shortage of staff cars, mixed-up or missing hotel keys, conflicting appointment schedules, etc.—so when we were airborne crossing the Himalayan Mountains, I called (the plane had a great communication system for 1985) Ambassador John Gunther Dean in New Delhi to review logistics and avoid a repeat.

Time spent on the plane was not wasted. Using the voluminous India briefing books that my staff and I had prepared, I briefed the secretary on the issues his counterpart, the minister of commerce and industry, was likely to raise, or the issues that Baldrige had indicated he might address. On the Indian side, of most interest were preserving multinational sources of foreign aid and sustaining access to capital markets. Baldrige would address intellectual property protection, opening India's consumer markets to global products such as Pepsi, and the administration's request that India purchase American-made airplanes and engines.

There was an interesting mix of personalities on the plane. William P. Clark, the former National Security Advisor and Secretary of the Interior and a close Reagan confidant was, for reasons I never knew, on board to Beijing. Under Secretary Lionel Olmer had announced his intent to retire after the trip, so he and his replacement, Bruce Smart, were on board. Smart had previously been chairman of the Continental Corporation, a Fortune 500 company, and it was obvious to all that he and the former Navy intelligence officer were two very different people. Smart would have a difficult time working in government.

Most of our brief time in India was spent in meetings, where we made some progress promoting our aviation sector, but no progress on the intellectual property or consumer market issues. I remember some collateral events better. Several of us would go out running, always carrying bananas to toss to the monkeys to keep them from jumping on us. Sometimes we would go out for a walk and blobs of grease would magically appear on our dress shoes followed by young boys offering $1 shoeshines. I had warned the twenty-five staffers on the trip not to brush their teeth with tap water; no one took my advice, and all wound up in extremis as they left for Helsinki (the secretary's final stop) and then back to the U.S. I made my way home commercially.

RAJIV GANDHI, INDIA PRIME MINISTER

For Prime Minister Gandhi's Washington visit a month after our India trip, my staff and I updated the briefing books for Secretary Baldrige and President Reagan. I participated in a meeting between Baldrige and the prime minister and afterward had a memorable discussion with the prime minister about flying. I asked him if he were still an active pilot and he said no. He asked if I were still flying, and I said no. He said, "Well, you have to give up something with these big jobs." I laughed and said that his job as prime minister of then 750 million people (at that time) was a bit larger than mine.

A stop in Tokyo on the way to China and India with Secretary Baldrige.

With Secretary of Commerce Baldrige, left, in India. The photo border inscribed, "To Jim Kelly with thanks from one of the young fellows in the foreground."

ALGERIA (AGAIN)

CHADLI BENDJEDID, PRESIDENT OF ALGERIA

In the time between my visits to Iraq and India, April 1985, I was called to Secretary Baldrige's office to brief him on our current economic relationship with Algeria. It was my first such meeting with the secretary (and before the India briefing), so in preparation for just such meetings I had asked the desk officers to prepare one-page country summaries. I handed the one-pager to the secretary who, having never seen one, asked me about it and said he would make it a requirement for all regions. I was off to a good start.

I understood I was briefing the secretary for his meeting that evening with Algerian President Chadli Bendjedid. I nearly fell out of my chair when he asked whether I had time to attend the meeting with him; I told him it would be an honor and later rode in his car to the Madison Hotel to meet President Bendjedid. Being relatively new to the department and the "cowboy" secretary I searched for common ground and told him that as a teenager I had been in horse shows and worked as an exercise jockey. I also told him I had worked in Algeria. The secretary didn't say much, leaving me wondering whether I had said *too* much.

However, as we entered the president's hotel suite Baldrige introduced me as having lived and worked in Algeria. Bendjedid had done his homework and it turned out he loved horses as much as Baldrige did, so for about half their time together they compared riding experiences. Later in the meeting, I told the president about some of my experiences in his country—all the time wondering to myself, how did this transition from engineer to diplomat come to pass? One thing did indeed lead to another.

SAUDI ARABIA

On several occasions, I visited Saudi Arabia and our ambassadors there, first Walt Cutler and then Hume Horan. Horan had been born in Iran of an Iranian father and an American mother, and in addition to speaking Farsi spoke perfect Arabic. He happened to be in office when United States intelligence discovered Saudi missiles hidden from our satellites in desert caves and was tasked with informing the king of our discovery. The king petulantly asked

In Riyadh with Ambassador Hume Horan presenting photos to the Saudi Vice Minister of Commerce of him and Secretary Malcolm Baldrige taken shortly before Baldrige's death in a rodeo.

for his replacement. Walt Cutler, who had preceded Horan, was pressed into service again.

My previous experience in the Kingdom and my friendship with the Alireza family gave me entrée not only in country, but also to the Saudi Ambassador to the United States, Prince Bandar bin Sultan, dean at the time of the diplomatic corps in Washington.

Every so often, Prince Bander invited me and other administration officials to dinner at the ambassador's residence in McLean, Virginia. After dinner one evening in 1988, he asked me to intercede with Secretary Baldrige on a matter concerning Saudi steel rod sold in the United States. The problem the Saudis were confronting stemmed from several complex trade practices: subsidies, countertrade, dumping, and countervailing duties.

The Saudi Arabian Government "subsidized" the production of basic steel rods that had been purchased by German companies as "countertrade" for machinery and equipment they sold to Saudi Arabian state enterprises. The steel was subsequently shipped directly from Saudi Arabia to the United States and sold at cost, below the going American market price, "dumping." American steel producers then sued the Commerce Department for not imposing "countervailing duties," a tariff that would raise the price of the steel to equal or exceed the American market price.

Following up, I arranged a meeting where Secretary Baldrige explained to the ambassador that the United States steel industry, already downsizing under attack from Korea, didn't need underpriced Saudi steel supplied by Germany and that if the shipments were to continue, trade relations among the three countries would suffer. The ambassador and the secretary agreed to accept what was here, but there were to be no more shipments.

I later testified before the House Foreign Affairs Committee about another controversial Saudi issue: Saudi men studying in the United States sometimes married American women and had children before returning to settle their family in the Kingdom. Some divorced their American wife and refused to endorse her Saudi visa or residence permit, banishing her from the Kingdom. They also would refuse to permit the children to visit their mother in the United States, for fear she would keep them. Unfortunately, there wasn't much we could do. The women, for better or worse, mostly worse, had married into a male culture they didn't really understand.

ZIMBABWE

During my tenure, there was concern across our government about the slowly deteriorating situation in Zimbabwe, formerly Rhodesia, which had transitioned to black rule in 1980. I knew that Pittsburgh's H. J. Heinz Company had a major tomato-growing project underway there, likely due to the relationship established between Heinz Chairman Tony O'Reilly and Zimbabwe President Robert Mugabe on the rugby field. It was easy for me to include Zimbabwe in one of my 1986 Africa trip itineraries, and I did so, responding to a request of the finance minister (we frequently received invitations from smaller countries who were keen to have high-level American visitors).

David Miller was the American ambassador to Rhodesia (I had heard he was from Pittsburgh and had worked for Westinghouse), but unfortunately was not in country, so I stayed at the Harare Holiday Inn, arriving early, where I was shown to the Presidential Suite—it was a mess of empty liquor bottles and full ashtrays. The room clerk told me that a delegation of Iran Mullahs had been there the night before with an assortment of women. I would have expected the Iranian delegation's hypocrisy, but I did not expect that Iran and Zimbabwe were connecting.

I first met with Agriculture Minister Denis Norman, a WWII Spitfire pilot, who brought me up to speed on the Heinz project. He invited me to visit parliament which, as of the country's independence from the UK in 1980, consisted of a Senate of forty and a House of one hundred. Ten Senate seats and twenty House seats were reserved for white Zimbabweans (the agreement that established this quota was terminated the year after I left and ended white representation). Norman introduced me to Ian Smith, the well-known former prime minister and, at the time, leader of the Opposition. Like Minister Norman, he had been a Spitfire pilot in the Battle of Britain.

One evening, I managed to visit a couple of white-owned farms with our CIA station chief. White farmers were coming under increasing attack by black insurgents, known to be operating on Mugabe's orders, who meant to force the white famers off their lands. Several of these farmers were Jewish and had seen the worst in Europe and were not about to give up. There had been frequent firefights between the farmers firing from armored pickup trucks and the insurgents firing from the bushes. For the white farmers, it was a battle they were destined to lose. It wasn't long before most of the farmers lost their land and moved to South Africa or left Africa altogether.

Before leaving Harare, I had a meeting with the very capable black finance minister who candidly expressed concern over Mugabe's plans to further restrict white participation in the government and to "nationalize" certain large farms. I wasn't surprised when the minister later defected to Canada.

On my return to Washington, I gave my desk officers and those at other departments a bleak assessment of what I saw, forecasting that white participation in the government would soon be a thing of the past and land reform (confiscation) would follow. I also reported the same to the appropriate people at the Heinz Company, which eventually sold its interest in the project to the government.

SOUTH AFRICA

Modern South Africa is larger than most people think. With a population of approximately sixty million people today, the country is about the size of France. It was established in 1910, eight years after the Boer Wars, by a peace treaty between the Dutch and English at the expense of the black population. Formal apartheid, classifying people by race, a legal system of economic, political, and social discrimination, was imposed by the White National Party in 1948 and was not completely dismantled until 1994 with the election of Nelson Mandela as president of a democratic government.

During the mid-80s, the population was twenty million and included five million whites who, in the main, supported a white government considered morally bankrupt by most of the world. The remainder of the population was black or "mixed race." Throughout the Reagan presidency, the administration's overarching objective was to preserve black employment while negotiating with the white government to encourage peaceful change.

Over time, administration policy came to be known as "Constructive Engagement" and its governmentwide implementation became the responsibility of Chet Crocker, Assistant Secretary of State for Africa. The center pole of that policy was support of American companies that were employing blacks, but that were under shareholder pressure to leave.

The domestic pushback against "Constructive Engagement" was intense. Numerous local governments, universities, cities, and states believed that the best way to cripple apartheid was by selling off pension fund shares of U.S. companies in South Africa and driving down their value unless they promptly left. The unfortunate result was that U.S. banks like Chase Manhattan and brands like IBM, who chose to shut down operations in South Africa, were forced to lay off their employees, black and white. The departure of such large American employers created further economic misery in the black community, which we were trying to avoid. My assignment was to support Crocker by describing the policy to the business communities in South Africa and the United States, and later to a congressional committee, but first, South Africa.

In January 1986, I was scheduled to speak about Reagan's South Africa policy to the mainly white Chamber of Commerce in Cape Town. The embassy representative who met me on arrival told me about the Space Shuttle *Challenger* disaster and suggested I comment on it in my remarks the next morning. I wondered what I could say, trying to figure it out because I was told my address would be televised.

The following morning, as I entered the hall with Counsel General Brown, a former African-American football player, I was still worried, and still scrambling to know what to say about the tragedy. America's efforts in space, particularly the space shuttle program, were seen as belonging to all men and all nations. The launchings and landings of the space shuttles were internationally watched. As such, I suspected many in my audience had heard about the explosion.

They had. But so too had the Afrikaans preacher, who spoke before me and delivered a eulogy I knew I couldn't top. It remained for me to affirm the administration's deepest sorrow, and then change horses to spell out the administration's support for American companies in South Africa, and the administration's dissatisfaction with progress toward the end of Apartheid.

Knowing I would eventually be asked back home to address not only Reagan policy, but also conditions in South Africa, I traveled around the country to gain firsthand impressions, first visiting Soweto, the largest black township in the country. It had been the scene of the 1976 riots that resulted in several hundred dead, and I observed the government making limited efforts to build schools and public housing in very crowded conditions. I also toured coalmines, talking to management and black workers alike, and taking particular interest in Pittsburgh's Joy Manufacturing, which provided mining equipment. Later, I would appear on Pittsburgh's KDKA TV to support the administration (and indirectly Joy) and to oppose proposed City Council legislation to penalize firms, like Joy, for being in South Africa.

In Johannesburg, I was invited to speak to a businessmen's luncheon and was surprised to see Richard Aguirre across the table, my friend from Thunderbird who had alerted me to Kennedy's death. In all my international travels I always ran into Thunderbird grads, but Dick was the only one from my time in Arizona.

Obviously, those of us seeking an end to Apartheid were not popular with the South African Government. While I was in Johannesburg, the government tried to compromise me by stashing an attractive blonde in my hotel room. I retreated before entering the room and went to the manager requesting that he ask the young lady to leave. The South African Government knew as well as I their scheme didn't work, so neither of us mentioned it.

I visited KwaZulu, the semi-independent Zulu homeland on the east coast, where I met the only black minister in the apartheid government, Prince Mangosuthu Buthelezi, prime minister of the nation's six million Zulus. I had met him in Washington and knew that he was a favorite of President Reagan and the American foreign policy apparatus, so I wanted to review our latest activities supporting the peaceful end of apartheid. He was prescient in his view that the rapid end of Apartheid with little preparation would leave the country collapsing under debilitating corruption, something that unfortunately occurred, and intensified after Mandela's death.

On my return to Washington, I testified before the House Foreign Affairs Committee with Chas Freeman, Crocker's Principal Deputy. We had met in China where he was Deputy to the Chief of the Liaison Office, George H.W. Bush. He was later appointed Ambassador to Saudi Arabia by Bush before the first Iraq War. The two of us spoke on behalf of companies training and employing blacks, but any sense we made with the committee was overshadowed by boisterous anti-administration comments by a well-known black congressman from California.

With Mangosuthu Buthelezi, prime minister of South Africa's 6 million Zulus.

MOZAMBIQUE

At the conclusion of my KwaZulu, South Africa, visit with Minister Buthelezi, I took off for Maputo, the capital of Mozambique, from Nelspruit (now Mbombela) Airport (often called *H.M.S. Nelspruit* because the runway was the size of a British aircraft carrier). I had rented a single-engine plane with a pilot from missionaries who had painted "Jesus Saves" on its side. After takeoff, I told the woman pilot I didn't think the VOR, a critical radio-navigation system, was working. She said not to worry because they seldom had electricity to power the VOR stations in Mozambique. We would fly by visual flight rules (VFR).

I alighted from the "Jesus Saves" plane in my diplomat's dark blue suit and red tie with Buthelezi's cane and was received by the U.S. ambassador and Graca Machel, Mozambique President Samora Machel's wife and the future wife of Nelson Mandela. She recognized the cane and asked after Buthelezi. I guessed he had gifted a few of them.

Mozambique in 1986 was a turbulent socialist country with an AK-47 on its national shield. The country had constantly come up in my discussions with South Africans who feared its ideological spread across poorer South African communities. It had won independence from Portugal in 1975 and much like the Pieds Noirs in Algeria, the Portuguese (including Pennsylvania Senator John Heinz's wife, Theresa, and her father) were ejected with limited possessions. The government then pursued a path of alignment with the Soviet Union, much to the detriment of its fishing industry, which was exhausted by the Communist so-called allies.

The ambassador and I called on various ministers as I got a sense of the country and looked for opportunities of potential interest to American companies, especially opportunities that could be implemented with USAID support to improve relations with the West.

Because the departed Portuguese had maintained the country's infrastructure, and because of an ongoing civil war, the central government did not fully control the area outside the capital, where most power was generated. Electricity in the capital was a sporadic luxury. I got my exercise hiking up ministry stairs, one with eleven floors, because there was no electricity for the elevators. I remarked that they most probably had the healthiest ministers in Africa. I found nothing that would be of interest to American companies, but years later USAID would play a role in restoring the nation's electricity grid.

Shortly after my visit, President Machel was killed in a plane crash inside the South African border, first blamed on the South African Government then on crew error for not following procedures on approach to Maputo. Our intelligence community believed the Soviet crew of the President's Tupolev Tu-134 plane, not expecting to leave Zambia when they did, had been drinking heavily before takeoff.

NIGERIA

A final example of the way we sometimes assisted American businesses concerned Caterpillar Inc., the Illinois heavy construction equipment manufacturing company. Their Washington offices had approached me to tell the story of their providing equipment to the government, and not being paid $500,000 ($1.4 million today). They had not been given any reason for the non-payment and asked that we investigate it with our Nigerian counterparts.

It just so happened I was planning to visit Nigeria during one of my Africa visits to support American companies there. After visiting the oil fields, the ambassador and I called on the trade minister, who had formerly been an artillery officer. Rather than get into a discussion about the overdue payments, I talked about our mutual interest in military history. The minister much preferred that line of discussion and, as an afterthought, approved the payment to Caterpillar.

Janet and I married August 1,1987, the same date as my son and best man Jim's birthday. He was an upcoming high school senior in England and was charged with picking up the ring I designed with a London jeweler and smuggling it to Washington. With the ring went my promise not to fly anymore (I did get dispensation later to qualify in a glider).

We had planned several days of wedding events with friends and family, but Secretary Baldrige died unexpectedly the week before, following a rodeo accident; I visited his office and helped his assistant pack some of his gear. Our wedding plans were compressed to a ceremony and Georgetown dinner the following Saturday.

Baldrige's death was a severe blow. Almost twenty years older, he had the same common sense, leadership skills, and elegance I observed in my father. I considered him a friend and learned as much as I could by carefully observing the way he handled himself and how he made thoughtful decisions.

As I was coming to grips with Baldrige's death and the impending next year's end of the Reagan Administration, I decided it was time to figure out what was next for me. It was clear Vice President George H. W. Bush would run and likely succeed President Reagan. I had no desire to become a political hanger-on, nor did I want to join the downtown lobbyists, so I began thinking about what I wanted the next stage of my life to be. I even called Drew Lewis to seek his advice, and I learned a lesson I applied when mentoring others: "It's your job to figure out what's next, and when you do, I'll be glad to help."

About that time, Janet and I had a conversation with a psychologist friend of hers who, hearing some of my background, said, "Janet has never been a risk taker, but you certainly are!" It was the first time I had heard that and as I look back, Janet's friend was right on. I had never really thought of myself as a risk taker, but obviously I had overruled common sense and taken some bold ones: transitioning from business to politics, from politics to business, and from business to government, each step of the way better than the one before.

In my mid-forties, I wasn't averse to taking a further risk, and with a year left in the administration I knew I had some time to figure out my next move carefully. As with my decision to go to Thunderbird, taking the easy road was not in my DNA, and I began to think about what my career and I needed to differentiate us from others with remotely similar experience.

The answer, not immediately clear, was in front of me. The government had just begun to install desktop computers and as I sorted through the floppy disks that came with my early-version Wang, I realized I knew nothing about computers or the technology that drove them, and furthermore the people around me didn't know anything about them either. I started to think that instead of waiting for something good to happen, I would use any and every opportunity to find a door to the world of computer technology.

Near the end of my service in the administration, and as is usual for international policy positions, I made parting visits to the countries where I had been most active: Saudi Arabia, Iraq, Algeria, and India. The Indian trade minister and I had a head-to-head when I insinuated that he had not always been honest with me regarding India's theft of American intellectual property. He just laughed and said, "As a poor country we sometimes have to do what we have to do for our people." I asked him to rethink that policy, but of course knew he wouldn't.

During my Saudi visit, the ambassador and I presented photos taken of Secretary Baldrige and Minister of Commerce Al-Zamil to the minister in memory of his close working relationship with the secretary.

Algeria took its last swing at me when one of the embassy residence staff stole money from my wallet while I was in the shower. He bought some wine, got drunk, and nearly burned the gatehouse down.

My deputy, who had been born in Ireland, suggested that since I had never been to Ireland, I should take time off to visit it on the way home from Algeria. Our U.S. ambassador to Ireland, Margaret Heckler, had followed Schweiker as Secretary of Health and Human Services. Prior to that she had been a Congresswoman from Boston representing the same district as my grandmother's brother. She kindly hosted a dinner with some of the government cabinet members at the residence. The next day I was a guest at a hunt where I was surprised by the presence of guards required to protect cabinet members from the terrorist-designated Irish Republican Army (IRA).

Looking back on my experiences in the administration, my strongest memories are of my hectic lifestyle while Janet and I settled into our relationship and marriage, of my accomplished staff, and of a lifelong friendship. Irishman Peter Cashman was my deputy, David Savastuk and later Sean Gallagher served as my administrative assistant. The three regional directors and the country desk officers were, if I say so myself, the best in the department.

Unfortunately, the mid-'80s witnessed the beginning of the AIDS epidemic and, before it was clinically identified, two of my staff required extraordinary time off. At one point I had a disagreement with a more senior political appointee over extended leave I granted one of the two who, in fact, would later die. Rough waters were smoothed by one of his staff, Charlie Black, Ambassador Shirley Temple's son and a graduate of Tuft's Fletcher School.

Finally, there is the story of a colleague with whom I have been close friends ever since (he would later serve on my SynXis Board). Alex Good joined the administration from California and when we met, he was Principal

Deputy Assistant Secretary for Economic Policy and we had adjoining offices with a connecting door. It seemed every time I had an important meeting with overseas visitors, Alex would come barreling through the door, as enthusiastic as Kramer on *Seinfeld*, suddenly realize there were visitors, and sheepishly withdraw. Finally, I placed a couch across the door. We worked closely and sometimes traveled together. Around the time of my son Jim's 16th birthday, Alex gave him his Porsche keys for a run around the block, something I am sure neither will forget.

My experience in the administration had been everything I expected it to be, and more. It gave me an inside view of the many effective actions our government can take on behalf of American business that I used extensively throughout the remainder of my career. It enabled me to engage with a level of American and foreign businessmen, and foreign government officials, that I previously could only dream about. And finally, it led to the next phase of my life where my knowledge of government would open the door to my learning about computer technology.

1988–1990 WASHINGTON, SCIENCE APPLICATIONS INTERNATIONAL (SAIC)

As my service in the administration wound down, we were having dinner with my friend Jim Grossmann and his brother Bill, an All-American swimmer at Virginia Tech who had been our freshman-year coach while he completed his Ph.D. in Mathematics and Aeronautical Sciences. He asked me what my plans were after the administration, and I said I was giving that a lot of thought.

I felt I had done well developing international business in a complex engineering environment and noted that technology was moving in the direction of computers and software, areas that I needed to understand better. At that time, and for much of his career, Bill worked for Science Applications International Corporation (SAIC), one of the largest defense technology firms in the United States. Though it was headquartered in La Jolla, California, SAIC had a significant presence in the Washington, D.C., area, under the direction of its vice chairman and executive vice president, David Heebner.

Shortly after my dinner with Jim and Bill, I received a call from Mr. Heebner. He had heard from Bill that it might be a good thing for us to meet. He invited me to the Washington-area SAIC offices, which were in McLean, Virginia. When we met, a couple of weeks later, I outlined my mostly international experience in and out of government, and expressed my interest in learning more about, and working with, computers, software, and advanced technology.

After meeting with Dave several times, he suggested I meet with SAIC's founder, chairman, and CEO, Dr. Robert (Bob) Beyster. I did so with some trepidation because, as Dave explained, Dr. Beyster thought there was enough business in the States without having to go overseas. I found this a bit hard to understand, as "International" was part of SAIC's brand name. As well, they were doing significant work in Saudi Arabia. That work included three Command, Control, Communications, and Intelligence (C3I) centers that were later used in the Iraq wars and whose design and construction funded SAIC's accelerating growth.

SAIC at that time was the largest, perhaps most prominent, employee-owned company in the United States. Dr. Beyster was a keen proponent of employee ownership to the extent that he started the Foundation for Enterprise Development with the intent of fostering employee ownership. When we did meet, our discussion was more about employee ownership than about foreign markets for SAIC. However, I was able to make the point that within the company there certainly had to be capabilities that, if sold overseas, would enhance the company's reputation and global standing without "giving away the store," his biggest concern.

Dave told me that even though Dr. Beyster felt little reason to hire someone to develop international markets, I had passed muster, kind of a strange dichotomy. He made me an offer as Vice President, International Programs, reporting to him, with a start date as soon as I could break from the Reagan Administration.

This was my first time out of the gate as a vice president, so I was keen to move quickly, but doing so was easier said than done. My government responsibilities covered a multitude of countries, including Saudi Arabia, where SAIC had been especially active. At the time, unlike today, using a government position for personal gain was a clear violation. In fact, one of my colleagues in the administration, the deputy assistant secretary for promotion of the American automobile industry had, while in office, sent a letter to foreign auto manufacturers, promoting a new association that he would lead. He was dismissed, while the rest of us political appointees were instructed to be ultra-careful in seeking our exit from the administration.

With the help of outside counsel and a review of SAIC activities, I was able to confirm as much for myself as for anyone else that there had been no overlap between SAIC interests and what I had done in government. I made the decision to resign, took some time off, and headed across the Potomac River midsummer of 1988.

The Apple Macintosh personal computer (PC) had been introduced by a spectacular Super Bowl advertisement in 1984 at a price of $2495. It was not until the 1990s that decreasing prices and increasing ease-of-use made minicomputers and PCs consumer-friendly and commercially viable and led to the development of distributed computing and the World Wide Web. Before then most largescale transaction computing was done by sizeable and expensive mainframe computers. As I became familiar with SAIC's capabilities, one specific mainframe computer program caught my attention. SAIC had won a billion-dollar contract to build a Composite Health Care System (CHCS) for the military. The system tied together radiology, laboratory, pharmacy, and scheduling, among others, to a single interface, accessible by anyone on the system, something that is quite common today, but was then very innovative.

I first asked why we couldn't sell that system to the American healthcare industry. I was told that SAIC, accustomed to government business, had no idea how to field a commercial marketing and sales force (which the EPIC Corporation later did with its ubiquitous computerized electronic medical records system).

Nevertheless, I thought that if we could support the entire United States military healthcare system, we should be able to support the healthcare system of a medium-sized country. Although IBM hardware had not been preferred for the U.S. Defense Department application, I told IBM healthcare executives of my interest in marketing the system overseas.

They introduced me to Jacques Maisonrouge, a member of their global advisory board who had recently retired in France as chairman of the IBM World Trade Corporation. Maisonrouge thought the system might work in France and introduced me to Jean De Kervasdoué, former head of the French hospital system and a principal advisor to the minister of health. In turn, Kervasdoué enlisted the help of Dr. Alain Pompidou, the son of former French President Georges Pompidou.

With this dynamic team, we decided to introduce SAIC to French healthcare executives by holding a reception at the Automobile Club of France in Paris during the 1989 Paris Air Show. The show drew technologists of all types from all over the world, so it was also an opportunity to present SAIC's many other capabilities to an international audience while sourcing potential global partners. Wanting to be sure of maximum attendance by senior French military healthcare decisionmakers overseeing a potential point of market entry, SAIC's well-known and well-liked board member and former Nixon secretary of defense, Mel Laird, was asked to host the reception. It was a pleasure to work with Laird on details for the reception, and at the same time attend the air show with Dave Heebner. It turned out that my friend Parkman Clancy from Pittsburgh was also at the show meeting with various oil officials from Francophone African countries.

After observing the crash of a MiG 29 during one of its delicate "cobra" maneuvers, we watched the U.S. SR 71 spy plane take off. Dave remarked, "Not bad for a thirty-five-year-old plane." We later heard that the Soviets changed the topic of their MiG 29 press conference from "what a great plane" to "what a great ejection seat"!

I was particularly taken by the German exhibit of a Grob G109 glider and determined that I would qualify in that plane when we got back, something I did shortly after. Unfortunately, the French trip was cut short by my stepfather's unexpected death, and we returned to Pittsburgh for the funeral and spent as much time as we could with Mom.

The outcome of marketing the SAIC CHCS system was an important lesson for me about something I had not fully recognized. In what I suppose you might call textbook fashion, I had early on identified a technology that later proved to be of global interest, and I had put together a dream marketing team in a country where there seemed to be strong interest. Finally, I had staged an event that effectively introduced the technology and the local team to prospective customers and partners. All those efforts came for naught because I had forgotten what is commonly referred to as "inside" sales.

Many companies with substantial domestic, but limited international, sales, like SAIC then, leave international marketing to a separate division while the responsibility for sales and execution remains with the domestic division. That had been the case at Dravo, where I worked closely with the barge and boat building division in selling the China contract. In the SAIC case, what that meant was that when I identified a capability of likely interest to foreign buyers, I had to convince the division "owning" that capability that it should devote effort to making the sale and executing the resulting contract. There were three problems that required the inside selling I wasn't doing effectively.

First, the chairman of the company never messaged his support for international activities, even the profitable Saudi contracts. Second, none of the divisions had budgeted time or money for international travel, generally more consuming on both accounts. And third, the corporate team assigned to the Pentagon CHCS project found they preferred stay-at-home opportunities with a customer and place they understood as opposed to six-hour plane rides to another continent and a customer and culture they had never experienced. For them, there was no working outside their comfort zone and the opportunity was lost for lack of the financial and human resources needed to bring it to contract. It was a lesson about "inside" selling I later took with me to BDM.

IRAQ (AGAIN)

The Iraqi Embassy contacted me after my return from the Paris Air Show, early 1989, and invited me to Iraq to discuss their defense needs. This was certainly because they knew me from my time in the Reagan Administration, and they knew that SAIC was building the C3I (Command, Control, Communication, and Intelligence) facilities for Saudi Arabia. The mercurial nature of President Saddam Hussain had been fully recognized by this time, and the majority Shia Iraqis were not on the best of terms with the Sunni Saudis, although the Saudis fully supported Iraq in its war with Iran. Dave agreed I should make the trip anyway, if only to scope out the military situation in Iraq.

When I arrived, I was met at the Baghdad Airport by what must have been most of the general staff, in uniform. After several meetings, it became clear they were indeed looking for C3I facilities like those in Saudi Arabia. I then met with the recently appointed U.S. Ambassador April Glaspie. I had met her previously as I was leaving the administration and she was taking the Iraq posting, a somewhat controversial appointment because Saddam was known not to cut women any slack. April was a career State Department employee with solid Mid-East and Arab language credentials whom I had briefed before she took up her assignment on what I knew to be the interests of the Iraqi military.

On my return to Washington, I briefed Dave and together we briefed the intelligence community and senior officers at the State Department. On the one hand, it might have made sense to provide Iraq with a limited capability whose strengths and weaknesses we would know, but on the other, American and SAIC complicity with Iraq might not be viewed favorably. We declined to provide any C3I systems to the Iraqis but were not surprised later to discover they had been provided by France and Germany.

SAIC's founder, Dr. Beyster, practiced a management technique that I, and others, found hard to fathom. He would encourage different groups in the company to pursue the same sales opportunity, without telling them, thus creating misunderstandings when different SAIC business units found themselves competing with each other. Not only were SAIC employees often dismayed, but customers had a hard time understanding the rationale, especially in the international environment.

Beyster had another way of short-circuiting international business. Based on my experience in France, I was beginning to think of other marketing approaches when our European representative, who lived in London and reported to me, suggested the acquisition of a British healthcare company through which to market our CHCS solution to the U.K. National Health Service. Contrary to our French approach, using British healthcare professionals to market and implement the solution would minimize the need for American travel. We reached agreement to acquire the target company and I headed to La Jolla with Dave Heebner to present the idea to Dr. Beyster.

I suppose I might have been called a "young Turk" at the time, but Beyster had a group of "younger Turks" whose job was, pure and simple, to say NO. My career up to that time had been in marketing and I was presenting the acquisition as a door to the British healthcare system. The people around Beyster were reviewing it strictly from a financial perspective and, on that ground, were running circles around me using acquisition accounting terms I had seldom, if ever, heard. Try as I might, I made no headway and the potential acquisition was rejected without any hope of resurrection, even though I had Dave's support along with two influential members of SAIC's board, Mel Laird and Barry Shilito, the former head of Teledyne. It was not lost on me that I needed to learn acquisition accounting.

With Dr. Beyster's cold opposition to a plan favored by three other board members, including my boss, I began to wonder whether any international opportunity could pass muster with him. On my return to Washington, I received a call from Mogens Bay, the International President of Valmont Industries. Valmont was a large pivot irrigation system and tubular light pole manufacturer based in Omaha, Nebraska. Both product lines used the same steel-fabrication method. Today, Valmont has around eleven thousand employees and yearly revenues of $3.5 billion. In 1990, the company had 4,500 employees and revenues of $790 million. Mogens Bay, who was originally from Denmark, had previously been with the Danish East Asiatic Company that handled Dravo logistics in China, where we worked together for three years in the late '70s. We had stayed in touch while I was in the Reagan Administration, and he even recruited one of my staff to Valmont's Omaha office.

Valmont had several Mid-East irrigation projects on their books, including one large one in Iraq, so Mogens and senior Valmont management thought I might be a good addition to their international staff. The vice president of corporate development invited me and Janet to visit company headquarters in Omaha. It didn't take long to decide that giving up Washington for Omaha was not in the cards, so we decided not to pursue an offer.

Shortly after, Mogens called with another proposal: Go to Brussels, Belgium, as Valmont's vice president, Europe responsible for making acquisitions to add to existing operations in Austria, Spain, and France. Also, Valmont felt that with my experience and contacts in Iraq, I might be able to help grow the irrigation business there even though it was not within my geographic area of responsibility.

I told Mogens about my recent experience at SAIC, not being able to convince the CEO of a worthwhile acquisition. I said that if I were to engage in making acquisitions for Valmont, I needed a specific course in acquisition accounting and integration. An offer was therefore made that included going first to the University of Michigan for such a course; it was coupled with a sizeable salary increase, stock options, and the title. Most importantly, I saw it

In Saudi Arabia on the Mobil Oil "Pegasus" with Dave Heebner, right, and Larry Delaney, center. I worked closely with Dave at SAIC and later with Larry at BDM.

as an opportunity to learn something I knew nothing about, but intuitively felt would be important to moving up in my career, mergers, and acquisitions.

Janet and I decided I would resign from SAIC, accept the Valmont offer, and relocate to Brussels. I explained to Dave I thought that SAIC was just not ready for prime-time international activities beyond the existing work in Saudi Arabia. I think he agreed with me, although he didn't say so. He and others later had their own issues with Beyster regarding corporate succession that ultimately brought about Beyster's retirement and a division of the company into two publicly traded units, precisely what Beyster did not want. Dave and I remained close friends and he would later play a significant role in my career and company.

Of my various mentors you have met, Dave Heebner is right up there with Drew Lewis. I used to love our morning meetings (his glasses steamed from the hot coffee), when we kicked around where we were—and where we were going. As an individual, he spoke only when he had something meaningful to say; as a technologist, there were few better. He had been involved in submarine and tank design, and there was no one who could hold a candle to his underwater acoustic expertise. For him, ethics were a be-all, end-all in everything. They became so for me, especially in a later situation that was challenging directly, professionally, and personally.

1990–1992 BRUSSELS, VALMONT, IRAQ (AGAIN), AND WAR

We put our Washington house on the market in spring 1990 and I headed to the University of Michigan for the course on acquisition accounting and then to Valmont headquarters in Omaha to come up to speed on company operations before moving to Brussels.

Valmont had four lines of business: irrigation equipment, tubular metal light poles, fluorescent lighting transformers (ballasts), and computer equipment for the farm community. I was to look for acquisitions to add to our irrigation businesses in Graz, Austria, and Madrid, and a recently acquired light pole company in Vichy, France. Parenthetically, I was to visit Iraq to see whether, with my contacts, I could help expand the irrigation business there. My responsibilities were not to include the computer retail business being divested or the ballast business that included the recent acquisition of GE's Illinois ballast manufacturing facility.

Janet and I decided she would stay with the Washington house until it sold, and I would take a small interim apartment in Brussels until she could join me. So after my classes at the University of Michigan and orientation in Omaha, I headed to Brussels with a Washington stop at the State Department Iraq desk, where I learned that Iraq's current disputes with Kuwait over oil reserves were on the top of the Department's watch list.

After a month or so in Brussels, I found a small apartment on the well-known Avenue Louise, and an office on the same street a block or two toward the center. In mid-July 1990, I headed to Iraq to assess the irrigation business before returning to Omaha for a companywide meeting—during which all hell would break loose!

IRAQ (AGAIN)

Before arriving in Iraq, I contacted the former Iraqi ambassador to the United States, Nizar Hamdoon who, by this time, was Tariq Aziz' deputy foreign minister. Nizar and I had always had a close personal and professional relationship, perhaps because I admired his being one of the most intellectual Iraqis I had met; he had studied architecture with an eye for art and modern design. During one of my earlier visits with him and his wife at their house in Baghdad, he presented me with a memento of our friendship, a page torn from a four-hundred-year-old Koran written in Arabic and Hindu.

We had not seen each other for over a year and agreed to meet for dinner. He said his driver would pick me up at my hotel and take me either to his office or to the restaurant. That evening the driver came by and took me to the dimly lit rear entrance of the foreign ministry and up the back stairs to Nizar's office.

After a brief discussion about friends and families, I turned the conversation to current events, expressing concern over Iraq's issues with Kuwait. Nizar did not respond, but suggested it was time to head out because he had reserved a table at a good restaurant beside the Tigris River and didn't want to be late. I quickly remembered that in Iraq anyone could be listening. In the car, I tried again, but realized that Nizar didn't even consider the car safe.

Although we were seated at a table some distance from others, Nizar still fended off my efforts to discuss Iraq-Kuwait issues. The tense situation between the two nations was ascribed to three principal conditions: Iraq could not repay the $14 billion in loans Kuwait had made Iraq during the Iran-Iraq War; the Iraqis believed the Kuwaitis were "directionally drilling" from their oil fields into the Iraqi Rumaila oil field reserves; and the Iraqis believed Kuwait was depressing oil prices, and therefore Iraq oil-production income, by exceeding their OPEC quotas.

As dinner ended, Nizar suggested we take a walk along the levee. As we got some distance from the restaurant, I raised the issue of the oil directional drilling. Nizar's response ignored that issue and reverted to an age-old question related to the British-drawn border between Iraq and Kuwait: "We intend to keep the Faw Peninsula and take Bubiyan Island," he stated.

The peninsula had been lost to Iran in the Iraq-Iran War and reclaimed in 1988, while nearby, the Bubiyan Island was Kuwaiti territory. Nizar asserted that these islands belonged to Iraq and were important to sustaining future oil exports and that Iraq would do whatever necessary to keep them, and as well, was going to restrict the directional Kuwaiti drilling, which Iraq believed illegal.

It was not in my purview to speak for our government, but I told him I personally thought it would be unwise to threaten Kuwait. Today, we know my advice was a dead letter.

The next day I briefed Ambassador April Glaspie and her staff, telling her, and later the State Department in Washington, about Hamdoon's remarks concerning the two islands but making no prediction as to future Iraqi actions. She in turn told me that Saddam had recently appeared before the Parliament claiming to have secured components needed for the ignition of an atomic bomb, an issue that would reappear before the Second Iraq War.

I immediately returned to Washington to see Janet and brief the State Department before going to Omaha and returning to Brussels. While I was in Omaha, August 2, Iraq invaded Kuwait, obviously short-circuiting any Iraq marketing plans. I was not sorry about that because I figured I had plenty to do in Europe, but I was unhappy to see Saddam set in motion what I expected would be the ruin of a country so many of us had tried to help.

My view is that Saddam's son-in-law, Hussain Kamel, whom I had previously met and who would later be killed by Saddam, lost control of his Republican Guards as they undertook a devastating program of looting and destruction in Kuwait City. The Iraq Army was eventually pushed out of Kuwait and all but destroyed before being rebuilt for the subsequent Iraq War.

Although I had no further official or unofficial contact with the Iraqi government after the Gulf War, there was an element of American policy after the later Iraq War (2003) where former colleagues and I, along with Ambassador Hamdoon, expressed concern to our government over the rules imposed on the Ba'ath Party by Ambassador Paul Bremer. Paul had been ambassador to the Netherlands and, when I met him in 1988, was Coordinator for Counterterrorism. After working with Reagan and a stint with Kissinger, and with no Middle East experience that I knew of, he was appointed Administrator of the Coalition Provisional Authority of Iraq.

Paul was a smart guy and his history with Kissinger and Reagan gave weight to his ruling that members of the Iraqi military, and members of Saddam's Ba'ath Party, be prohibited from holding government positions. I could only wonder whether he had read about the essential rehabilitation of some Nazis after WWII. In Iraq, in my view, he laid the foundation for the failure of the Iraqi government and the emergence of ISIS, populated by out-of-work Ba'ath Party officials and former military personnel.

BELGIUM AND HOLLAND

The path Janet and I took to living in Brussels was stranger than fiction. We sold our Washington house and took a nearby Adams Morgan apartment as part of the payment. In completing the sale, our house came up as being owned by my son, a student with no credit. Things got stranger still. A banker in Houston had used my Social Security number (mistakenly?) on a million-dollar loan to a James Kelly that was in default. We hired a lawyer to sort it all out and got the help of a woman in a credit agency who had the same birthday as me and decided to set the rules aside to reveal information we needed to solve the problem.

Settling into our Brussels apartment, we were surprised to be in a small earthquake with the bed rocking and the blinds shaking. When everything from the move, and the earthquake, finally settled down, we found ourselves in a cosmopolitan neighborhood amidst wonderful Belgian restaurants. And if that were not good enough, we were in easy driving range of French Champagne country and Paris, where we could visit our friends Mel and Andy Searls from Dravo and the Commerce Department. Mel was now minister counselor in our Paris embassy.

For what would now be the Valmont European corporate office, I hired an assistant who had grown up in Ostend, Belgium. Her grandfather had been mayor. During WWII, he had surrendered the house to the Germans while the family was forced to live in the basement. Through her family stories, I came to understand what it was like for one Belgian family to live literally under the Nazis, listening to their every footstep for five long years.

Once the office was set up, I began the search for potential acquisitions with a process I had gleaned from discussions with Mogens Bay and at the University of Michigan. Success, I learned, would be determined by the strength and breadth of a contact network of bankers and mergers and acquisitions (M&A) specialists I would need to establish across Europe to help identify targets. Contrary to real estate, very few companies advertise they are consciously for sale; if they do, there is likely something wrong. So what you rely on your contacts for is the identity of companies that, for some hopefully minimal shortfall, may be convinced to join you to enjoy greater success. I often heard it took over one hundred targets to find a potential acquisition, and that was before the integration issues. I'll get to that part further on.

After a few dead ends, I connected with Dutch banker Roel van der Heide in Amsterdam. Roel introduced me to the manufacturing company Nolte Mastenfabriek, which was in the village of Maarheeze, not far from Eindhoven, the Netherlands. They manufactured streetlight and sign poles. That company was but a tiny part of a larger conglomerate, Stork B.V., and therefore suffered from a lack of corporate management attention and capital.

As Roel and I spent time with the company and its management, I became more confident Stork would sell Nolte to focus on its other, larger businesses, and that Nolte would prefer to be part of a similar, but larger, American company sharing greater resources. I concluded this would be an excellent candidate for my first acquisition recommendation and put together a file with all the relevant financial information noting the company's long history and profitability. I also pointed out that its product portfolio of streetlight and sign poles would give Valmont a larger share of the European market, but not compete with the French subsidiary. After brief negotiations, Valmont and Stork senior management agreed to the transaction, and today it remains a significant part of Valmont, Europe.

Speaking of the French subsidiary, I learned an important lesson working with its managing director and former owner. Although he and I generally communicated in French over the phone, he once sent me a letter in English explaining what he had been doing: "I have been hardly working…etc." It was amusing but clear to me that I had best not try writing back in French.

POLAND

While living in Brussels, I happened one evening to be in Warsaw on my way home from Romania, where I had looked at an integrated manufacturing company. Coincidentally, my college friend Jim Grossmann was there with a friend who was accompanied by the son of a Florida family whose cattle-breeding business he represented. Although the son, who was in his early 20s, had set out to be a professional golfer, he was in Warsaw to observe what he could of the family business. I knew the friend from my government days in Iraq, where I was able to introduce him to the Iraqi agriculture minister who then bought Florida cattle by the 747 load.

As there didn't appear to be much demand for cattle in Warsaw, the cattle dealer asked at dinner whether anyone had an idea what might sell in Poland. Cattle and vodka already were abundant; good beer, wine, and whiskey, however, were not, so a half-joking motion was made to explore the beer business. On my friend's behalf, I made a call to Pittsburgh's Iron City Brewery and connected them. It was a relationship just waiting for someone to bring them together!

Iron City had tried to enter the export market and, having failed, had two leftover containers of beer that they would sell for the cost of hauling them away. The Central European Distribution Company (CEDC) was formed. The son became the CEO, the family representative became executive vice president, and Jim Grossmann and I signed on as outside directors with little thought the venture would succeed. The rest is history.

CEDC went forward to add premier brands like Johnnie Walker Whisky and Foster's Lager. Not long after, CEDC went public on the Nasdaq exchange with a valuation of over a billion dollars. Alas, I did not ride the rocket to the top; I sold out early, while the son and representative went on to be multi-millionaires. The company was eventually sold to a Russian conglomerate.

Valmont, unlike CEDC, was experiencing severe difficulties. It had bought General Electric's Illinois-based florescent light ballast business, even though it was generally understood then that GE didn't part with businesses that had a future. Shortly after purchasing the GE division, management decided to open what was called a Maquiladora facility in Mexico to produce a better product with advanced digital technology at lower cost, the result being a debilitating strike at the Illinois plant, and its eventual closure.

Living in Europe, I was blindsided when senior management was forced to exit the ballast business and make cost-cutting adjustments throughout the company, including Brussels. The corporate vice president of business development took responsibility from Mogens for my office. Shortly before Christmas, 1991, he came to Brussels to let me know he was closing the office, laying off my assistant, and returning the leased computers and furniture—and ending my employment. It was not long thereafter that he, the CEO, and several others were fired, and Mogens Bay was named CEO, but by then we had closed the office and I had begun the process of moving on.

This was absolutely the most difficult and scary time of my life. Only then did I realize what it must have been like for my father when his Middlesboro mining partner died, and we returned to Pittsburgh. I was in Belgium with an "American" salary package and a work permit tied to Valmont employment. The chances of finding a similar arrangement with a European firm were slim. I was going to have to find something in the States, and I was going to have to find it from Belgium. I knew it wouldn't be easy, that it would take time, and that at my age (fifty) I would need to make a good choice.

Instant internet email saved me! Fortunately, just before we left for Brussels, Janet's soon-to-be former company decided to upgrade their computers and she was able to buy one of the early Apple Macintoshes at a small fraction of its original $2495 cost. Using a dial-up modem, our apartment telephone line, and a Belgian internet provider, we sent and received emails a couple of times a day. Email wasn't as ubiquitous then as it is today, and that too probably helped; people carefully reviewed their emails. If I sent one in the afternoon, I'd usually have a yes-no-maybe response the next morning. Even so, job hunting was easier said than done. However, over the course of six months and several hundred emails, I made two interview trips to the States and wound up with two offers and one in the wings.

This time in between was a time of reflection. I repeatedly asked myself why I had taken the assignment in Brussels and why it didn't work out. Although I had had a sincere interest in learning about manufacturing and expanding my global mergers and acquisitions experience, I came to realize I had accepted the position for the wrong reasons. The reality was that I was escaping SAIC. To get out of that job quickly, I bought into an improbable career path.

I had a memorable conversation with Mogens as I was shutting down the office. It was perhaps because he had not yet been named the new CEO, but he said I should consider myself lucky to be outside the painful reorganization that was about to occur. He also told me I would come out of the layoff experience better for it. It was hard to believe at the time, but over the next year I would see that he was right. Why?

Mogens was a Dane I had worked with in China and was the only "internationalist" I could relate to in the home office; the rest were serious Midwest manufacturing executives, which I was not. In Europe, I was the Lone Ranger, out of range with Mogens and other senior management. My assignment was to search for acquisitions that manufactured products for which I had little intellectual curiosity and as I found out with Nolte, once the acquisition was made, I had no responsibility for its integration or management. I would take all of this into account in my next position. Indeed, I was lucky!

1992–1996 WASHINGTON AND GERMANY, CARLYLE'S BDM INTERNATIONAL

The Carlyle Group, headquartered in Washington, D.C., today employs 1900 people in twenty-six offices on five continents and manages $325 billion in assets. It was founded in 1987 by Steve Norris and David Rubenstein with Bill Conway and Dan D'Aniello and named after the New York hotel where Norris and Rubenstein came up with the idea. In 1989, former Secretary of Defense and National Security Adviser Frank Carlucci joined the firm, later becoming chairman. Early investors included the Richard King Mellon family office of Pittsburgh.

In 1992, as I was conducting my job search from Belgium, the group was establishing itself as a major buyout firm; it purchased undervalued companies by adding debt to the target company's balance sheet to cover some or all the purchase price, and then improved the company's performance before selling it or taking it public. While I would not work directly for Carlyle, I would find the next pages of my story written within their most significant early acquisition, BDM, and later in my own company, SynXis, with the help of one of their founders.

Carlyle had acquired BDM in September 1990, the initials standing for its three Fordham-educated scientist founders: Braddock, Dunn, and McDonald. A defense contractor deriving most of its income from government consulting, BDM was run by Earl Williams, the longtime president and CEO, who was hired by the three scientists to manage the company. Williams had moved BDM from New York City to Tysons Corner, Virginia, a short distance from my former employer SAIC.

BDM had been a private company, then public. Then it was acquired by Ford Aerospace, a division of the Ford Motor Company where, incidentally, Drew Lewis was on the board of directors. It was Drew who brought the potential acquisition of BDM to the attention of Carlyle, something I learned years later from Steve Norris, who also told me it had been the Pittsburgh Mellon family that initially helped capitalize Carlyle.

There were similarities but also major differences between BDM and SAIC. Both companies were significant high-technology defense consultants focused on some of the most sophisticated weapon systems, but while SAIC was an independent employee-owned company, BDM had been part of a public company known for making cars. SAIC, with sales of a billion dollars, was nearly three times the size of BDM.

The Loral Corporation had acquired Ford Aerospace in 1990. BDM was separated from the transaction and sold at the same time by Ford to the Carlyle Group because BDM oversaw certain Loral contracts for the Defense Department and the government would not permit it and Loral to have the same ownership.

BDM employees were ecstatic about the Carlyle takeover. First, it restored their independence (from Ford), and second, it represented an opportunity for increased future compensation, especially if the company were to go public again, which was understood by all to be the likely Carlyle plan.

In 1992, two years after the acquisition by Carlyle, Earl Williams, who had always had a desire to get into politics, announced he would leave BDM and seek the governorship of Virginia. By that time, Frank Carlucci had become chairman of both Carlyle and BDM.

SAIC's Dave Heebner, my former boss and mentor, had known and been friends with Earl Williams for years. Once it was announced Williams would leave the company, and that management changes would follow, he suggested that Williams and I meet. And so, in the spring of 1992, during one of my returns from Brussels in my job hunt, I met with Earl and learned that the search for a new BDM CEO hadn't gone far, about twenty-five yards from Carlucci's tennis court to Phil Odeen's house in McLean.

Phil Odeen would start in mid-June as president and CEO. Williams offered to set up a meeting between us and suggested I could work with Odeen to increase international business in support of Carlyle's goal of making the company more global and therefore more valuable for an eventual sale or public offering by extending its reach into foreign markets.

Phil Odeen was an interesting and smart guy with strong credentials in government and the private sector. I knew that he had served in senior positions in the Department of Defense and had worked on arms-control issues with Henry Kissinger during the time Kissinger was national security advisor. From 1973 to 1978 Phil, a golf lover, was vice president of Wilson Sporting Goods before joining Coopers & Lybrand, eventually becoming Vice Chairman, Management Consulting Services. He left Coopers & Lybrand to join BDM.

Earl Williams followed up and arranged for me to meet with Odeen, where I stuck my neck out and started by describing my unsuccessful SAIC healthcare systems experience in France. I told him the experience taught me that few American government contractors were comfortable pursuing business outside the United States. I then told him I felt the fastest and best solution to grow BDM's international business might be to go the route of a foreign acquisition, mentioning my Valmont acquisition training and European experience. Contrary to the swift rejection of my healthcare company acquisition recommendation at SAIC, Odeen thought for a minute and expressed interest in the idea. I was surprised. Little did I know it would consume me for the next three years.

A short time later, I received an offer to start about two weeks after Phil as Vice President, International, reporting to him with the broadly defined responsibility of increasing the company's business outside the United States. This was undeniably a tall order considering that 85% of the company's business and experience was with the Federal Government; very little of the remainder was overseas. The increasing government contracting rules and accounting regulations, hard for foreign customers to understand, made international business complex and expensive, thus another reason to pursue an acquisition.

Not only was I up for the challenge; I loved it. Here was the magical combination of the three elements I understood and craved: high technology, important government involvement, and an assignment in the global business world. And not to be overlooked, I would be working with a team headed by Phil, a CEO who not only liked my idea, but encouraged me to pursue it. I would work for him for four years. It was an extraordinary opportunity.

Janet and I moved from Brussels to Alexandria, Virginia, where we rented an apartment. Because politics is never far from my mind, I signed up as a delegate to the Richmond Republican gubernatorial convention to help Earl Williams secure the party's nomination. Unfortunately, he was outdueled by George Allen. Janet and I spent a year in our apartment before buying a house in Bethesda, Maryland, not far from the beltway. For a few years, until traffic in Washington went berserk, I would have an easy drive to BDM in Tysons Corner.

Early on, I learned a memorable lesson about Phil from one of his former Coopers & Lybrand employees whom Phil asked me to meet. While chatting, I asked him to tell me about working for Odeen. He explained he had once taken a contract proposal to Odeen, vice chairman at the time, who volunteered to sign it. The fellow thanked Odeen but said he would handle it. The proposal was rejected for lack of evident senior management buy-in. So the lesson: Pay careful attention to Odeen's suggestions—they are usually winners!

Shortly thereafter, Odeen called me to his office and mentioned that he had heard from a U.S. Navy Admiral friend that the German Federal Ministry of Finance aimed to sell a prominent government-owned defense firm based in Munich. He "suggested" I contact a couple of Germans who the admiral seemed to feel had a line on the sale and gave me their numbers.

That evening, I was to travel to Atlantic City for an Air Traffic Control (ATC) conference (we had strong ATC capabilities for which there would likely be international demand). Needing another set of ears, I called on my German-speaking friend and former SAIC colleague, Dr. Larry Delaney, who was now a consultant. I asked him to go with me and scheduled a call with the two German intermediaries for the next morning from our hotel.

The two individuals were Jens Fischer and Peter Limberger. Fischer was somewhat of a political animal, having been press secretary for former Chancellor Helmut Schmidt. Peter Limberger was more of a dealmaker, always looking for an opportunity. Their role, to me, was always a bit of a mystery. I suppose each of them recognized the skills of the other and when it came to their attention that the German Federal Ministry of Finance (BMF) was prepared to sell the company, Industrieanlagen-Betriebsgesellschaft mbh (IABG), they made it their business to find a buyer.

In our call, it was agreed I would make a trip to Bonn, the capital of the former West Germany, which was still the location of many ministries. They would later be moved piecemeal to Berlin, the capital of reunited Germany. I was to be briefed by Peter, Jens, and government representatives from the office of Theodor Waigel, the minister of finance under Chancellor Kohl. Waigel had been charged with overseeing the sale. Within short order, I was on a plane.

General Siegfried Schulz, a former chief of staff of the postwar German Army, met me when I arrived. I learned a fascinating bit of history on the way to my hotel, but first the general received a ticket from the local police for not wearing a seatbelt. He did so with great humility. He then explained to me that my hotel, the Rheinhotel Dreesen, had been Adolf Hitler's favorite. He went on to say that Hitler and British Prime Minister Neville Chamberlain had met there in September 1938, when Hitler proposed conditions for the annexation of the Sudetenland, part of the Czechoslovakian Republic. The agreement was confirmed later that month in Munich, and American foreign policy has wrestled with armed incursions ever since.

I was able to confirm during that first trip that the Finance Ministry was, indeed, selling IABG, and that Jens and Peter knew well enough what it would take to execute a transaction. I informally enlisted them as agents in the process. Little did I know that the government of the Free State of Bavaria, and plenty of others, would oppose the German Federal Government's plan to sell off a government-owned defense firm to a then somewhat obscure, privately held firm headquartered in the United States.

That trip was the first of a series of trips I made, often joined by Dr. Delaney, from Washington to Bonn, Munich, and Berlin. Part of the Ministry of Finance was still in Bonn, part in Berlin. Some months, one or both of us could spend an entire week traveling the circuit Munich-Bonn-Berlin-Munich. The objective was to figure out just how BDM and IABG fit together, what the cost of the acquisition should be, and what were going to be the problems needed to be overcome in an American-German acquisition.

When I think back to those years, 1992-1995, I recall the number of issues stemming from BDM being American. The questions flew at us from the German employees, from the German media, and from the Bavarian State Government itself: *Why would the German Federal Government be willing to sell to Americans one of its premier defense research facilities known for its roles in the European Space Program and development of the Eurofighter jet? Why would they sell us the company testing Airbus aircraft, having new models onsite alongside the Eurofighter in hangar-like test facilities? And why sell us the company that tested German automobile components, shock absorbers, and brakes, for the likes of BMW and Mercedes?*

At first, it appeared the German Federal Government was privatizing not only former-Communist, East German entities, but also certain government-owned companies in West Germany that appeared to have future negative budget implications. Remember, this was a time when every Deutschemark was needed to cover the costs of reunification. Higher costs, which would have to be bankrolled by the government, were certainly in IABG's future: A majority of its two thousand employees, especially the higher-paid engineers and scientists, had been hired in the early 1960s after the company's founding and were approaching retirement, the $200-million cost of which was unfunded.

Once it became known the transaction was being considered seriously by the Federal Ministry of Finance, opposition mounted far and wide. In Germany, the Bavarian government was frequently at odds with the Federal Republic of Germany. In this case, Bavaria's opposition to the sale was expressed by the Bavarian Minister of the Interior, Edmund Stoiber. Although the German Finance Minister Theodor Waigel was Bavarian and open to selling the company to Americans, Stoiber preferred a Bavarian solution.

Added to the Bavarian government's opposition to the deal were the voices of top German newspapers who hounded the Federal Government asking why an American solution was necessary. After that, opposition to the American-German buyout came from multiple interested international entities, including the Dutch government, the French government, and then the French firm Airbus. These parties wanted to know why Germany would consider selling the company designated as its European Space Agency (ESA) partner, and why also it would sell the organization testing Airbus aircraft to a company often working with Boeing. Another question was why BDM, with no foreign operations experience, would want to undertake a difficult and time-consuming acquisition on another continent. Was BDM possibly a spy for Boeing?

The question as to why BDM would want to make the acquisition had arisen in my discussions with Phil and members of the board, including Conway and Carlucci: If the intent down the road was for BDM to grow and go public, and it was, BDM with operations in the European community would be a far more attractive investment. The answer to the other question—was BDM a spy for Boeing—was a definite no. Nevertheless, aside from the Bavarian desire for German control, the Dutch, French, and Airbus concerns about BDM spying for Boeing had to be dealt with. All three lobbied the German government with the argument that BDM would simply be a conduit to Boeing of Airbus secrets. And as members of the European Space Agency, they assumed BDM would not continue IABG participation or support for the Agency, sometimes viewed as a NASA competitor.

Bill Conway, one of Carlyle's founders, had an astute focus on the here and now, and made a couple of trips to Germany, as did Phil, with outside legal and accounting advisors. The issue at hand, for them, was the unfunded $200-million pension liability. They concluded that the best approach would be to acquire the company for the assumption of that liability. Yet that would solve only one of the problems. Next up, we would need to deal with the political aspects of the acquisition.

FRANK CARLUCCI, SECRETARY OF DEFENSE

PAMELA HARRIMAN, U.S. AMBASSADOR TO FRANCE

Phil decided I would accompany Carlyle and BDM Chairman Frank Carlucci to meetings with Airbus and government officials in France and Germany. I would also accompany Phil to meetings with his friend Pamela Harriman, the

U.S. Ambassador to France, and to meetings with our ambassador to Germany, Robert Kimmitt. In all these government and private sector meetings, we delivered a consistent message: A Chinese wall would be built around the Airbus activities and no related information would be given to Boeing; we would continue IABG's role with the European Space Agency.

With our unwavering assertions of privacy for IABG, and with further reassurances from Harriman and Kimmitt, France and the Netherlands, while never endorsing the transaction, at least agreed not to oppose it. As for Bavaria, well, they were Bavarians and continued their opposition, even against their fellow Bavarian, German Minister of Finance Theodore Waigel. Eventually, Minister Waigel accepted our assurances and signed off on the transaction in which BDM acquired IABG, its two thousand German employees, and a $200-million pension liability.

An important step in the process was the addition of Dr. Walther Leisler Kiep to the Supervisory Board (the equivalent of the American Board of Directors, not to be confused with the Management Board, comprised of members of the management team). Kiep had been a CDU (Christian Democratic Union) member of the Bundestag (Parliament) and was considered one of Germany's most distinguished statesmen. He was a dynamic promoter of German-American relations and headed the prestigious Atlantik-Brucke (Atlantic Bridge), an organization that promoted transatlantic cooperation. We also managed to recruit to the Supervisory Board Gerhard Buck from Bad Reichenhall in Bavaria. Gerhard's family had been active in industry and was favorably regarded on both sides of the Atlantic.

A memory, on the lighter side, concerned Frank Carlucci. Impressive as it was to travel first class on Air France with him, I managed to tip a glass of wine his way. If that weren't bad enough, I had to wait longer than usual for my bag in Paris while he fumed in the car; he was in Europe for a few days while I was there for weeks at a clip and there was no way I could do that with an overnight bag. Sorry, Frank. The good news was that wherever we went, we stayed in a superior hotel with a pool so Frank could swim to strengthen a recently repaired rotator cuff; I joined in.

Now that the acquisition seemed to be a go, it was time to find the right people to run it. As luck would have it, I was in the right place at the right time to recommend the new leader, and hire the go-between, of the new

BDM-IABG asset. When Earl Williams stepped down, his long-time chief operating officer was Bill Sweeney, a physicist with abundant self-confidence. About the time we were completing the agreement to secure IABG, Phil Odeen felt he wouldn't need a COO and so relieved Bill. To me, Bill represented the history of BDM and although he was sometimes hard to work with, I enjoyed talking with him, so I stopped by his office to say goodbye while he packed boxes.

As we were speaking, it occurred to me Bill might be a good fit as the senior BDM manager at IABG. After all, he was a big guy with supreme confidence, a physics Ph.D., and whose mother was of German descent. Aside from the fact that he didn't speak German, what was there not to like about Bill as a prospective American head of IABG? So I wandered over to Phil's office and left him with the thought that he might consider keeping Bill on and engaging him in helping wind up the acquisition process, which he promptly did.

I met Jim O'Toole shortly before that. As previously mentioned, he was one of the West Point quarterbacks in the 1968 Penn State game I attended with Senator Schweiker. He had been introduced to me by Tony Calio, an executive (later president) at Hughes Space Systems and a friend from the Reagan Administration, where he was Undersecretary of Commerce and NOAA Administrator.

Jim drove from the Pentagon, where he was ending his Army service as a lieutenant colonel. He had graduated from West Point in the class with Ambassador Kimmitt and served with distinction in helicopters in Vietnam (where he was shot down) and Germany. His wife, Gail, was also a West Point grad and had served in Germany in helicopters.

With German-language skills, and an aviation and technical background, Jim also had a terrific personality that I thought would serve him well as a go-between, helping both BDM and IABG accommodate each other. I made him an offer, which he accepted, although there were days in succeeding years when he perhaps wished he hadn't because of the strain of working with the demanding Dr. Sweeney. Of course, Sweeney took issue with my hire saying that BDM should hire more senior ranks, but I pointed out that as a quarterback of the West Point football team, Jim was known to, and likely knew, all the senior officers in the Army, including those who had served in Germany.

IABG had been known as having a strong environmental group, and after reunification it became one of the organizations directing the remediation of multiple environmental issues in the former East Germany. To strengthen IABG's environmental management team, it was decided that Dr. Larry Delaney, my friend and colleague from SAIC who had helped with the acquisition process, would join IABG, first in Munich and later in Berlin. He would direct many environmental remediation activities of IABG following the departure of the Russians from East Germany. For example, IABG contracted with the government to clean up a small valley about a mile long, perhaps five hundred meters wide and two hundred meters deep full of scrap Russian tanks, railcars, and road vehicles as shown in arial photos.

In another example, IABG consulted on removing asbestos from the building previously used as Communist Party headquarters in East Berlin. In other parts of East Germany, IABG accumulated, disarmed, and destroyed discarded artillery ammunition, some of which had rusted together. Leftover hand grenades were detonated in a large steel chamber. After destroying several missiles, our employees gave me a Soviet gyro guidance system for my desk. Although not strictly environmental, IABG deactivated a neighborhood STASI switchboard in former East Berlin that had enabled the infamous East German security agency to tap neighborhood residences.

For what I considered one of the worst environmental issues, Dr. Delaney and I visited Chemnitz, a city formerly in East Germany not far from the Czech border. It was the site of the Wismut Mining Company, which had been the primary source of uranium within the Soviet bloc. In 1991, the mine came under the control of the unified German Government, and IABG assumed part responsibility for remediating it. Our biggest concern was that houses near the mine had been built with cinderblock made with radioactive tailings.

It was incomprehensible that the health problems suffered by people in the area were never perceived by the East German government as connected to the radioactive building materials—or perhaps nobody cared. Perhaps they felt that if they could operate the mine and build cheap houses, everything was working out fine. Larry and I couldn't help but feel sorry for those people for whom remediation would not change their history.

While working with IABG, I had opportunities to meet with senior German military officers and remember especially Eberhard Eimler. He was a retired general, formerly head of the Luftwaffe, and Deputy Supreme Allied Commander Europe. We met in Washington, where I showed him several WWII German aircraft at the Smithsonian National Air and Space Museum. At the museum's Silver Hill facility, where planes are restored, we saw the Enola Gay as it was being worked on and were able to climb around inside.

Eimler told me that at age thirteen and traveling with his mother during the war, they had run from a train car being strafed. He still carried the bullet that ricocheted to the ground in front of him because it reminded him how lucky he was. At one point, he invited me to a dinner with Adolf Galland, the famous WWII German ace who, near the end of the war, bravely told Hitler all the things he didn't want to hear. Unfortunately, Galland died shortly before we could have that dinner.

Among its businesses, IABG was an advisor to the German Army on certain aspects of the Leopard Tank, which Germany sold to friendly governments. At one point, I accompanied a delegation to Madrid, where I met the Spanish army chief of staff who came from Galicia, where I had lived in the '60s. He was amused to find an American who had lived in his region now working with Germans selling tanks to the Spanish.

KOREA (AGAIN)

Although I was heavily focused on the IABG acquisition and its activities in Europe, I remained responsible for global marketing and simultaneously pursued other international engineering opportunities such as one for the Hanjin Shipping Company in Korea. Hanjin, one of the largest shipping companies in the world, was also the parent of Korean Air, and both entities relied on a single logistics system said to be neither fish nor fowl: The airline seat-reservation system had been converted for use in arranging containers on ships. With Dr. Robert Burger, head of BDM's Army logistics programs and recipient of the first Penn State Computer Science Ph.D., we contracted for a purpose-built logistics system for the shipping company. Bob later left BDM to join my SynXis, which brings me to that point in the story.

V. THE ENTREPRENEUR

1996–2005 WASHINGTON, SYNXIS STARTUP

By 1996, when AOL (America Online) was riding high, it was clear the internet would play a major role not only transforming communications but also transforming business. Having been so heavily involved in the mechanics of the IABG acquisition, I realized I still knew little about this emerging technology that would likely be important to BDM and, thus, to me, so I went out of my way to accumulate books and articles that explained it. As I developed a deeper understanding of internet technology, I began a process of thinking about what could be done to develop and own useful products beyond what we knew at the time: dial-up connectivity, email, games (solitaire), and limited search (no Google to speak of).

It was difficult to think of building and owning products within BDM because companies with its history were usually paid on an hourly basis and, in the end, owned nothing. A good example was EDGAR (Electronic Data Gathering, Analysis and Retrieval System), which was built by BDM for the easy retrieval of Securities and Exchange Commission (SEC) documents. I once asked one of the executives involved in its development whether they had thought about building the system and charging a users' fee instead of charging time and materials it took to build the solution. The answer, "We don't do it that way," caused me to think harder about the internet, and about a company to build and *own* internet products.

From time to time, I had worked on air-traffic control problems with BDM's Denver and Boulder offices and had become friends with Jerry Myers, a sharp technologist living in Denver who previously was associated with AT&T, and had been marketing communications services to our government clients. In talking with Jerry, I raised the idea of creating a company to build business products for the internet. I didn't have experience with consumer products, and I didn't want to make products and not own them, a la BDM. So what was it that I *could* do?

After a lot of back-and-forth and time on the phone, Jerry affirmed my thought process and agreed to join me to explore funding a company to build B-to-B (business-to-business) solutions *yet to be identified* using internet technology; for the time being we would call it something like "Internet Solutions Company."

I then contacted Bob Sterling, an entrepreneur I had met through Bill Grossmann in my days at SAIC. Bob had been one of the initial investors in PictureTel, a Zoom forerunner that enabled televised telephone conference calls over landlines. PictureTel was peaking at that moment with over $500 million in sales. He said he thought he could raise $700,000 to fund the internet product development company I loosely described.

In August, Jerry and I, with Denver BDM software developer Tharun Reddy, put together a barebones business plan and decided to start the company with headquarters in the Washington area and a software development team in Denver, where Jerry and Tharun would be most comfortable recruiting other developers as needed. Investor Bob Sterling would serve as chairman, me as CEO, Jerry as executive vice president, and Tharun as the principal developer. Bob had 51% of the shares, Tharun 5%, and Jerry and I 22% each. Suffice it to say that had I known then what I know today, the share splits would have been different.

I then sat down with BDM CEO Phil Odeen and explained it was time for me to "retire" from BDM and head out on my own. I think Phil was surprised to see me go and a bit skeptical, but also, I think he understood my observation that I had learned lessons from him, from Dave Heebner, and from others, and that it was now time for me to apply them.

But first, an interruption: On the day we had decided would be the first official day of the new company, August 15, 1996, I was called for jury duty! I knew from the local news that the jury was being impaneled for a trial involving four mean characters, a couple of whom had committed murder during a robbery, and there was no way I could start the company from the jury room.

I arrived at the courthouse at 8 A.M. that day wearing my conservative dark blue suit, white shirt, and red tie. Immediately that morning, the entire jury pool was sequestered and told the trial would likely take a month. I was not called to the courtroom till 8 P.M., at which point I took a seat in the witness box and the judge asked me to read a list of reasons on an easel why I might be disqualified.

The first question was whether I was a lawyer. I told the judge that I was not a lawyer but had been a member of the Pennsylvania Legislature that obviously wrote laws, and I told him I had headed the Judiciary Subcommittee on Corrections and had visited Pennsylvania prisons.

The judge said he found that interesting and asked me whether I learned anything from visiting the prisons. Looking around the room packed with guards and directly at the four defendants, I said, "Yes, all the inmates told me they were innocent!" The defense attorney quickly stood up and asked the judge to excuse me, which he did!

Excused from jury duty, it was important that I get to work. Janet was still working at the *Washington Post*, but we didn't have what we should in the bank, so I got busy immediately. While Bob Sterling went about speaking with potential investors and setting up a Delaware corporation, I boarded a plane for Denver, where Jerry Myers, who had also resigned, said he had found several developers in Boulder willing to take a flyer with us.

Jerry picked me up at the plane and we drove to Boulder for a meeting with the new team. The leader squirmed in his seat and told us that after further consideration they had decided not to join us but to continue doing what they were doing. From then on, I would always say that recruiting a first-rate team is the hardest and most important part of the entrepreneur's life. Jerry and I drove back to Denver and discussed our limited options over a long dinner before I went to my hotel for some sleep.

I remember waking up wondering how I had gotten into this situation. Recognizing this, I then began focusing on how to get out of it, "focus" being an essential tool in the entrepreneur's toolkit. First, I had a prescheduled meeting with a smart young advertising firm.

While Jerry tracked down software developers, I worked with the advertising firm to come up with stationery and descriptive marketing language, everything but the name. As the staff left at the end of the day, I recall sitting on the floor paging through a huge dictionary trying to come up with a word that would prompt a brand name. Leafing through uncommon Greek words transposed into English, I found the word "synaxis," meaning a "gathering of the faithful for liturgical purposes." Yep, we needed a lot of prayer!

I called Bob and proposed the name, but shortly after, he called me back to say the name was already registered by a small company in Boston. I suggested we drop the "a" and call the company Synxis. Bob moved quickly to determine nobody owned it and to register it.

Over time we learned that people had a hard time pronouncing it, so we capitalized the "X" and that helped, most people learned to say syn-X-is. Eventually we colored the X red, and that seemed to encourage uniform pronunciation.

Jerry, searching for software developers in Denver, contacted previous BDM developers and identified a group of three who had left BDM and established their own company. We met with them and found that they had had some experience in the bed-and-breakfast industry in California that was to come into play later, but for the time being they were more interested in identifying projects calling for the use of a new software language, Smalltalk, in which they considered themselves world-class developers. While at BDM they had attempted to apply it to Defense Department work even though it was apparent Java would be the preferred software development language of the future.

Jerry and I described our potential investors and interest in building internet products, leaving the door open to the use of Smalltalk if it could be justified. We did not have a customer yet, so it was a hard sell, but they agreed to join us when the level of investment became clear, and when there might be a prospective customer on the horizon. With a *potential* team and *potential* investors, I decided to return to Washington to work on the third part, finding the *potential* customer. Such, I discovered, is the life of the entrepreneur: solving equations of multiple unknowns.

In the seminars I conduct at the University of Pittsburgh graduate business school, I ask, "Which is the most important: investors, customers, or employees?" In nearly all cases the students respond with customers or investors first, perhaps because those are their areas of least familiarity. To the contrary, I have always felt that with a great team one can find the investors and customers, which is exactly what happened in our case.

The company headquarters was in my basement for the time being, so that was where I returned from Denver to begin, as we used to say, "dialing for dollars." As I settled into the task at hand, my colleague from the BDM Hanjin project, Dr. Robert Burger, stopped by to say, much to my surprise, that he had resigned from BDM and wanted to join the effort. Bob, recipient of the first Penn State Ph.D. in Computer Science, had significant software-development management experience and was a most welcome addition to the team that now consisted of five for sure, and three provisional software developers.

One of my first calls was to Alex Good, my close friend from the Reagan Administration, whose office abutted mine at Commerce. After the administration, he had joined the Jones Day Law firm, then became president of MTel International, a global paging company, before becoming president of Bell Atlantic International. From that position, he was promoted to Bell Atlantic's corporate head of strategy, number three in their management hierarchy.

Bell Atlantic was evaluating options for the future of their *Yellow Pages*. Google was not a common search solution in 1996, so the telephone companies all had the idea that the digital search engines of the future could include the *Yellow Pages* and they would no longer print and deliver literally tons of multiple local business directories Little did we or they know.

Alex introduced me to Majid Naderkhani, Chief Information Officer of Bell Atlantic, who was responsible for figuring out how to put the *Yellow Pages* online. There seemed to be two options: present a digital representation of the pages as they appeared in print, or display an alphabetical list of the usual categories with the merchants listed below. Bob Burger and I explained to Majid that we were prepared to do either, or both.

There was one conversation I never forgot: When Majid pointed out that most of the phone companies relied on the COBAL programing language, by that time considered ancient, I asked whether he had software documentation manuals that described how the systems were built and revised. After Majeed said, "Are you kidding?" I asked him how they kept track of system functionality. The answer: "Tribal knowledge!"

After several technical meetings that included one of our three *prospective* developers, we were able to assure Bell Atlantic that whatever choice they made about depicting the *Yellow Pages*, we could handle it. After brief negotiations we signed a $400,000 contract and our three developers signed on and began looking for Denver office space in LoDo (Lower Downtown) while Bob Burger initiated a search for an office in Court House (Arlington), Virginia, across the river from Washington and near the Bell Atlantic executive offices.

Shortly thereafter, Bob and I settled into a small single-room office in a shared facility that became our "headquarters," while the software development team took space in a restored building across from Denver's Union Station.

During the discussions with Bell Atlantic, it was clear that whatever solution we developed for them, or for any subsequent yellow-pages publisher, we would not have the muscle to own it; we considered ourselves the proverbial flea on the elephant's back.

Not long after that, I was in Denver and initiated a discussion separate from our *Yellow Pages* assignment with the team asking what product ideas they had. They told me they had started a reservation solution for a small group of bed-and-breakfast hotels in California but stopped when they were owed over $50,000. I resolved to investigate the idea of an internet-based hotel reservation system, and I also decided to go after the $50,000 receivable we had assumed when the developers merged their company with SynXis.

First, the receivable. It just so happened that the California fellow who owed the $50,000 was in the process of raising money for another venture and when he heard we had filed suit against him in a Virginia court, he was quick to pay up rather than explain to prospective investors why he was being sued.

Second, the hotel reservation system. As the developers explained the reservation process, it sounded complex and arcane, something that could and should be simplified on the back of the internet. I vowed to investigate the idea while they handled the Bell Atlantic development work.

Serendipitously, Janet was writing a story for the *Washington Post* about the reopening of the restored Willard Hotel, not far from the White House and well known on the Washington scene since Abraham Lincoln's time. The Willard was an InterContinental Hotel and through Janet's contacts I was able to speak with the brand's reservation manager. He told me his biggest problem was "selling the last room."

Reservations at the time were made in one of three ways: by phone or fax to the hotel or its chain's 800 number, through a travel agent, or with one of the burgeoning internet sites like Travelocity. The common denominators for travel agents and internet sites were four Global Distribution Systems (GDSs) built by the airlines in the '80s: Sabre by American, Galileo by United, World-Span by Delta, and Amadeus by the European airlines.

The GDSs each displayed to their member travel agents and internet sites (for example, Travelocity with Sabre) approximately the same auto rental, airline, and "available" hotel inventory, with some bias shown their founding airlines. The fee for a travel agent to connect to a GDS was $100,000, so it was not common practice for travel agents to connect to more than one. In turn, travel agents usually charged hotels 10% of the reservation stay plus a GDS transaction fee. That could cost hotels as much as $12–$25 per reservation.

The largest problem for the hotel, aside from the cost, as described by the InterContinental reservations manager, was the difficulty of allocating inventory across the four GDSs to "sell the last room." For example, let's say a one-hundred-room hotel allocates eighty rooms to the four GDSs (twenty each) and twenty to the front desk telephone. These are moving targets. The hotel reservation manager, or sometimes night staff, needed to constantly reallocate available inventory among those reservation sources, especially the GDSs, in order not to be shown as "sold out" in any of them when, in fact, rooms were available. This process was never well-enough executed to enable "sale of the last room" because there was nearly always a room left over in one GDS or another, or at the front desk.

As an example, a Sabre travel agent books all twenty rooms of the Sabre GDS allocation of our hypothetical hotel for a wedding. Unless some inventory is moved from the other GDSs or the front desk to Sabre, all other Sabre-connected travel agents will see the hotel as fully booked during the wedding when in fact there may have been up to eighty rooms available. This explains why travelers found they could not book a hotel with one agent but could book it with another using a different GDS, or with the front desk.

It occurred to us that if we could connect the hotel to all four GDSs simultaneously and thereby expose the entire inventory to all GDSs, their travel agents, and connected internet sites, on a first-come, first-served basis, that would resolve the problem of "selling the last room." It also occurred to us that with the appropriate user interface, the system could permit large and small hotels or chains to display their entire inventory directly to potential guests on their website and thereby enable consumers to book directly avoiding travel agent and GDS fees.

Software as a Service (SaaS), where a solution is centrally managed and paid for on a monthly or yearly subscription basis, was increasingly popular.

We took it one important step further for our most important innovation: We opted to charge a fee only for a successful reservation, as opposed to a subscription fee for processing prospective or booked reservations. In effect, we were productizing a service, our second-most important innovation. It meant hotels could use our system, which included connectivity to the GDS and internet sites, to display availability to all sources of reservations and only pay a fee if a reservation was made on the system.

This was a novel concept that cut the hotel's cost of a reservation in half. We reasoned that the savings it generated—without a subscription—would support strong early sales of our system, as it would cost the hotel nothing to try us. Thus, we separated a couple of software developers from the Bell Atlantic project and began to document the requirements for a hotel reservation system that 1) connected to all four GDSs, their travel agents, and internet sites; 2) charged only for the reservations booked; and 3) could power the hotel's website.

Among my first tasks was helping Bob Sterling raise the money it was going to take to build the entire system. This was an especially difficult task because we couldn't estimate the total cost or time required until we fully documented the requirements, a process that precedes all software projects, and that would take time and money above and beyond our Bell Atlantic project. One thing we knew for sure was we were going to have to come up with $400,000 to connect to the four GDSs. This was well beyond our Bell Atlantic/*Yellow Pages* revenue.

Initial contacts with investors always brought up the obvious question: "What do the *Yellow Pages* and hotels have in common?" The question behind the question was: "Is the hotel product a diversion from the profitable *Yellow Pages* assignment?" Our first answer, not to be too serious, was that hotels were listed in *Yellow Pages*, and *Yellow Pages* were in most hotel rooms. But then we explained, more convincingly, that our contracts in the *Yellow Pages* service business would sustain us as we sorted out our approach to a unique product of significant importance and value to the hotel world, which consisted of 75,000 hotels in the United States and 450,000 worldwide.

Our initial $500,000 investment in SynXis, in addition to what Bob Sterling had raised, came from a group of Washington executives who had more faith in the *Yellow Pages* business. It was going to take a far greater investment than that to build the hotel product. So Bob Sterling successfully approached Sequoia Capital in New Jersey. He also opened the door to a personal investment by George Soros in New York. We also met with Fred Whittemore, chairman emeritus of Morgan Stanley, the executive who had taken Morgan Stanley public.

In our meeting with Mr. Whittemore, known for financing Broadway plays, not software companies, he unexpectedly asked me to describe the technology as opposed to the usual questions about the business model. At that time, we had begun to architect the product using object-oriented languages, including Smalltalk, that we eventually discarded in favor of Java and other subsidiary languages. Without thinking, I used the term "object-oriented programing" during the conversation and Mr. Whittemore asked what that meant.

One of my rules has always been "Make the complex simple." Although I usually left questions like that to the developers, none were in the meeting. Without backup, I soldiered on explaining that object-oriented programing represented both a *class*, like automobile, and an *object*, the automobile including its attributes like model and color, that could be reused in the development process. In essence, object code enabled accelerated development using "objects" (code) previously developed and in a library. That seemed to do the trick and a few days later Bob Sterling received a check for $400,000. This, of course, coming from the former head of Morgan Stanley, had a positive effect all around.

By this time, we had added a room to the Virginia shared office suite for a developer for the Bell Atlantic project and increased the Denver staff by ten developers. Bob Burger and I would, for a short time, be alone with the one developer in the Court House office while most of the employees were in Denver. The Denver office was remarkable in that it was in a space that in the 19th century had been a house of ill repute with a tunnel connecting to the nearby Oxford Hotel, where I usually stayed. I never found the tunnel.

The Denver office was not far from the new Rockies baseball field and about a block from the Wynkoop Brewpub, where we often adjourned after work to play pool. A young woman waitress befriended our team, and we reciprocated by hiring her as our receptionist. Sitting at the front desk while handling calls and visitors, she eventually got to know the product so well she became the first member of our quality-control group.

Continuing to shake the money tree, we had multiple discussions with one investment group, Edison Partners Venture Capital Group, New Jersey, though with their office in Washington. Their questions and comments reflected a strong interest in the *Yellow Pages* side of our business, and little interest in the hotel product. I suppose that was because we were already making money providing services to Bell Atlantic—and soon the other regional telephone companies—but had miles to go in development of the hotel product.

During those discussions with Edison, out of the blue a publishing executive returning to his home in Annapolis from a London posting got in touch looking for investment opportunities. On the advice of his brother-in-law at the Washington investment firm FBR, he connected with Edison Partners and together they offered to acquire our *Yellow Pages* business for $7 million. We sold it to them but kept the name SynXis.

On the one hand, this was good news because it gave us additional resources for the hotel reservations business and enabled our team to focus on developing the product. On the other hand, we lost a revenue stream and Edison insisted that Bob Burger and a couple of our top developers go with the business. By that time Jerry Myers had left the company to cope with a serious personal issues and Burger had become my closest confidant. Of the original staff, only Tharun Reddy, in Denver, and I were left.

Edison renamed the business and went forward with the other regional telephone companies. Unfortunately, Google's search engine would kill the *Yellow Pages* business a couple of years later. Our former *Yellow Pages* services group disappeared with them.

As we moved forward with the hotel product, I hired an experienced small-firm controller, Kevin Cheetham, as SynXis's CFO. He and I were to work closely together over the next six years as we added other key players in the Washington headquarters: Sally Payze in operations, Carol Levitt in marketing, Bernard Ellis for strategy, Geoff Mitchell (my old friend from the Middlesboro, KY, debate team) as in-house counsel, and Larry Murray for personnel. As we grew, we moved the Court House office to Tysons Corner and took the top floor of the building next to the McLean Hilton.

It was difficult to predict the development stages of the hotel system, what it would cost, or how long it would take before we could bring our first hotels online. Our objective was to release the system in its most basic, yet workable, form, much like what Microsoft did, to be "first to market" and thereby support our fundraising efforts by demonstrating a working product.

Often, I could tell that venture capital groups found my being in my 50s, about twenty-five years above the norm for most startup CEOs, a problem, although they didn't directly say so. Suffice it to say that in the end the product and business case spoke for itself, and we ultimately raised about $20 million from a variety of sources. However, at one point we were facing a payroll with $37—yes, $37—in the bank. Such is the life of the entrepreneur.

We hosted the system first in our Denver office and later in a secure facility in Washington. We scoped out Hawaii as our first installation, not only because the prospective client was keenly interested in it for his three hotels, but also because the internet in those days slowed with distance. Choosing Hawaii enabled us to demonstrate superior system speed across multiple "hops." After the Hawaiian hotels, we began to find and "load" additional hotels on the initial basic system, paying close attention to potential partnerships in the United States and Canada with the many multiple-hotel management companies.

A hard part was finding the right sales manager. Our first was a misfire, recommended by Priceline, with whom we were trying to partner. We hired the fellow and then found discrepancies in his resume that, because of Priceline's recommendation and our hasty hiring decision, we had missed. I could not accept his remaining on. Unfortunately, his firing precipitated a disagreement with the SynXis Board, some of whom were more interested in a potential deal with Priceline than the poor ethics of the new sales manager.

My relationship with the SynXis Board of Directors waxed and waned over the eight years of my management. The early board consisted of Chairman Bob Sterling; a representative of the initial Washington investor group, Zim Putney; Dave Heebner from SAIC; George Soros' representative, Stewart Paperin; and John Whitman, husband of New Jersey Governor Christine Todd Whitman, from Sycamore Ventures.

In the case of the fired sales manager, it was Dave Heebner who stood by me to say that fudged resumes were not acceptable in an ethical business. Fortunately, that view prevailed among a majority, and the new sales manager was let go having spent a very short time on the job. I was later subpoenaed to testify in his wife's divorce suit that revealed more problems than we knew and confirmed that people who fudge their resumes fudge a lot of other things.

It wasn't long after that that Dave was diagnosed with prostate cancer. To make matters much worse, his treatment was delayed because of his having contracted MRSA. We went to New York City together to visit specialists I knew, but it was just too late. As we were walking, I remember him saying, "Seventy-four is just too soon." Indeed, it was, and he died a few months later.

Dave's death was an enormous loss, personally. Working for him at SAIC and with him on my SynXis Board, we had bonded deeply. Our relationship was as close as a father-son relationship as I had had since the death of my father forty years before. I was devastated. Dave was the one board member who knew me well, and knew what I wanted, something not always the case with the other board members, who flew in and out for quarterly meetings; it was thus also a loss for the company. It was also a loss to the SAIC community, who recognized Dave as a force behind the growth of the company. And last, it was a terrible loss for his wife, Lynn, whom Janet and I loved.

At his funeral, I walked arm in arm with Lynn behind the caisson carrying him to rest in Arlington Cemetery, when an AWACS (Airborne Warning and Control System—a multi-engine aircraft command center with a large radar dome) flew low over the cemetery. I remarked to Lynn I had never seen one in Washington. She said she had received a message from President George W. Bush in the morning, saying that one would fly over Arlington in Dave's honor since he had played a major role in its design.

As development of the hotel product continued, so did my fundraising activities. Thinking it would be good for future system marketing to have international investors, I began looking to Europe, Milan, and my former colleague Alberto Gnesutta in particular. He and I connected with a Texan who had married an Italian and stayed in Milan to create his own investment firm. Through this gentleman, SynXis received an investment by two individuals who were added to the SynXis Board, a young KLM chief 747 pilot, and KLM's former CFO.

I was actively evaluating opportunities in the European and Asian markets with senior staff and had decided to establish an office in Europe. Kevin Cheetham and Geoff Mitchell went on a fact-finding trip to Dublin and Amsterdam to evaluate tax laws and prospective sites. One evening, they were at dinner in a Dublin restaurant discussing SynXis when a fellow at the next table introduced himself and, following some conversation, said he might be interested in investing. His name was Domhnal Slattery. It didn't hurt the discussion that the SynXis CEO was named Kelly. He suggested he would like to meet me when next I was in Europe.

The Milan Texan suggested we schedule a quarterly board meeting in Italy, which we did, including a reception at the Villa d'Este on Lake Como. I took that opportunity to corral my friend Alberto to drive us across the French Riviera to the Cap Ferrat Hotel, where we met with Domhnal Slattery. After leaving GE Capital, he had made his fortune by creating one of the world's largest aircraft-leasing companies, which served all the major airlines. As best I could remember, after three bottles of Cristal Champagne among us, he agreed to invest. He and his brother, John, now head of GE Aviation, turned out to be fun investors. He had a voice like Pavarotti and wasn't shy about exercising it, once serenading a young affianced couple in Bobby Van's Irish restaurant in Washington.

Alberto and I made our way, slowly, back to Milan, stopping in Monaco to meet another investor and share another bottle of Cristal. I was beginning to think the startup business wasn't so bad after all.

Back at the firm, it was becoming apparent that our second sales manager was even more contentious than the first. At the time he signed on, we had three Dutch directors. (This becomes important.) I was chairman and CEO. But Bob Sterling had left the board and Dave Heebner had died. We first added a well-known industry expert, John Russell, and then Steve Norris (formerly of the Carlyle Group), along with Larry Hough, the former head of Sally Mae and SATO, the Federal Government travel agency. Including Whitman, Putney, and Paperin, it was now a board of ten, which was too many for a company our size. As well, most members had no technology startup experience. I would change both were I to have a do-over.

The second sales manager had been born and raised in Holland. He had come to the States and in his first assignment managed the Washington Sheraton (later the St. Regis). From there, he had formed, with a Houston hotelier, the Lancaster Group that managed both the Lancaster in Houston and the Jefferson on 16th Street in Washington. For reasons I discovered later, via a phone call from his former partner, that partnership had fallen apart over his personal use of corporate assets, including the guest limousine and hotel landscapers. He was also having an affair with the marketing manager, which resulted in a messy divorce and then marriage to the marketing manager. Of course, none of this was on his resume.

After he had been with us for a while, he decided he could do a better job running the company than I was doing, so he began a backdoor campaign to oust me, using Dutch language email with the Dutch directors. Fortunately, Director Steve Norris and several of our senior employees were solicited by him and told me of his intentions. I called him in and fired him, which led to another inquisition by the board, primarily the Dutch directors, who wanted him reinstated. The Dutch emails were translated for me by my Amsterdam banker friend, Roel van der Heide, and shared with the board. Eventually, the Dutch directors acquiesced on the basis that the manager be paid $10,000 to finalize a sales agreement he said he was negotiating with a large Spanish hotel group, something he never did.

Although the company, by any measure, was succeeding—we were loading increasing numbers of hotels on our system each week—two undercurrents, in my opinion, brought about the sale of the company. The first was the Dutch directors' hardheaded, continued press for the former sales manager's reinstatement. In fact, I think they had lost money on other investments and saw an opportunity to cover some of those losses by insisting SynXis be sold. Not having gotten their way concerning the company management was, in part, an excuse. They may have been smart investors, but they were shortsighted board members.

The second undercurrent concerned Director Larry Hough, who opened a channel with friends at Sabre Corporation, Dallas, Texas. Larry made a case to the SynXis Board for selling the company to Sabre. On the one hand, I felt we were just getting started and did not think it was time to sell the company. On the other, I was wearing thin trying to synthesize widely differing views of the company's future, the Dutch on one side and the Americans on the other. Seeing the writing on the wall (and reading it, as I liked to say) I decided to step aside.

Larry became CEO and negotiated the sale at roughly twice the total invested in the company. Although he had hoped to continue as CEO, it didn't work out. Sabre named the number-two executive of competitor Pegasus in Dallas as CEO, and the Washington office of SynXis was soon closed. Eventually, nearly all the core members of the original team left or were changed out. In recognition of my founder's role, and perhaps also connecting with my service in the Reagan Administration, the team gave me an eagle engraved in glass with a monogram attributed to Reagan: "It can be done!"

Something like 2% of startups prosper, so after the success of two startups, the online *Yellow Pages* and the hotel reservation system, I was asked to speak in seminars and classrooms. As talking points, I put together a ten-step primer covering what I thought were critical steps in establishing a successful software company. I always emphasized No. 3, which stated that personnel decisions, often difficult in a startup among friends, must be made quickly or the company will fail (see Appendix A).

I was also asked to describe my management style. As I have said before, most people like to do what they are good at, but that only holds if they are honest with themselves. Just because they say they are good at something is not a qualifier. As a manager, I was always partial to team members who demonstrated knowledge of the job coupled with an intense desire to do it, and I always tried to hire people smarter than I was.

While running SynXis, I spent time each month just walking around our offices in Washington, Denver, Boston, and Amsterdam, making sure I knew what everyone was thinking, and that they were satisfied with their "seat on the bus." I always felt it was my responsibility to help our people do their job and if ever they expressed a need, I tried to accommodate them, or at least be clear in telling them why I couldn't. In this way I honored our strong team for who they were.

Intuition is a large part of who I am, and I've always believed that intuition cannot be taught; it is the sum of your experiences. By the time I created my companies, I had more experience than most people I knew. My intuition fortified me and gave me confidence.

SynXis was officially sold to Sabre in January 2005, and today is a division of Sabre Corporation, Dallas, Texas, providing central reservation services to over fifty thousand hotels, including such brands as Wyndham and Hyatt, with revenue exceeding $350 million.

While CEO of SynXis, I was invited with other leaders to spend a week at the Army War College, Carlisle, Pennsylvania, studying leadership lessons learned by the military during war. With a keen interest in military history and principles of leadership, I was quick to accept the invitation. There was an unexpected side benefit in that Lynn Swann, the Pittsburgh Steelers Hall of Fame wide receiver, would also be there.

Earlier, I had attended an Army-Navy game in New Jersey with my former BDM colleague, Jim O'Toole, where I met his West Point classmate, the Commandant of the War College, Major General Bob Ivany, who had served as a military aide to President Reagan in his first administration. A few days after the game, General Ivany invited me and other leaders of diverse businesses to attend the War College, describing the week as a learning experience in the classroom and on the nearby Gettysburg Civil War battlefield with Army officers. We would study command lessons learned, notably the importance of effective top-down communications.

The example I remember so well was that while Confederate troops had little idea why they were in Gettysburg, Lincoln made clear to Union troops through his generals that they were fighting to save the Union by blocking a Confederate advance on Washington. Neither Confederate President Jefferson Davis nor General Robert Lee had clearly communicated to their forces an understanding of the bigger picture, their Washington objective, or why they were in Pennsylvania, which contributed to the loss of the three-day battle. After my experience at the War College, when asked about other companies, I usually started by saying, "An organization reflects the person at the top, and how well he or she communicates the organization's mission, or doesn't."

At the War College Leadership Conference, it wasn't all serious study. Attendees were given a room and a parking space, so when I arrived, I found a space with my name posted in large letters, right next to a space with the name Lynn Swann. I quickly realized that the soldiers standing around knew who Lynn Swann was and had assumed that the adjacent Jim Kelly parking space might be referring to the famous former Buffalo Bills quarterback who shared my name, Jim Kelly. As Lynn arrived, I was quick to point out he was the real deal; I wasn't.

Our last session was memorable. Various colonels described the formulation and importance of battle "after action reports (AARs)" and each of us was asked whether and how we used them in our business. None of us wanted to answer the question without first hearing Lynn Swann, and his tales of leadership. He started off talking about his career as a broadcaster but didn't get very far before we stopped him and said, "Give us something about the Steelers."

"Okay," he said and proceeded to tell us about an after-game Monday morning when Coach Chuck Noll reviewed game films. The coach showed a play where running back Franco Harris gained eight yards. The coach then asked quarterback Terry Bradshaw to name the play. Terry, smoking his usual cigar, repeatedly asked the coach to run the film again while he did his best to remember the number of the play. Finally, he said, "Coach, that's a 32 (Franco's number) something-something," to which Noll responded, "Terry, we don't have that play." To which Terry responded, "We do now, Coach!" It was an unexpected lesson in improvisation on a different battlefield.

Lynn's description of that instance was not the only thing we learned about the '70s Steelers. The huddles must have been crazy with Swann, John Stallworth (the other Hall of Fame wide receiver), and Franco Harris all asking for the ball. "Shut up!" was Terry's response while he devised the play, sometimes from the playbook, often not!

In the summer of 2003, at the height of my involvement with SynXis, my mother died in Boston at the age of eighty-eight. After my stepfather Erwin's death in 1989, she had lived in Pittsburgh with my brother and his wife, then briefly alone, and finally decided to move to Boston to live near my sister and her husband.

She had been a heavy smoker from the age of sixteen, and we had a scare when she had entered a Boston hospital a couple of years earlier, around New Year's Day, 2000. I had flown from Williamsburg, Virginia, to be with her and suggested she might just be a little better off if she stopped smoking. She did and lived another three years.

My mother's early years were spent in a large well-known family in Springfield, Illinois; she grew up with a silver spoon. Her great-grandfather, George Chatterton, had jewelry stores in Springfield and New York, and had made Abraham Lincoln's jewelry and watches (now in the Smithsonian). Her grandfather of the same name owned the opera property in town (now the site of the Lincoln Library). Her great uncle, Richard Yates, had been Lincoln's friend, a congressman, Civil War governor, and senator from Illinois. Her cousin, Governor Yates' son, had also been governor in the 1890s and a congressman at the time she attended school in Washington. She was her father's only child, age fifteen when her mother died.

As the daughter of a successful executive in the 1930s, Mom did not experience the Depression as did many others her age, and throughout her life she had a hard time managing money, either what she inherited, or what she and my stepfather, Erwin, had from operating the kennel.

My relationship with my mother ran hot and cold, seldom in between, but there is no doubt she was an influence in my life. Although my mother and my sister got along well, my sister often said Mom would never be a candidate for Mother of the Year.

Raising children was not a priority for her, as it is with so many parents today. That doesn't mean we weren't loved; she just wasn't very expressive and seldom gave us feedback, unless we did something we shouldn't. All this added to my sense of being on my own after my father died in 1960 and it likely set the mold for my close-kept emotions.

Not much of a cook while I was in the nest, she later gave us several exceptional recipes, including those for vichyssoise and popovers, my favorites. She was a voracious reader with a top-notch intellect and an inquiring mind, which I like to think my siblings and I inherited. All three of us were constant readers since before the first grade. My feeling is that in her later life, after her own mother's early death, attending four different high schools and college, the Second World War, the move to Kentucky, my father's death, and then her father's death, my mother was content to slow down. She would read by the pool she and Erwin installed, do her Sunday *New York Times* crossword puzzle, attend horseraces with Erwin near Pittsburgh, and handle epic gatherings of the family on vacations and holidays. In all that, she succeeded amazingly.

She never looked back, always forward. I never knew about Great-Uncle Yates, other than having seen his portrait and his statue on the capitol lawn in Springfield with my grandfather, until I read a book by Stephen Ambrose that mentioned that Yates had recruited Grant at the outset of the war and was with him at Vicksburg. I asked Mom, "Are we related to this guy?" Shortly thereafter I received a FedEx package with a stack of documents having to do with Governor Yates, including an 1863 hand-drawn Vicksburg battle map.

I went to Vicksburg with some friends to check out the battle map and locate an old house in the Mississippi woods, from where it was said Governor Yates had addressed the troops; I also wanted to establish the provenance of the map. We came across a cenotaph dedicated to Illinois soldiers that featured the faces of President Lincoln, Governor Yates, and General Grant. Under Yates were written his words: "God forbid that I should say aught in malice against the South. I look beyond the blue waves of the Ohio and upon the green hills of Kentucky and there is the grave of my mother."

I called my mother to tell her what I had seen and read, the governor talking about his mother, who was Mom's great-great-grandmother.

Her response, "So what?" clarified her perspective: The past was the past. As I thought about it, I had to admit that I hadn't spent much time looking to the past, either (until now).

During my visit with her shortly before she died, she said my father was there with her, and she told me how proud she had been of my career. That surprised me. Although she never failed to give me "guidance" and, in certain instances, help in one form or another, she never gave compliments. My sister later found a stash of notes, photos, newspaper articles, and letters about me that she had collected. I was surprised but realized that neither one of us was very good at expressing our feelings to the other.

2003–2014 BLACKSBURG, VIRGINIA TECH BUSINESS SCHOOL

With the early success of SynXis in the hotel industry, and my recognition as a Virginia Tech graduate, I was asked to give several seminars on the emerging "Electronic Distribution in the Hotel Industry" at the Virginia Tech Pamplin Business School Department of Hospitality and Tourism Management. The department had recently moved from the School of General Sciences and was keen to modernize its offerings in a more businesslike context. The seminars focused on how information technology was changing an age-old business and primed students for interviews with the likes of Marriott Corporation and Hilton Hotels, both located in the Washington metropolitan area.

I usually spent time with one or two faculty members after the seminars and on one such occasion was introduced to Richard Sorenson, the long-serving dean of the business school. We had a conversation not only about the hospitality and tourism industry, but also about my international experience. Subsequently, when the dean invited me to join his advisory board, I sensed he was more interested in my international experience than in my travel-and-tourism seminars.

The board met at least once a year and various committees carried out assignments requested by the dean between the meetings. In my case, and after I had become acclimated with other members of the board, the dean asked me to become chairman of the board's International Committee. Although the committee included several members with international experience, it had not been particularly active, other than recommending more foreign language studies.

My charge was to increase student *and* teacher awareness of the importance of international business studies within the business school curriculum. Virginia Tech, not far from Roanoke in Southwest-Central Virginia, had mostly students from Virginia high schools and although many came from urban areas around Washington and Richmond, there were others from small towns in Virginia whose world consisted of fewer than five thousand people. International business was far from their minds.

One of the top professors was assigned to work with me and I suggested we do a competitive analysis of what other schools were doing for their students, particularly those considered direct competitors like Penn State and the University of Virginia. We also took a close look at the University of South Carolina, often considered a top competitor with Thunderbird.

The study we presented to the committee and later the full board revealed three elements important to international business studies existent at the other schools, but not at Virginia Tech:

- Professors with advanced international business degrees qualified to teach international business courses at the undergraduate level
- A minor degree in Global or International Business
- A minimum foreign language study requirement.

The board agreed to recommend the adoption of all three elements to the dean and the university. Fortunately, I was later able to meet with University President Charles Steger to secure his buy-in. Shortly after, a "Minor Degree in International Business" replaced the "Global Business Certificate." The requirements for it included a semester of language study, not necessarily for the purpose of fluency, but rather to understand that people organize their thoughts differently in other languages. Finally, two "International Business" courses were added, as was a dedicated professor of international business. Our International Committee staffer was elevated from adjunct status to fulltime support of international business coursework. Little did I know that this work would later drive an assignment for me at the University of Pittsburgh.

2005–2008 WASHINGTON, FLIGHT EXPLORER

The second half of 2005, I was approached by a banker who had once pitched SynXis on finding a buyer. He had not been selected because terms with Sabre already had been established, but he thought he could earn a fee pitching me for another opportunity. He asked if I would be interested in building a company incorporating software technology for tracking and reporting airplanes in flight, an application that today is very common, but then wasn't. As a former pilot, I had a leg up on the subject, so there was little question whether I would be interested.

The technology and its early development team resided within a company called Flight Dimensions International, which itself was a subsidiary of Northern Virginia defense contractor Dimensions International. Dimensions International was in the process of being sold by its owner, Robert (Bob) Wright, to Honeywell International. Mr. Wright was interested in taking the technology out of the transaction and developing it separately from Honeywell. The banker asked me to meet with Mr. Wright prior to my leaving the States to visit friends in Italy.

Bob was from Columbus, Georgia, and had an unusual resume: An Ohio State optometry grad, he was a highly successful businessman, an African-American, and a Republican. He had served three terms on the City Council, and in 1980 came to the attention of the Reagan team and played an important role marshalling black voters in that year's presidential campaign. He then served in President Reagan's first administration as Associate Administrator for Minority Small Business in the Small Business Administration (SBA), after which he founded Dimensions International. His biographer once asked me to describe him and being something of a Lincoln student, I said that with his sense of humor and practical, lowkey way of looking at things, he was about as close as I was going to get to someone like Lincoln.

When we met, Bob explained that an airplane-tracking system named Flight Explorer had been developed inside Dimensions International with its initial deployment managed by a former Air Force four-star general and pilot. The software development team was located near Atlantic City and the FAA Technical Center and was engaged in building out the Flight Explorer Aircraft Situation Display (ASD) product combining existing tracking sources to display an airplane's flight path and location. A separate office near Atlanta had begun to oversee development of a related product, a satellite-based cockpit communication and datalink system. The ASD was in limited use, the datalink system was not.

Bob had already floated the idea with the banker of selling the Flight Explorer ASD separate from Dimensions International, but it was not sufficiently developed for a meaningful offer. It was therefore Bob's intent to exclude the Flight Explorer product, technologies, and staff from the Honeywell transaction and create another company called Flight Explorer to oversee the further development of the ASD and the datalink system. I was asked to be the new company's CEO.

As Bob explained it, my first job would be to ramp up software development and marketing of the ASD, which initially was used mostly by private pilots and business aircraft. The technology had gained attention when Dimensions International's subsidiary, Flight Dimensions, produced a map with the tracks of the four 9/11 weaponized aircraft. Previously, aircraft operators had only a snapshot of a plane's location from FAA radar reports, or from reports by ARINC, a private Annapolis firm with some two hundred towers sprinkled around the country. There were no digital displays, common today, that showed an aircraft's position and its flight path, past and future.

My second job would be to advance the development of the data downlink system, which Bob had been convinced would have enormous potential, perhaps even beyond that of the Flight Explorer ASD. The software development team in Linwood, New Jersey, was primarily responsible for the ASD while the team in Peachtree City, about an hour from the Atlanta Airport, was responsible for the datalink system.

I was excited by the opportunity. Bob and I worked out the details of my arrangement and in October we met with the twenty-five or so Dimensions

International/Flight Dimensions/Flight Explorer employees in person and by phone and it was announced that a new company named "Flight Explorer" and headquartered in Northern Virginia would be started to further develop and deploy Flight Explorer technology with Bob as chairman and me as CEO. After a few weeks' overlap with the Air Force General and visits with him to the offices in Linwood and Peachtree City, he stepped away and I took over.

Fortunately, the transition was more efficient than the SynXis startup. We had a small team needing only a few changes and additions. We had a product that had been deployed to a modest number of users by our small sales force, and we had temporary space in Dimensions International's building until we could find our own. The second product would be the problem area, which I found out as I made my first solo visit to our Peachtree City office.

When I had been in Peachtree with the Air Force general during my orientation, I heard what I assumed to be over-the-top claims about the development state of the satellite downlink product, and about the commercial arrangements made for its near-term deployment. The presentation had been made by an individual with the title of executive vice president who was the development lead of the second product and head of the Peachtree City office. Unfortunately, he was also the source of problems that almost knocked us off the rails before we started.

I let the manager know before my departure for Atlanta that I wanted to spend time with him to understand the new product. When I arrived, he was not in sight, and it was with some difficulty that I found him at the Atlanta Airport on board a World Airways MD-11 aircraft. He was, by himself, installing a prototype and integrating it into the cockpit avionics. This shocked me; people doing what he was doing were supposed to be trained, licensed, and monitored. As far as I knew, he had a pilot's license, but was neither a licensed mechanic nor certified in flight electronics.

I returned to the office with him, where we reviewed the state of the technology and the various contracts he had signed. As for the technology, I was right: Their descriptions of it had been overblown, and the technology was far from prime time, not even marginal; it had hardly progressed from the idea stage. As I surveyed the state of this supposed world-class application, I began to review the contractual commitments that already had been made by Flight Dimensions. These were contracts we, Flight Explorer, were expected to fulfill.

The contracts I found had not been reviewed by counsel. More important, these signed contracts obligated our new company to provide a working system in short order to three airlines: Lufthansa, World Airways, and EOS, a startup business-class airline in New York.

Bob and I were stunned. We had just started a business that already had signed commitments in the aggregate of millions of dollars for a product and services that we clearly could not deliver within the specified time, if ever. My first step was to investigate the manager's background to get a better understanding of why and how he could have unilaterally put the company in this position. I asked my high school friend and former SynXis counsel, Geoff Mitchell, who would provide outside counsel to Flight Explorer, to research what was known about the manager.

While that investigation was underway, I invited staff from Peach Tree City and Linwood to my first team-building, all-hands meeting and dinner in Linwood. That evening, my interior radar pinged. I had recently read an article that said you could make an accurate character assessment from the way a person treated restaurant staff. In this case, I watched the Peach Tree City manager sorely berate a young woman server who appeared to have just arrived from Eastern Europe and was trying her best to handle a new job and language. It was not a good omen, nor was it pleasant to have to watch. Him, I would have to watch.

In the days after the dinner, as we put together all the pieces, the results were shocking. First, there were twenty-six liens against the manager in multiple states, largely for having skipped on house rental or purchase payments. His company credit card showed personal purchases of tires, personal restaurant meals, and home furnishings exceeding $35,000. His former employers revealed he had been fired in every case for a variety of causes. One firm I ran into at my first aviation conference said their former manager's company credit card account included personal expenditures of $16,000, for which they were suing him.

I fired the individual, and we joined his previous employers pursuing him through, believe it or not, his next two employers. It seems that he was such a "successful" liar the following employers couldn't believe he had done what previous employers accused him of doing, until they had their own experiences. Eventually, he was convicted of a felony.

Having resolved the management issue, I decided to focus on the commercial development of the flight-tracking product for the airlines, not just the private pilots and a small number of aircraft operators. However, that did not resolve the issue of the datalink product agreements or the question of what to do with the partially developed prototype. My first contact was with Lufthansa operations staff, who were understanding and readily agreed to rescind the agreement without penalty.

Needing to address our promises to the other two airlines, I sought out firms working on similar technology and met with a Boston aviation software development company called Wingspeed. They appeared to have significant experience in the aviation and software worlds and had gone much further in their development of a similar advanced satellite datalink product. Although their product was not quite ready for prime time, they were more than pleased to add two new customers and assume the remaining two contracts if it were agreeable to the two airlines.

I met EOS in New York, and Bob and I together met with World Airlines in Atlanta, explaining up front and openly what had happened, that we would provide them with the ASD product for their operations, but that we could not deliver the second product on time. Given the alternative of working with Wingspeed, both airlines agreed to transfer the agreements to Wingspeed. Unfortunately, building the satellite downlink product was more difficult than anyone really knew and Wingspeed was never fully able to commercialize it either; the company later failed.

While later visiting Linwood, I came to see that the head of the office, who was also the original architect and lead software developer of the ASD product, was superior technologically, but not so good communicating and leading. With software version releases there is always contention over their timing: Is the latest good version ready for prime time or should more time be spent to make it better? Our office head and lead developer invariably spent too much time developing the best next version and holding up the better one that could maintain our competitive lead and move us up a notch in the marketplace. Secondly, he didn't have sufficient people-management skills to handle a team of software developers who were known to be cranky. I pulled everyone into the conference room to develop a plan to move the product forward, particularly in the commercial aviation world, and to make some personnel changes.

Once we had a plan, I made three significant, somewhat intuitive, adjustments. The first was to elevate one of the youngest software developers to head the office and lead the team, which he handled with aplomb. It wasn't easy for him because he had joined the company only recently, and few expected the new kid on the block to suddenly be in charge. But I thought he had a presence and a way about him so that things would work out, and they did! There was an added benefit in that his wife, an Atlantic City show dancer, owned a talent management agency and referred one of her fellow dancers to us for a receptionist job. We hired her and as was the case with the receptionist at SynXis, she advanced over time into more responsible and senior positions.

My second move was to recruit an aviation graduate and pilot who had previously been in touch with Dimensions International and had expressed interest in the flight-tracking product. After a short back-and-forth, he came on board essentially as chief operating officer and contributed to all areas of the company.

The third move was to hire a top sales lead. It was largely through his team's efforts that we penetrated the airlines, adding the likes of Jet Blue, American, British Air, Delta in Atlanta after their merger with Northwest, and finally, Qantas (Air Services Australia), along with two China airlines. The woman who had previously been sales manager became the chief administrator of the company and did an outstanding job.

As soon as we found space, we moved out of the Dimensions International building in Alexandria and set up shop in a building in Tysons Corner, also in Northern Virginia. Our offices were on the ground floor and most, including mine, had a window to the outside parking lot.

One afternoon, when I was on a landline phone, I heard the fire alarm and saw people gathering outside and assumed they were participating in the usual fire drill. The windows in my office were slanted inward, top to bottom, and I started to see water cascading down them into my office. I told whomever I was speaking with I would call them back, grabbed one of my model planes, and retreated just as the ceiling collapsed. I had the habit of keeping a clean desk and little paper in my office, something I learned from Drew Lewis, so it was only the furniture that took a beating; the desktop computer survived! The fire resulted from a fellow upstairs overcharging his electric model car. In a month or so I was back in my office.

In early 2008, Bob Wright and I were having lunch. A year before that we had hired an Air Force Academy grad, Ph.D., and industry technology expert to expand our ASD technology offering to include tracking taxiing aircraft (easily done today); he had been working on the subject matter for years and claimed it was nearing prime time.

Bob asked me what I thought it would cost to implement the product addition alongside the relatively successful path we were on. The team had prepared a budget and time-to-release estimate of $4 million and two years. I gave this information to Bob, adding that I thought it was a high-risk project, principally because our competitors, like today's well-known Flight Aware, were backed by private equity and venture capital firms with deep pockets and could afford to spend more to deliver the product sooner. Bob suggested we give some thought to determining what the company was worth now that we had added significant customers and staff.

The outcome of lunch was that we decided to explore valuing the company and opening conversations with prospective buyers, the first task being to identify a banker or bankers who could help us. I will not be so bold as to say that we could see the September 2008 market crash. It was rather a simple question and answer whether we could justify the additional investment in an uncertain result that could simultaneously disrupt our successful focus.

Initially, I thought Bob would want to use the banker he had first engaged to sell the technology separate from his Dimensions International, the same banker who had approached SynXis, the fellow who had recommended me to Bob. Unfortunately, the fellow had, unbeknownst to me, insisted on and received an over-the-top fee for bringing me to the table, a step that soured his relationship with Bob. I was surprised because the banker knew our objective was to build and eventually sell the company, which would have resulted in a significantly larger fee on the backside. In the end, we engaged a banker who had recently returned from years in the UK and Germany engaged in aviation mergers and acquisitions. He understood the space well, so it only took a couple of weeks to bring him up to speed.

His first conversation was with Carlyle, and we made a presentation. I had not met the people we presented to while I was at BDM and would have been surprised if they knew any of my history there; I didn't see any point in mentioning it. In any event, we received an indication of a forthcoming offer well below our expectations, and so moved on.

We then entered discussions with a large European aviation services group that, after a preliminary evaluation, made an offer one and a half times the Carlyle offer. Of course, the ultimate sale would be dependent on completion of a due-diligence process.

In the meantime, we would keep working to grow Flight Explorer. Two of our first clients, British Air and Qantas, had been international airlines. With the growth of Chinese aviation, it became time to make a pitch in China, so I arranged to meet our sales vice president and our in-country representative in Beijing and to take Janet with me because she had never been there.

We met at what was then called Raffles Hotel, which contained the remaining part of the Beijing hotel where I had lived off and on between 1977 and 1980. We hosted a formal Chinese dinner for industry leaders there and although Janet had a bit of trouble with the menu, she managed to make her way through with a little help from the sommelier.

There was one interesting event beyond presenting Flight Explorer to the China market. We were invited to the U.S. Embassy Residence to have lunch with Ambassador Clark (Sandy) Randt and his wife, Sarah. Ambassador Randt was a fraternity brother of President George W. Bush and spoke fluent Chinese.

The invitation was largely due to my previous history in China and our relationship with Mel Searls and his wife, Andy. Mel had preceded Ambassador Randt as head of the Hong Kong American Chamber of Commerce and later was First Secretary and Commercial Counselor in our Beijing Embassy. In between, Mel and I had worked together at Dravo and the Commerce Department, and he and Andy were in Paris when we were in Brussels. Long before Mel's untimely death in 1995, the four of us had been fast friends. Andy had maintained her contacts within the China-expert community and when I told her of our upcoming trip to China, she kindly alerted the ambassador.

While we were at lunch, an aide entered the dining room with a landline phone and announced that the *Washington Post* was on the line. This was a time just prior to the 2008 Olympics and the *Post* was anxious to explore various issues, some probably not complimentary to China. The call was interrupted, and the line went dead three times before the ambassador could say a word.

Finally, he stepped into the courtyard to use his cellphone, with the same result. He remarked that he would not likely be able to talk to the *Post* that day, but if he did, he certainly knew someone else was listening.

Sarah kindly took Janet shopping at the famed Pearl Market, where she had her first experience with Chinese high-pressure sales techniques. The young, attractive saleswoman, when Janet told her she would not make the purchase, said, "You're breaking my heart!" Amusing, and tough to resist.

While in Beijing, I attempted to continue discussions concerning the sale of the company. Noting that Chinese authorities were monitoring the ambassador, I could be pretty sure they were also monitoring me for having been at the residence, but also to gain business intelligence helpful in negotiations with us. As much as we tried to camouflage our discussions, the Chinese were probably able to interpret my telephone calls with Bob Wright and our banker, but regardless, we were able to move ahead in their market and signed Air China and China Southern.

During this time, the potential European buyer expressed concern over what it thought the Committee on Foreign Investment in the United States (CFIUS) might say about their acquiring a company building sophisticated aviation software. CFIUS is an interagency committee of the United States Government that reviews from a national security perspective concerns about foreign investments in U.S. companies.

In our case, the European buyer was worried that CFIUS would challenge the acquisition, which presented a conundrum because the buyer wanted advance CFIUS approval of the sale, something CIFIUS doesn't do. They review the sale after the fact and seek to nullify it through due process if there is evidence the buyer's acquisition will be injurious to the United States.

To open a new front and add a little pressure to the European firm's decision-making process, I made a call to Sabre Airline Solutions executives (different from the hospitality executives who made the SynXis acquisition) I had met shortly after setting up Flight Explorer. That had only been an exploratory meeting in which nothing was concluded, but during which a Sabre executive had said that if Flight Explorer ever gained any market traction, they would be interested in working with us.

I called the executive to say that we would be interested in exploring a relationship and—oh, by the way—others were taking a close look at working with us. It took a nanosecond for the executive to figure it was a competitor and that they better move quickly. They did!

Janet and I had long planned a late summer cruise in Europe, and I remember standing by the ship's rail watching for Italian shore lights and checking the signal strength on my phone for opportunities to make calls. Eventually I was able to confirm that Sabre was pleased with the due diligence they had begun prior to my departure and wanted to proceed, offering a third more than what the others had been considering and more than double the Carlyle offer.

In a final interview with a Sabre Group vice president, I was told that they already had another subsidiary that had the same excellent look and feel as Flight Explorer, SynXis! He had not been involved in the SynXis acquisition, so he was not aware of my role there. It confirmed what I have said earlier: A company reflects the man or woman at the top, good or bad. He went on to say that he had never interviewed a CEO with such a depth of knowledge of so many of his employees at all levels. Knowing our team members well and what motivated them had been an essential ingredient of my success as CEO at both SynXis and Flight Explorer.

Janet and I returned to Washington and proceeded directly to the Tysons Corner lawyer's office to meet Bob Wright and sign the papers selling Flight Explorer to Sabre. The following weekend, the market began to tank into the 2008 recession.

I won't claim that Bob and I were prescient; the decision to sell was made in early 2008 because we could not support an unpredictably high cost and timespan to develop the next level of technology ahead of well-funded, large-market, consumer-based competition. Leave that to people with deeper pockets. It just so happened that our decision wasn't executed until that fateful week in September. I later heard from a Sabre executive that had the market begun its decline a week earlier, Sabre most certainly would not have acquired Flight Explorer at that time.

Shortly after signing all the documents, I drove to Linwood to meet the acquisition team and introduce them to our developers, and then I returned with them to Washington, where they began the process of integrating Flight Explorer. As for me, I had little interest in joining Sabre and everybody knew that, but I did agree to a three-month consulting contract under which I was asked for minimal advice on what would be best for both parties in the integration process. Today, Flight explorer is owned by CAE, Inc. (Canadian Aviation Electronics) and has an installed base of 5000 commercial systems.

2009–2012 WASHINGTON, LIFEDOX

After the sale of Flight Explorer in 2008, with thoughts of my retirement Janet and I traded a boat we had had for several years for a larger boat. We were members of the Annapolis Severn River Yacht Club, where I served one year as commodore, and we spent nearly every spring and summer weekend cruising to different Chesapeake Bay port cities.

On one of the cruises to Baltimore, during lunch on the dock, a friend from Northern Virginia told me he was focusing on what he might do after his approaching retirement from a large accounting firm where he had headed one of the practices. His wife and Janet had been friends at the *Washington Post*. Interesting to me, the conversation then turned to recent medical technology developments, something I had been following.

One of his clients had been MedStar Health Hospitals, which was headquartered in Washington. The MedStar chain included two well-known hospitals, Georgetown and the Washington Hospital Center. The CEO had just retired, so we thought it might be interesting to sit down with him and explore opportunities in healthcare based on the assumption that coming from his position in the industry his expertise would be helpful and his support meaningful.

Back in Washington and a couple of weeks after our dockside discussion, we had dinner at the hospital executive's Maryland horse farm, where we discussed creating a group for the purpose of exploring ways to develop advanced medical technology. One of the technologies we discussed was the need for a patient-based medical record that would enable patients to take their records with them from provider to provider, state to state, and even country to country.

At that time, and more so today, medical records were created and held by the hospital or the patient's medical provider. A patient going from one provider to another had then, and continues to have today, an arduous process transferring records between providers.

Simply put, the inertia in this system restricts patient mobility among providers and is one of the many reasons medical costs are high these days. Another consequence is that hospital systems "own" the patient records, and as more and more doctors leave private practice to join those hospitals, they find it difficult to change employers because their patients are tied to the hospital holding the patient's record.

After dinner with the retired hospital executive, the three of us formed a group to pursue the idea. We then met with an orthopedic surgeon with a history of developing software for IBM medical systems. He was very interested in the concept of a patient-based electronic medical record but raised the question of what technology would be most appropriate.

DR. ROBERT KAHN, A FOUNDER OF THE INTERNET

My boating friend from Baltimore had also been the engagement manager for a contract with the Corporation for National Research Initiatives, headed by Dr. Robert Kahn. Kahn and his co-designer, Vint Cerf, have been credited with the development of the foundation of the internet, the TCP/IP Protocol (Transmission Control Protocol/Internet Protocol) while they were at DARPA, the Defense Advanced Research Projects Agency, at the Pentagon. A dinner was arranged with Dr. Kahn to explore what technologies would be most suited for the medical record concept.

Dr. Kahn told me at dinner that he and his wife Patrice Lyons had been neighbors and friends of Senator Schweiker and Claire. Small world, once again! After pleasantries, he told us about the Digital Object Architecture technology he was developing to power defense industry applications. To his way of thinking, the technology was super secure and would therefore conform with HIPAA (the Health Insurance Portability and Accountability Act). He also assured us it would scale to millions of users and that his team was capable of economically building a prototype. We decided to take a next step.

During my work in the hotel industry, I met a fellow member of the Virginia Tech business school advisory board. He had risen through the ranks to become CEO of a large hotel group, had left, and was now interested in pursuing new opportunities. Seeing him as a potential CEO for the new venture, I suggested he join us for an afternoon discussion about the possibilities of building and delivering this new concept.

At that meeting, it was agreed that we would develop the basic requirements documents for the system. Dr. Kahn's team would develop a budget to build out the technology, the former hotel executive would serve the venture as CEO, and my boating friend as CFO, while the hospital president would be chairman of the board on which I agreed to serve. I had no interest in again taking on the pressure of an operating role. The net outcome of the meeting was that we agreed to proceed with a company we called LifeDox and to seek the investment that would be required to fund it and Dr. Kahn's development team.

Dr. Kahn came up with a budget that in the early stage was minimal, but eventually reached over a million dollars. As development of an iPad app proceeded, the CEO entered discussions with an individual who had been working with a South Florida aviation company providing air ambulance services to Jamaica. The individual suggested Jamaica would be a perfect testbed for the product because patients being air transported to the States using the electronic record could arrive with their medical information on an iPad. This solution would overcome the need for difficult communications back and forth with island doctors, or for redoing medical tests already done on the island.

After we worked on this product for more than a year, I began to see that we were on the wrong side of success. First, the Jamaican contact started to go haywire making weird, somewhat helter-skelter demands that left us wondering not only what his real end game was, but who he was. Our chairman's wife was slowly dying of cancer, so he was understandably inactive at a time when we needed input and help from his industry contacts. Moreover, Dr. Kahn's team started identifying programmatic issues that were obviously going to be difficult and expensive to fix.

I had been going along with the effort and leaving the day-to-day stuff to the CEO, but he had limited startup experience. As the only one who had been through a successful startup, I felt pressure from the team to step into the daily effort, pressure I resisted because, frankly, I was depressed, something I regretted not having shared.

A lot of people look forward to their retirement and plan carefully for it, but I was not one of them. For fifty years, I had been following one path after another assuming, as Drew Lewis had said, that the future would take care of itself. Shortly after we sold Flight Explorer, and even in the time between Syn-

Xis and Flight Explorer, I had suffered depression from early wake-up till mid-morning that, no matter how hard I tried, I could not shake.

In multiple discussions with one or another well-known Washington psychiatrists, I explored the whys of this, and how to alleviate it, succeeding after several years. There is not an easy answer to depression!

More recently there has been a lot written about executives having difficulty distinguishing between their business persona and their "real" self, but I never thought of myself in that way. In fact, one doctor said, "You know who you are, and that contributed to your success." The doctor then said, "At this point in your life, after years as the guy in charge, it must be hard not to be. You ought not to take on new assignments unless you are responsible and can see the all-around benefit." I took that lesson to heart.

Although it wasn't easy, I shortly thereafter began taking a lower profile in LifeDox, which eventually failed. There was no single factor in the venture's demise. Although it was becoming clear that the software would not scale to millions of users without a huge investment, it was more a matter of lack of focus: None of the parties to the venture, including me, was willing to take fulltime responsibility, which is the essential ingredient required of everybody in a startup, especially one built by a group of friends.

We wound down LifeDox, and I took the opportunity to visit London and tour Normandy (again) with a couple of friends, including the one from the boating and LifeDox world. He and I met our wives in Paris, leaving the memories of LifeDox far behind. It was perhaps my first step in defeating depression by focusing on my future and something other than work.

VI. FINALE

2014–2016 WASHINGTON

In 2013, Janet retired from the *Washington Post* and, with three of her former colleagues, decided to start an online publication for "women of a certain age." I was enlisted in the effort, and we approached a Baltimore advertising and PR agency that helped with the naming process and the initial rollout of *My Little Bird*, or rather *mylittlebird.com*. Initially, a small contract with Janet and one of her colleagues to edit a *Washington Post* fashion publication helped push *My Little Bird* out of the nest and nine years later it is still flying.

In mid-2014, I convinced Janet that we should downsize and that it was time to leave what had become a much younger suburban community. Born and raised in New York, Janet was always a city person, so I suggested we move to an apartment building in Washington next to the zoo on Connecticut Avenue. It seemed to have an excellent location, an interesting group of urban dwellers, and a plush bar where to meet them, but it would only be for two years.

2016–NOW WASHINGTON TO PITTSBURGH AND ONWARD

In early 2016, I spoke with Andy Lewis, kly asked about my going out there, but Andy suggested I might not want to see the Drew I had known for forty-eight years and who had been so helpful to me. I made the trip anyway.

Drew had been my mentor for most of those forty-eight years and made much of this book possible. I called the facility and indicated I would be visiting Drew in a day or two. The facility was a couple hours' drive from Phoenix, so I had plenty of time to think back about our work together in the Schweiker campaign, his help in my joining the Reagan Administration, and the multitude of personal meetings and phone calls.

When I got to the facility and his room, he was just returning in a wheelchair from lunch. I knew it was difficult for him to speak, but for once I wasn't asking him to. It was my turn, and I was more interested in expressing my gratitude for all he had done for me, which I did, trusting he was able to process what I said. It was a sad and silent return to Phoenix.

A few weeks later I attended Drew's funeral in Worcester, Pennsylvania, at the same Schwenkfelder church where we had buried Dick Schweiker, alongside Claire, the year before. As I made the walk from Drew's grave to Dick's, perhaps thirty-five yards, I couldn't help but think of their incredible careers, what they had meant to me, and sadly, that they hardly spoke with each other in their final years.

Schweiker had died the year before, on Friday, July 31, 2015. His longtime assistant, Elsie May, had called me with the news the following morning. Monday, I sent an email to Elsie Hillman, who had introduced me to Schweiker, to make sure she had received word. By return email from her assistant, I learned that Elsie died that day, Tuesday, four days after Dick had passed away. Although I had been able to spend time with Dick and his family in his last years, telling him of my appreciation for our having worked together, I regretted not being able to do so with Elsie as well. We had often exchanged emails and I was somehow sure I would see her again in Pittsburgh.

With Dick's death, and Elsie's, and now Drew's, I felt the passing of a generation of greats in my life. It became a time of great reflection for me.

After a couple of years in the Washington apartment next to the zoo, I had begun to realize that with the demise of LifeDox and the beginning of the Trump campaign, I was no longer playing in the Washington mainstream. I also understood that Janet could continue *My Little Bird* from just about anywhere, so I resolved to do more than hang out evenings at the apartment house bar. With Janet's buy-in we began discussions with friends' friends in Connecticut, New York, Philadelphia, and Pittsburgh about what I might be able to do to stay busy in those locations. It was my friend Jim Roddey in Pittsburgh who came up with the best answer.

JAMES RODDEY, ALLEGHENY COUNTY EXECUTIVE

Jim Roddey and I had been introduced by a mutual Pittsburgh friend in 2005, after I left SynXis and before I knew about Flight Explorer. He had worked with Ted Turner in Atlanta and had moved to Pittsburgh to acquire an outdoor advertising company. He then entered Republican politics and led the restructuring of county government, and after doing so became the first elected Allegheny County Executive, extremely hard to do for a Republican. He and I related easily in the intersecting worlds of business and politics.

Jim had visited Washington in search of funds to acquire a Pittsburgh-based company managing prison healthcare systems and felt that my connection with Carlyle, my having raised capital for SynXis, and my legislative prison oversite experience could be helpful. Working together, we secured venture funding from a firm in Miami and put together an offer to buy the prison healthcare company. We had been told by the owner that the company's CEO had an option to purchase the company but had decided that he would not. Unfortunately, the CEO changed his mind and moved forward with buying the company and we were excluded. A short time later I moved on to Flight Explorer.

In 2016, I reconnected with Jim in Pittsburgh, and he introduced me to several Pittsburgh business and university executives, including the assistant dean at the University of Pittsburgh Katz Graduate School of Business. When I told the dean of my experience at Virginia Tech, helping to enhance their international coursework, he asked me to consider becoming an executive in residence at Katz to create a value proposition around a goal that all the Katz fulltime MBA students engage in a meaningful international experience. I would also serve as a resource for students and faculty, starting at my convenience. This opportunity, combined with the fact that my brother, cousins, and earliest friends were in Pittsburgh, encouraged Janet and me to consider a move to Pittsburgh.

We looked for a house in the Shadyside neighborhood near both Carnegie Mellon and Pitt and, after a brief search, bought and remodeled a house in that neighborhood. We moved in in December and I began my assignment at Pitt in early 2017. Later that year, I delivered the "value proposition" to the assistant dean and the dean of the business school. Since then, I have advised students interested in international careers and served on boards of directors working with student teams managing simulated global companies.

Our move to Pittsburgh has had, as you might expect, its ups and downs. A large part of the reason for moving was to spend more time with my younger brother Kevin, who retired in 2018, but he died in January 2019, before he could even get his retirement RV rolling. Shortly after that I lost my youngest cousin, Tom Flannery who, aside from being a good friend, had been a big help to me on personnel matters at SynXis.

On the bright side, in the three years before he died, my brother was able to connect with a daughter, Katharina, in Berlin. As a teenage Army private stationed in Germany, Kevin had had an affair with an English teacher that resulted in a daughter some months after he had been sent home. For various reasons, the father and daughter did not connect until 2016. My sister Molly and I have been delighted to have Katharina and her family as a part of ours, and we find ways to spend time with them each year.

Reconnecting with former Shady Side classmates has been a joy. They have managed to come up with stories that I long ago forgot. At our age, it's hard not to reminisce, at least occasionally.

There are also some new friends in the Pittsburgh mix, especially for Janet, who has managed to accumulate quite a few in a very short time. In the months after we arrived, we were fortunate to have dinner with Max and Peggy King. Max had been editor of the *Philadelphia Inquirer* before taking the helm of the Heinz Foundation and subsequently the Pittsburgh Foundation before writing a biography of Mister Rogers: *The Good Neighbor: The Life and Work of Fred Rogers*. I told a few of the stories you have seen here, and Max strongly suggested I write them down. Whenever I have seen him since then, he has asked me what progress I was making.

At Max's urging, I decided to pull out an outline I had constructed years ago and start writing. When I sent twenty pages or so to Max for his opinion, he said, "Dig deep and keep writing." With this encouragement, I "dug deep and kept writing" and that is what you see. In my most recent Max sighting, he asked what I had discovered in the process. I told him frankly that writing is hard. "Ah," he said, "you're learning."

And so it is, and yes, I am. But by writing this book I hope I have first told stories of interest, especially to students trying to figure out what is ahead of them. They will see here that there is no easy way or single way to make an interesting life. It requires action. It requires reaching out to shake that unfamiliar hand, it requires getting on that plane, picking up that phone, and believing enough in your dreams to step out into the unknown. It requires making wise choices and the enlistment of helpful mentors like Elsie Hillman, Drew Lewis, and Dave Heebner, people I honor in telling these stories.

Each story leaves a record of a not-so-normal life and demonstrates what awaits students, internationalists, businesspeople, and entrepreneurs willing to step out of their comfort zone and be a part of the world in the 21st century.

APPENDIX A

TEN-STEP SOFTWARE ENTERPRISE STARTUP ROADMAP

Mission: Is the enterprise mission documented in a business plan defining products, services, and markets that is fully understood by everyone in the organization and are they totally aligned with it? There should be no "If we build it, they'll buy it!" Remember that companies rich in product drive high multiples and those serving diversified government and private-sector domestic and international markets even higher.

Structure: It is important to make sure that all "housekeeping" items are carefully reviewed. Is the corporate form appropriate to the business and will it be attractive to potential buyers/investors in a transaction? Is it properly documented, i.e., charter and shareholder certificates and board meeting minutes? Are financial records up to date and can enterprise deliver three years of audited information? Has a relationship been created with an attorney who understands the company and is quick to give knowledgeable advice when called on? Is all IP catalogued and properly documented; are patent filings in order? Are employee contracts fully documented with non-compete clauses and ownership plan references? Have employee backgrounds been reviewed for any surprises and documented? Are contract files complete and up to date? Has insurance (i.e. D&O, E&O) been considered and procured?

Management: Are the right people in the right seats on the right bus going in the right direction? If not, changes must be made expeditiously and not incrementally. By far, personnel issues are the hardest part of effective enterprise management, and few managers handle them effectively. Do the CEO and the CFO have a clear understanding of each other's position? That is the most important relationship on the management team, and it will be tested by the board, by employees and by customers, all of whom have different expectations of these two teammates and will seek to play one against the other. Additional key management considerations may include:

- Make the complex simple.
- Have partners confirm concepts.
- Be first in large markets.
- Invest incrementally.
- Seek early revenue.
- Use transaction pricing when possible; it drives incredible value.

Funding: Close attention should be given banking and shareholder relationships to make sure the enterprise has access to sufficient capital when and where it needs it, for example, for acquisitions. If the owners are not up to contributing additional capital, relationships need to be developed with outside sources of debt and equity. Consider establishing and drawing on as large a line of credit as permitted in order to build a credit history and banking relationship. Then consider an investment, likely a minority investment, from a firm or firms with sound knowledge of the business's industry, but also capable of assisting in raising additional capital if required and in helping to organize an exit event when appropriate.

Software Development: This is the lifeblood of the company. Is the IP fully in the enterprise's hands and is the development process documented? Even though outside contractors may assist, weight will be given to the enterprise that is most self-reliant. Is there a serious process, such as a product review board, in place for effectively matching development priorities to market requirements so that the process is forward looking and without room for helter-skelter, last-minute changes without serious consideration by the team? Developers are known to do their best creative work in a calm environment and, like everybody else, do not like surprises.

Marketing and Sales: The marketing and sales team should be fully occupied seeking new customers while staying engaged with existing customers at all times. Contact between salespeople and developers should be minimal; any such contact should be by the sales VP through the management vehicle for setting development priorities. Sales personnel compensation plans are of necessity complex in the software world; management must make a special effort to adjust and readjust the plan to maximize sales productivity. Finally, remember that the enemy has a vote; the sales team needs always to be mindful of real and imagined competition. Many times, a supposedly minor player became an industry leader because their competition wasn't paying attention to them!

Pricing: Second to the issue of personnel is pricing. The best brains in the enterprise need to take the time and make the effort to carefully price all products and services of the organization. Prices too low or too high will result in an early death of the organization, and failure to review pricing often will only enable competitors.

Partners: Having partners in the processes of the enterprise is essential to its success, because partners can be so helpful in verifying need, defining requirements, supporting concept tests, helping with pricing, and in spreading the good word within their respective communities. They are also an important source of information about the competition that may not be aware of the relationship and therefore are less guarded about competitive information. Product development with partners should be an enterprise rule.

Delivery: Has someone other than the developers vetted the software and is what is being delivered to the customer within the expectations of the customer? In the initial stages of the enterprise sales or support undertake this function, but as the organization grows it is important to invest in quality-assurance personnel.

Support: If a customer has an issue, are his/her options clear? Does the organization have a disaster recovery plan in the event of a catastrophe (software fault or major delivery error)? Everyone in the organization should know their battle station when things go bad, as they are bound to do once in a while.

INDEX OF NAMES

Agnew, Spiro vii, 78
Aguirre, Richard 36, 37, 148
Al-Bakr, Ahmed Hussan 135
Allen, George 172
Al-Zamil, Abdulrahman 153
Ambrose, Stephen 200
Annenberg, Walter 74
Arthur, Alexander 15
Aziz, Tariq viii, 134, 136, 163

Baker, Jim 119
Baldrige, Malcolm 129, 143
Bander Bin Sultan 144
Barr, Joseph 39
Bay, Mogens 160, 166, 168
Ben Bella, Ahmed 48, 51, 106
Bendjedid, Chadli viii, 142
Benson, George 4
Bentley, Patrick 49, 66
Beyster, Robert 155, 159, 160, 162
Black, Charlie 153
Blakeslee, Steve 68
Bradshaw, Terry 199

Brambilla, Pinin 121
Bremer, Paul 165
Brown, James 92
Buck, Gerhard 176
Burger, Bob 179, 187, 191, 192
Bush, George H. W. 109, 116, 119, 152
Buthelezi, Mangosuthu 148, 149

Calio, Tony 177
Camino, Paco 57
Carlos, Juan 57
Caracciolo, Stan 120
Carlucci, Frank ix, 169, 171, 175, 176
Carnegie, Andrew 4, 30
Carson, Jay 81
Carter, Jimmy 97, 99, 103, 109, 117
Casey, Robert Sr. (Auditor General/Governor) 97, 98
Casey, Robert Jr. (Senator) 97, 98
Casey, Robert 97, 98
Cashman, Peter 153
Cerf, Vint 214
Chaing Kai-shek 114
Chamberlain, Neville 173
Chatterton, George 199
Cheetham, Kevin 192, 194
Cheney, Dick 98
Churchill, Winston 96
Clancy, Parkman 84, 127, 157
Clark, Joseph 66, 67, 70, 72, 74, 75
Clark, William P. 140
Colby, William 134
Colson, Jack 17
Conmy, Jack 74
Connally, John 37
Conway, Bill 169, 175
Cooley, Jeanne 61
Cooper, Alice viii, 90, 93

Cordobés, El 57
Cordic, Rege 4
Cox, Archibald 99
Crocker, Chet 146
Cutler, Walt 142, 144

D'Aniello, Dan 169
Davis, Jefferson 198
Dean, John Gunther 139
DeKervasdoue, Jean 156
De Gaulle, Charles vii, 45, 48, 78
Delaney, Larry 161, 173, 178
DeMarcus, Gladys 21
Deng Xiaoping 109
d'Estang, Valery Giscard viii, 95
Devine, Sam 68
Dewey, Thomas vii, 78
Dole, Bob 99
Dominguin 57
Duggan, Robert 69

Eckstine, Billy 4
Eimler, Eberhard 178
Einstein, Albert 114
Eisenhower, Dwight 63
Ellis, Bernard 192
English, Pat (Aunt Pat) 39
English, Sherry 52

Faisal I 135
Faisal II 135
Fineman, Herb 95
Fischer, Jens 173
Flannery, Roger 8
Flannery, Rogers 29

Flannery, Tom 222
Fonda, Henry34
Ford, Gerald 19, 23, 32, 74, 92, 98, 99, 107, 119, 170
Foster, Bede 13
Foster, Polly 13
Franco, Francisco 55
Freeman, Chas 148
Friend, Bob 68

Gallagher, Sean 153
Galland, Adolf 179
Gandhi, Indira 135, 137
Gandhi, Rajiv viii, 135, 137, 140
Gandhi, Sanjay 138
Garner, Erroll 4
Glaspie, April 158, 164
Gnesutta, Alberto 121, 194
Gnesutta, Paola 121
Goldwater, Barry 63
Good, Alex 153, 187
Gordon, Shep viii, 153
Grant, Cary 34
Grant, Ulysses S. 200, 201
Grossmann, Bill 184
Grossmann, Jim 76, 128, 129, 131, 154, 167

Hall, Katie v
Hamdoon, Nizar viii, 133, 134, 137, 163
Han Xu viii, 109
Harper, Bob 90
Harriman, Pamela ix, 175
Harris, Franco 199
Haskell, Jay 86
Heckler, Margaret 153
Heebner, Dave 157, 159, 161, 162, 171, 184, 193, 195, 223

Heebner, Lynn 154, 157, 159, 161, 162, 171, 184, 193, 195, 223
Heinz, Henry 4
Heinz, John 96, 97, 98, 130, 150
Heinz, Theresa 150
Helm, Richard 222
Hill, Bruce 81
Hillman, Elsie vii, 62, 67, 77, 80, 81, 94, 96, 99, 117, 130, 131, 220, 223
Hillman, Henry 62
Hitler, Adolph 5
Horan, Hume 142, 143
Horne, Alistair 47
Hoover, Herbert 129
Hough, Larry 195, 196
Humphrey, Hubert 67, 75
Hussain, Saddam 134, 135, 158

Imprescia, Stelio 15, 17
Ivany, Bob 198

Jagger, Mick 92
Johnson, Lyndon 63, 98, 134
Johnson, Sam 35, 54
Juan, Don (Count of Barcelona) vii, 57

Kahn, Robert ix, 214
Kamel, Hussein 137
Kennedy, John F. 37, 62
Kelly, Grace 94
Kelly, James B. Sr. (Grandfather Kelly) 35, 94
Kelly, James B. Jr. (Dad/Father) vii, xii, 5, 6, 8, 10, 11, 12, 13, 14, 15, 16, 19, 20, 24, 25, 26, 28, 29, 30, 31, 32, 36, 37, 38, 39, 54, 56, 57, 61, 64, 78, 79, 84, 94, 95, 109, 114, 137, 142, 150, 151, 168, 194, 199, 200, 201, 222
Kelly, James B. IV (Son/Jim/Jimmy) 22, 77, 85, 87, 95, 103, 121, 126, 127, 128, 151, 154, 165
Kelly, John 94

Kelly, Kevin 6, 28, 29, 222
Kelly, Mary (Grandmother Kelly) 39, 62
Kelly, Megyn 30
Kiep, Walther Leisler 176
Kiesling, Bill 98
Kimmitt, Robert 176
Kiner, Ralph 7
King, Martin Luther 65, 66
King, Max v
King, Peggy 222
Kissinger, Henry 109, 171
Kline, Ernie 91

Laird, Mel 157, 160
Lang, Cindy 94
Lee, Ken 94, 95
Lee, Robert E. 10
Levitt, Carol 192
Lewis, Andrew (Drew) vii, 69, 70, 77, 79, 94, 95, 99, 119, 128, 130, 131, 152, 162, 170, 208, 215, 223
Lewis, Andrew Jr. (Andy) 219
Limberger, Peter 173
Lincoln, Evelyn 78
Lukanov, Andrey 125

Machel, Graca 150
Machel, Samora150
Macron, Emmanuel 47
Maisonrouge, Jacques 156
Mandela, Nelson 146, 150
Mao Zedong 108
Martha, Paul 92
May, Elsie 74, 76, 220
Mellon, Andrew 4
Mesta, Perle 134

Miller, David 145
Miller, Warren 14
Mitchell, Geoff 21, 24, 192, 194, 206
Mitchum, Robert 23
Mondale, Walter 131
Montgomery, Bernard 96
Morris, Jim 8
Mugabe, Robert 145
Mulcahy, Patricia v
Murray, Larry 192
Musial, Stan 7
Myers, Jerry 183, 185, 192

Naderkhani, Majid 187
Newhall, David 68, 72, 79, 82
Newton, David 136
Nicholson, Penn 21
Nixon, Richard M. vii, 15, 74, 75, 109
Noll, Chuck 199
Norris, Steve 169, 170, 195,196
Norman, Denis 145

Odeen, Phil 171, 177, 184
O'Connell, Fred 61
Olatunji (Tunji) 38, 39
Olmer, Lionel 129, 140
O'Reilly, Tony 145
O'Toole, Gail 177
O'Toole, Jim 177, 198
Oxenberg, Michael 117

Paperin, Stewart 193
Payze, Sally 192
Pearl, Richard 137
Phillips, Howard (Howie) 71, 72, 74, 75, 76

Placke, Jim 136
Pompidou, Alain 157
Pompidou, Georges 157
Power, Samantha 30
Putnay, Zim 193

Randt, Clark 210
Randt, Sarah 210
Radziewski, Marie-Claude 106
Reagan, Ronald 117
Reddy, Tharun 184, 192
Rhodes, Joe 86
Rickover, Hyman vii, 78
Ridgway, Mathew B. vii, 96
Riegle, Don 65
Robbins, Chauncey 62, 63, 65
Rockefeller, Nelson 63
Roddey, James ix, 221
Rogers, Fred v, 222
Ronstadt, Linda 92
Roosevelt, Franklin D. 5
Rose, Evans (Ev) 81, 82, 84, 96, 118
Ross, Chris 134
Rubenstein, David 169
Ruckelshaus, William 99
Russell, John 195

Sahnoun, Mohamed viii, 132, 133, 134
Salk, Jonas vii, 5, 12
Santorum, Rick 97
Savastuk, David 153
Scaife, Richard Mellon 69
Schlesinger, James 134
Schmidt, Harold 81, 82
Schmidt, Helmut 173

Schuette, Erwin 32
Schuette, Margaret (Marnie/Mom) 52
Schultz, George viii, 116, 134
Schulz, Siegfried 173
Schweiker, Richard S. (Dick) vii, 66, 69, 119, 130, 131, 220, 241
Schweiker, Claire 69, 70, 76, 119, 214, 220
Scirica, Tony 74, 86
Scott, Hugh vii, viii, 63, 76, 78, 96, 109
Scranton, Bill 67, 82, 83
Searls, Andy 165
Searls, Mel 138, 210
Shaffer, Ray 86
Shapp, Milton 87
Sheen, Fulton J. 4
Shilito, Barry 160
Siegel, Dick 68
Simon, Paul 92
Slattery, Domhnal 194, 195
Slattery, John
Smart, Bruce 140
Smith, Ian 145
Sorenson, Richard 201
Specter, Arlen 130
Stalworth, John
Starzl, Thomas 5, 239
Steger, Charles 202
Sterling, Bob 184, 185, 190, 191, 193, 195
Stewart, Jimmy 34
Stoiber, Edmund 174
Stokoweski, Leopold 1C4
Stuhldreher, Harry 39
Sullivan, Ed 4
Swann, Lynn 197, 198
Sweeney, Bill 177

Temple, Shirley 153
Thorbecke, Bill 104, 117, 126
Thorbecke, Sonya Stokowski 104
Thornburgh, Richard 69

Van der Heide, Roel 166, 196
Vilsak, Ray 7
Vincent, Stan 91
Viti, El 57

Waigel, Theodor 173, 174
Walgren, Doug 97
Walter, Greg 68, 75, 79
Warhol, Andy 92
Westinghouse, George 4
White, Theodore 114
Whitman, Christine Todd 193
Whitman, John 193
Whittemore, Fred 191
Williams, Earl 170, 171, 172, 177
Wright, Bob 209, 211, 212

Xi Jinping 109

Yount, Barton Kyle 34
Yates, Henry (Grandfather Yates) 10, 12, 29, 31, 32
Yates, Richard 12, 199
Yates, Richard Jr. 12, 199
Ye Fe 114

Zhou Enlai 109
Zhou Ju Mei 114
Zhou Peiyuan 114

ABOUT THE AUTHOR

Jim Kelly is a recent executive in residence at the University of Pittsburgh Graduate School of Business. He co-founded and was CEO of two software solutions companies after serving as international vice president of two defense technology companies. Prior to that he was Deputy Assistant Secretary for Africa, the Near East and South Asia in the U.S. Department of Commerce International Trade Administration, served three terms in the Pennsylvania Legislature and worked for Pennsylvania U.S. Senator Richard S. Schweiker on Capitol Hill. He is a graduate of Virginia Tech and ASU's Thunderbird School of Global Management in Phoenix, Arizona.

www.ingramcontent.com/pod-product-compliance
Lightning Source LLC
LaVergne TN
LVHW052308200926
848481LV00002B/501
* 9 7 9 8 8 9 1 2 7 5 8 1 2 *